THE STORY OF TWENTY-FIVE YEARS

HIS MAJESTY KING GEORGE V.

News Chronicle

STORY OF TWENTY-FIVE YEARS

Compiled by

W. J. MAKIN

*Celebrating the Royal
Silver Jubilee, 1910–1935*

With over 300 half-tone Illustrations

London
GEORGE NEWNES LIMITED
Southampton Street, Strand, W.C. 2

PRINTED IN GREAT BRITAIN BY
BILLING AND SONS LTD., GUILDFORD AND ESHER

ACKNOWLEDGMENT

THE compiler of this record of *The Story of Twenty-Five Years* wishes to express his indebtedness to many anonymous journalists for descriptive matter appearing in the newspaper files of the period. Also to the authors and publishers of the following books:

War Diaries. By Lord Riddell. (Ivor Nicholson and Watson.)
Intimate Diary of the Peace Conference and After. By Lord Riddell. (Gollancz.)
A Modern History of the English People. By R. H. Gretton. (Martin Secker.)
Ourselves 1900-1930. By Irene Clephane. (The Bodley Head.)
How We Lived Then. By Mrs. C. S. Peel, O.B.E. (The Bodley Head.)
King George V. By Sir George Arthur. (Jonathan Cape.)
England's Royal Family. By Colonel R. J. Blackham. (Sampson Low.)
These Hurrying Years. By Gerald Heard. (Chatto and Windus.)
King Edward VII. and His Times. By André Maurois. (Cassell.)
First War in the Air. By R. H. Kiernan. (Peter Davies.)
Celebrated Spies. By George Barton. (Page.)
A Brief History of Our Times. By Ramsay Muir. (Philip.)
The Encyclopædia Britannica.
By Air. By Sir Harry Brittain. (Hutchinson.)
The A B C of the B.B.C. By Sir Harry Brittain. (Pearson.)

Finally, the thanks of the compiler are due also to Mr. Ewart Williams for his help in the selection of the photographs and the reading of the manuscript.

WILLIAM J. MAKIN.

18, HENRIETTA STREET,
LONDON, W.C. 2.

CONTENTS

THEIR MAJESTIES KING GEORGE V AND QUEEN MARY

LIST OF ILLUSTRATIONS

CHAPTER 1

BIRTH OF A NEW AGE

Illness of King Edward VII.—His death—Proclaiming the new King—King George's youth—"The Sailor Prince"—His marriage to Princess May—Training him for the Throne.

I

A GREY-BEARDED man sat at a tea-table in a room in Buckingham Palace. He looked tired and ill. From his chair he could see the bright green of lawn and trees shaded by the sunshine of a May afternoon.

Fumbling for a cigar, he put it between his lips and lit it with an air of finality. But he had only taken a few puffs when he was seized with a paroxysm of coughing. Large brown patches appeared on the familiar face. His hands trembled.

The door opened quietly. A frock-coated medical man approached the coughing figure.

"Your Majesty!" he begged. "These cigars . . ."

Britain's greatest diplomat, King Edward VII., gazed with tear-dimmed eyes, brought on by the coughing, at his medical attendant and tried to wave him away. But the medical man had glimpsed something else. By the tea-table was a mass of official documents that the King had been perusing.

"Your Majesty," he again pleaded, "I implore you to rest."

With an effort, King Edward recovered his breath.

"No, no," he wheezed, shaking his head. "I shall work to the end. . . . Of what use is it to be alive if one cannot work?"

The medical man shrugged his shoulders. A gesture from the King and he withdrew. But no sooner had the door closed than the grey-bearded man, clutching the cigar between his fingers, was once again doubled by a fit of coughing.

This time it was a good four minutes before he recovered. He breathed noisily and painfully.

"If this lasts much longer," he muttered to himself, "I am done for."

An hour later he was receiving a high colonial official and discussing with an effort matters of State. As the official left Buckingham Palace, he was heard to remark: "I have seen a dying man."

Meanwhile, in another room of the Palace, other medical men had gathered. A Cabinet Minister. Also the King's Private Secretary. It was still the tradition in Britain that the illness of royalty should, unless terribly serious, be kept secret from the public. At the same time it was decided to send an urgent telegram to Queen Alexandra, who was at Corfu.

"It is best that the Queen return at once," decided the doctors.

Hurriedly, the Private Secretary composed a telegram, and, by means of official channels, it was flashed towards that island in the Mediterranean.

On the morning of May 6, 1910, the doctors examined King Edward. He

was very ill. The heart was failing. Yet the King was ominously calm. He refused to stay in bed. He dressed himself fully, and sat again in that room overlooking the Palace gardens. At one period he walked painfully to the other side of the Palace and looked down towards the Mall. A criss-cross of scaffolding and grey tarpaulin covered the huge mass that was to be a monument to Queen Victoria, a work in progress.

"I shall never live to see it unveiled," he nodded, a strange smile hiding itself beneath the beard as he thought of that great mother Queen who had chided him as Prince of Wales for his glittering, rather feverish, life.

What was it they had said of him? The dying man struggled to recall the whispers of those about him.

" . . . He likes the society of women who can talk, of Jews and people who can amuse him. And he really likes any public ceremony, and theatres and cards. . . . But he is a sensible man, and knows more about foreign affairs than anyone, and has quite advanced ideas. . . ."

King Edward chuckled. Yes, he had lived his period. Edwardian, they would call it. And many would look back upon it with regret. Few realised at the time that in that dying King was England at her zenith, her richest and most powerful. Even then the clouds were gathering on the horizon. And he, Edward, shrewdest of all the diplomats, had glimpsed them. His many journeys to the Continent had been in the nature of a preparation for the storm.

With a sigh, King Edward wandered back to his sitting-room. He tried to smoke one more cigar, but got no pleasure from it.

"I feel miserably ill," he confessed, laying the cigar aside.

At eleven o'clock he wanted to rise to receive his old friend, Sir Ernest Cassel, who found him in his sitting-room, dressed as usual. The King rose from his arm-chair to shake Cassel's hand, but looked as if he had suffered, and could not speak distinctly. But he still had his kindly smile.

"I am very ill," he murmured, "but I wanted to see you. . . ."

Once again in that other room the medical men had met. This time a public bulletin had to be issued. At the same time the Archbishop of Canterbury was summoned. Rumours began to be whispered through the streets of London. The King was dying; the King was dead. . . .

In the official residence of the Prime Minister, 10, Downing Street, Mrs. Asquith was handing a telegram to a servant. It was addressed to her husband, urging him to return at once. Even as the servant padded away, Lord Kitchener was announced. He entered the room.

"Have you heard the dreadful rumour?" whispered Mrs. Asquith.

Lord Kitchener jerked his head impatiently.

"Absurd!" he snapped. "You've only to look out of the window. The flag on the Palace isn't at half-mast yet."

And indeed the Royal Standard was still flying in the windy May sunshine.

The serious bulletin published at eleven o'clock cast a gloom over the luncheon tables of the West End. At Kempton Park a huge crowd of race-goers anxiously watched the board go up for the 4.15 race. The King's horse, Witch, was scheduled to run. Would it be scratched at the last moment? But

a cheer was raised when it was seen that the horse would run after all. And even greater and prolonged cheering greeted the finish of the race with Witch an easy winner. It was considered a happy omen.

Inside Buckingham Palace, the Prince of Wales received the glad news and hurried into the sitting-room to congratulate his father.

The grey-bearded figure nodded, and tried to smile.

"Yes, they told me. . . . I am glad."

A few moments later he slipped into a coma. Queen Alexandra, who had returned from Corfu, herself helped to carry him to his bedroom. He was undressed and laid on the bed.

"I will go on. . . . I will go on. . . ." he muttered determinedly.

But they were the last coherent words King Edward spoke. Even while he was still struggling against death a Privy Council had been summoned to proclaim his successor. And in accordance with tradition a regiment of Life Guards stood by, booted and spurred, ready for emergencies.

Groups of people began to drift towards the Palace. They clustered the railings and stared silently at those lighted windows where a king was fighting his last desperate battle. Some shivered in the cool night air. A woman wrapped a shawl round her baby. Dumb faces stared upwards.

At a quarter to twelve King Edward breathed his last. A member of the Royal Household came down and stepped across the gravel to the railings. His feet crunched nearer and nearer, a messenger of ill-tidings.

He faced the crowd through the railings.

"The King is dead," he said quietly.

A deep silence fell on the crowd. Men fumbled for their hats and removed them. A woman's sob seemed to shake them. The news, though not unexpected, was stunning.

"The King is dead."

That quiet announcement was already flaring and resounding throughout the world. Mr. Asquith, the Prime Minister, at the moment aboard the Admiralty yacht *Enchantress*, pitching full-steam ahead from the Mediterranean to England, received the news at three o'clock in the morning. He rose from his bunk and went on deck.

Above the pitching mast in the pale glow of the dawn, Halley's comet blazed across the sky.

"The King is dead; long live the King!"

King George V. had begun his reign.

II

At half past four the following afternoon, one hundred and fifty Privy Councillors met in the large hall at St. James's Palace. A silent, hushed assembly. No greetings, no handshakes.

Lord Crewe rose from his seat. A strange, tense silence held all who were present.

"The King is dead," announced Lord Crewe simply, "and it is our duty to proclaim his successor."

The Lord Chancellor and the Archbishop of Canterbury then went out of the room. In a few moments they returned. Walking between them was the Prince of Wales, whom Lord Crewe presented to the Council as King George V. After a few words the King took his seat on the throne and all those present knelt before him on a cushion,

2

swearing their loyalty, each in the manner of his faith.

That same evening Mrs. Asquith dined with Winston Churchill and Lord and Lady Crewe. After dinner Churchill rose, and, holding his glass on high, said: "Let us drink to the health of the new King." And Lord Crewe replied: "Or, rather, to the memory of the old."

The black velvet darkness of night was over England. In the Throne Room at Buckingham Palace, four Grenadier Guardsmen, their heads bowed over their reversed rifles, stood at the corners of the coffin in a long, silent vigil. . . .

At nine o'clock on the morning of May 9, 1910, an ancient and picturesque ceremonial was unrolled. A Guard of Honour of the First Life Guards clattered into Friary Court of the Palace, followed by the band of the Coldstream Guards with draped guns. Behind them rode the Army Headquarters staff in full-dress uniform. The red and blue garbed figures stood out against the grey stone background of the Palace.

A great crowd had assembled for the ceremony. A fanfare of trumpets drew all eyes to the balcony overlooking the quadrangle. The State trumpeters had raised their shining instruments. Figures in colourful robes and uniforms stalked on to the balcony. The group included the Duke of Norfolk, Earl Marshal, and Garter King-of-Arms and Pursuivants of the Heralds' College.

From a window of Marlborough House, opposite the quadrangle, three young boys and a girl watched this picturesque ceremonial. They were the children of King George. At another window, though unseen by the people, were the King and Queen.

After that preliminary fanfare of trumpets, there was silence for a few moments. Then the Garter King-of-Arms stepped forward, unrolled a scroll, and began to read in a loud, clear voice.

" . . . Whereas it has pleased Almighty God to call to His Mercy our late Sovereign Lord King Edward the Seventh, of blessed and Glorious Memory, by whose Decease the Imperial Crown of the United Kingdom of Great Britain and Ireland is solely and rightfully come to the High and Mighty Prince George Frederick Ernest Albert:

"We, therefore, the Lords Spiritual and Temporal of this Realm being here assisted with those of His late Majesty's Privy Council, with numbers of other principal gentlemen of quality, with the Lord Mayor, Aldermen and citizens of London, do now hereby, with one voice and content of tongue and heart, publish and proclaim:

"That the High and Mighty Prince George Frederick Ernest Albert is now, by the death of our late Sovereign of happy memory, become our only lawful right Liege Lord George the Fifth by the Grace of God King of the United Kingdom of Great Britain and Ireland, and of the British Dominions beyond the Seas, Defender of the Faith, Emperor of India, to whom we do acknowledge all faith and constant obedience, with all hearty and humble affection, beseeching God, by whom Kings and Queens do reign, to bless the Royal Prince George the Fifth with long and happy years to reign over us. . . ."

As the clear voice of the reader of the proclamation rang out, the troops stood at the salute and the men in the large crowd bared their heads. When the voice of the Garter King-of-Arms ceased there was a breathless silence. Then the Earl Marshal raised his gloved hand.

"God save the King!" he cried.

THE FUNERAL OF KING EDWARD VII. in May, 1910, saw the death also of an era.
The years that followed, with his son as King, were to create a new England.

EIGHT KINGS *attended the funeral of King Edward VII. At the head of the procession walked the new King and his eldest son, the sixteen-year-old Prince of Wales.*

"God save the King!" cried the crowd in unison, and the roaring sound of the National Anthem echoed from the grey stone walls surrounding the quadrangle.

Even as the crowd sang, the guns began to boom. A Royal Salute of forty-one guns was being fired from the bright green lawns of St. James's Park.

III

"Good old Teddie!" is how a crowd often boisterously received King Edward. If the new King was not spontaneously greeted as "Good old Georgie!" there was, nevertheless, an unqualified note of warm affection and absolute confidence which revealed the respect with which he stood in the eyes of the nation.

Throughout the year that preceded his coronation, King George was discussed, studied and written about with that democratic freedom which is the envy and amazement of Continental nations. The British public wished to know about their new King. And from this searching limelight of publicity there emerged a man, human, and, above all, likeable, who, throughout the years of trial and fortitude that were to follow, never lost the deep affection and loyalty of the nation.

King George was not so jovial as was his father, but he had more urbanity. He was approachable, friendly, and sympathetic in bearing. King Edward would sternly dismiss anyone whom he thought was presuming too far. King George would not hurt the feelings of even the most aggressive by a look of displeasure or annoyance.

Throughout his exacting Royal cavalcade King George has graciously received everyone who approached him, however ordinary. He has bent himself to listen with an air of earnest expectation, as if there was an important message about to be delivered, and when he has heard it he responds with a kindly comment and understanding smile. He has displayed certain simple and fundamental qualities of character which have not only endeared him to the people, but also achieved a more profound devotion than that accorded to his father.

It was at Marlborough House, in June, 1865, that the baby Prince George was born. That there is good, healthy blood in the family has been proved by the remarkable longevity of the present ruling house of England. No ruling member of it has lived for less than 67 years.

George I. was 67 when he died, George II. was 77, George III. 82, George IV. 68, William IV. 72, Queen Victoria 81, and King Edward 69. Our present King, George V., is 69, and, as was manifested on many occasions, it is hoped that he will be spared for several more years.

Although the blood of King George is mainly German, it can safely be said that no more English King ever sat on the throne. Despite the origin of the Coburg family, in its small principality on the fringe of the Thuringian Forest, that branch which came to England soon shed their German trappings. King Edward was essentially an Englishman, and both by early training and environment the young Prince George soon revealed himself as more English than the English. Today, King George is regarded as the very apotheosis of the English gentleman.

Actually the limelight of publicity fell more upon Prince George's elder brother, the Duke of Clarence, who was until his death in 1892 the intended heir to the Throne. Nevertheless, the training of the two young princes proceeded together and was of that rigorous character which prevailed in the Victorian age.

There are engaging incidents on record to give us a picture of Prince George as a boy. Mr. Hector Bolitho, in his new book, *Victoria, the Widow and Her Son,* gives us a glimpse of the 'sixties and 'seventies when the two young princes were growing boys.

Prince George was brought up in awe of his father, whose genial nature never lessened his sense of princely right. But the authority which Edward exercised over his sons was never relentless nor unsympathetic. The healthy spirits of boyhood were never treated brutally at Marlborough House. When Prince George and his elder brother were sent to the training ship *Britannia* they showed "as much healthy naughtiness" as their contemporaries.

There is one enchanting story of a day when the Prince was taken with his brother to Westminster Abbey. Dean Stanley had been asked to show them the treasures of the Abbey. Nobody could make the memorials of Westminster come to life again as Dean Stanley could, with his vivid historic sense. In spite of the charm of the Dean's stories, Prince George wandered away by himself. At last he was found in a dim little side chapel. He had scrambled on top of Queen Elizabeth's tomb, and, looking down at the effigy, he was saying, "What an ugly old woman!"

Prince George was twelve when he became the youngest cadet on board the *Britannia.* He was conscientious; the flame of duty, which was to be an inspiration of his reign, was already alive in him and was an inheritance from his Coburg grandfather. When he was a boy, there were already signs of the similarity in character. The signs were to increase as the years passed. But, in leisure, he was spirited and impish. On one occasion, a couple of marline-spikes found their way into the bed of an officer. A certain cadet was suspected. Then Prince George admitted that he was the culprit and he faced his punishment. His leave was stopped for one week.

Nevertheless, the record of Prince George was that of an efficient officer. He was devotedly attached to his calling, although, like Nelson and other distinguished sailors, he suffered from seasickness. No distinction was made between Prince George and his shipmates. It has been recorded that he was an excellent singer of comic songs and often regaled his shipmates with the latest.

Moreover, he early displayed that keen sense of humour which has remained with him until the present day. Once when his ship was in Turkish waters, a Pasha came on board to pay his respects to the grandson of the Queen of England, and son of the Prince of Wales. It happened that the Prince that day was having his turn in the duty of coaling, and when he appeared on deck from the stokehold, his overalls black and his face and hands grimy with coaldust, even the Oriental calm of the Pasha was ruffled at the sight.

It was when he was serving in H.M.S. *Excellent* that the future King met a certain "Jackie" Fisher, who was then Captain of the Gunnery School. Even in those days the future First Lord of

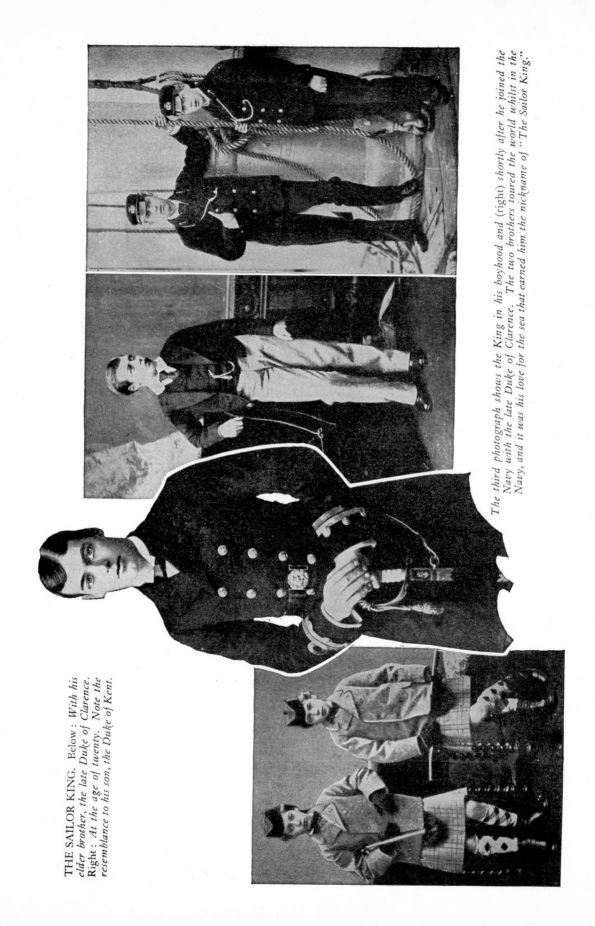

THE SAILOR KING. Below: With his elder brother, the late Duke of Clarence. Right: At the age of twenty. Note the resemblance to his son, the Duke of Kent.

The third photograph shows the King in his boyhood and (right) shortly after he joined the Navy, with the late Duke of Clarence. The two brothers toured the world whilst in the Navy, and it was his love for the sea that earned him the nickname of "The Sailor King."

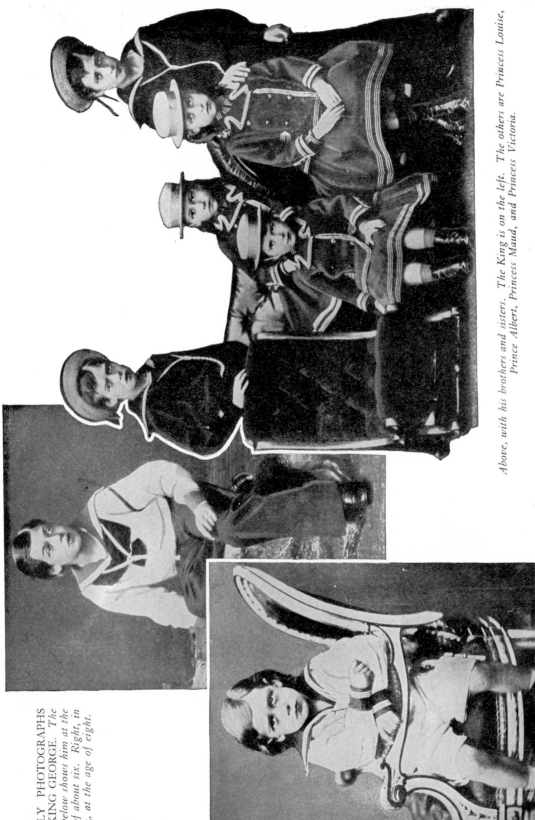

EARLY PHOTOGRAPHS OF KING GEORGE. The one below shows him at the age of about six. Right, in 1873, at the age of eight.

Above, with his brothers and sisters. The King is on the left. The others are Princess Louise, Prince Albert, Princess Maud, and Princess Victoria.

the Admiralty had a perverse temper and an eloquent flow of language, but Prince George appears to have recognised the real and outstanding ability of the man, and formed a real attachment that lasted until the death of Lord Fisher.

Eventually, the two young princes were transferred to the *Bacchante,* in which they toured the world. There was no hint yet that Prince George would become heir to the Throne, through his elder brother's death. He was, therefore, educated as a second son, with the consequent differences in aims and responsibilities. A sailor's life suited him; he was a man's man, and his character and tastes were of the mould that thrives in a wardroom or an officers' mess.

In the *Bacchante* the princes travelled as far as Australia and New Zealand. In Australia they descended a gold mine; they aimed with boomerangs and even ate minced kangaroo. In New Zealand they shook hands with dusky Maori chieftains who had fought against their grandmother's soldiers.

Prince George was at home on both land and sea. He wrote in his Journal: "After dinner much amusement, trying to sit on an empty corked bottle, on the deck, at the same time holding a candle in each hand, one of which was lighted, the other to be lighted from it, without rolling over."

While he was in Australian waters Prince George left the *Bacchante* to stay with an Australian hostess. She made a charming gesture which showed him that graciousness was to flourish as well as corn and wool in the new countries of his grandmother's empire. When he went down for breakfast he found a wreath of rosebuds about his plate.

They were, he was told, "For Sunday morning and in memory of England."

It was during this voyage that the world was startled by a statement widely published in the newspapers that the princes, landing at Bermuda, had each had his nose tattooed with an anchor. It was feared in the Royal Household that the story might be true, because of Prince George's addiction to pranks and practical jokes, for which he was known in the home circle as the "Royal Pickle." Once at a family luncheon at Windsor Castle, in his childhood, he incurred the displeasure of the severe, as well as august, Queen Victoria, and as a punishment was sent under the table until he was in a fit mind to behave himself. After a while he was heard to say, "Grandmamma, I'm quite good now." "Very well, then," said Grandmamma, "you may come out." Out he came, wholly naked and unashamed, having in his banishment divested himself of every bit of clothing. There was no knowing what a boy like that might be up to. Anxious telegrams were sent to the ship, and greatly to the relief of the country, as well as of the Royal Family, it was announced that the story was unfounded. What had happened was that the boys ornamented each other's noses with pollen from the brilliant orange stamens of the Bermuda lilies. From that day to this yellow noses are regarded as the height of fashion in the island, especially by the native ladies.

It was also while a midshipman that Prince George began his hobby of stamp collecting, which today is still one of his chief relaxations. It can be said that the present King George possesses one of the most comprehensive and valuable collections of stamps in the world. It was an excellent hobby for a boy to have chosen. Postage stamps do give a breadth of vision, with the vivid colouring, the heads of potentates, the pictures, and names of far-off places suggestive of romance. As the King once told the Junior Philatelic Society, it was a hobby he had pursued with "unabated interest" throughout the years.

Before he left home for this world voyage he promised his mother to read the Bible daily. The Pocket Testament League in 1912 wrote to Buckingham Palace asking if it was true that King George followed the practice of daily Bible reading. "It is quite true," Lord Knollys, the King's Private Secretary, replied, "that he promised Queen Alexandra as long ago as 1881 that he would read a chapter of the Bible daily, and that he has ever since adhered to this promise."

Always the watchful eye of Queen Victoria was on the young princes. When the *Bacchante* in which her grandsons were serving as midshipmen had been ordered to South Africa, Queen Victoria wrote to her daughter-in-law, Alexandra:

Darling Alix,

I am sorry Bertie (the future King Edward) *should have been sore about the boys; but I think he must have forgotten the arrangements and conditions and instructions respecting their going to sea.*

I, and even Bertie and you, only consented to their both going to sea for their education and moral training. This being the case—the Bacchante *going to the Cape, which was done in a hurry without one consultation with me (I disapproved)—and feeling how valuable these two young lives are to the whole nation, I felt bound to protect them against useless and unnecessary exposure in a cruel Civil War—for so it is, the Boers being my subjects, and it being a rule that Princes of the Royal Family ought not to be mixed in it.*

In any other war, should in time there be one (when Georgie be older), and his ship be obliged to take part in it, I would quite agree with Bertie.

Pray show this to him, as I am sure he and everyone would agree in this being the right course.

But even Queen Victoria could not control the adventures which the young princes encountered on this world tour.

The ship nearly drowned Prince George in the Pacific upon one occasion. They even survived the adventure with a mad nigger of Simonstown who almost killed them in a "spider" drawn by four beautiful white horses, which the Governor had sent over to drive them to Cape Town.

Mad with drink, we are told, the Malay drove headlong up hill and down dale, into the surf of the sea and out of it, crashed into a Cape waggon, and finished upon the spoke of one wheel at Government House, a jubilant man who was at least an optimist.

And in this same region, when sailing round the Cape of Good Hope, our future King and some of those who sailed with him in the *Bacchante* fell in with a phantom ship, and clearly observed that her spars and her sails shone with a fire as of gold.

At the end of the cruise, in 1882, the two brothers parted company. Prince Albert Victor was destined for the Army and the succession to the Throne; Prince George adopted the sea as his avocation. His Englishry was already marked. Truly he could say:

I travelled among unknown men,
In lands beyond the sea;
Nor, England, did I know till then
What love I bore to thee.

Prince George was given his first independent command—Torpedo Boat No. 79. This ship took part in the naval manœuvres of 1889 in some of the worst weather which has ever been experienced on our coasts.

Admiral Penrose Fitzgerald has brought to light an incident in these manœuvres which shows that the King was not only a capable but a very plucky sailor. Three torpedo boats, of which No. 79 was one, had a rendezvous with a senior officer in Lough Swilly. Prince George's little craft turned up in time, but had to report the grave news that one of its companions had engine trouble and had been obliged to cast anchor close to the Donegal coast. The commander of No. 79 reported that he had tried to tow the crippled torpedo boat, but his towing gear had broken. There was nothing to be done except to leave her with the third torpedo boat standing by and report at the rendezvous for fresh hawsers.

The senior naval officer wanted to go to the rescue himself, but with some misgivings gave way to the request of the plucky young commander of No. 79 to let him have another try. A less conscientious commander might well have rested satisfied after spending the previous night trying to assist his companion ship, and leave to a less tired crew than his own the task of dealing with the situation. The future King was, however, made of sterner stuff, so, equipped with a new hawser, he put to sea again in the teeth of a heavy gale.

The work of rescuing the disabled torpedo boat was a job requiring not only courage and initiative, but skilful seamanship, and one of those proud moments which the King must love to recall is when he towed the helpless ship to safety. The incident reveals that the King was in his true element when at sea, and there is reality behind the proud title "Sailor King."

For this achievement Prince George received the post of commander of the first-class gunboat *Thrush,* and later commander of the new second-class cruiser *Melampus.* This commission was designed to be the first of a series of important commands. There was no doubt of the keenness of Prince George. His ambition was that one day he would have the pride and joy of hoisting his Flag as an Admiral on the active list. He used to say how glad he was that he would not have to be King, as he wanted to remain a sailor.

Fate, however, decreed that this command of the *Melampus* was to be his last naval appointment as Prince George. In November, 1891, he was attacked by serious illness, which very nearly brought to an end his career.

The Prince was on a visit to the Curragh, where his brother was quartered with his regiment, the 11th Hussars. He returned to a small family party at Sandringham, but showed signs of being seriously ill. He developed fever and King Edward hurried him off to London, where the doctors diagnosed enteric fever. It was a long struggle, but Prince George came through. His vigorous and healthy constitution resisted the disease germs. But the young Prince had only entered upon the convalescent stage when another tragic event occurred in the English Royal

Family, which was to entirely change the outlook of Prince George.

In January, 1892, by the premature death of his brother Prince Albert Victor, Duke of Clarence, he came into the direct line of succession to the Throne. After sixteen years' continuous service afloat, his career at sea was abruptly terminated. He was raised to the peerage as Duke of York, and was introduced in the House of Lords by his father.

A new and greater career was opening for him.

IV

And so we come to the woman, the first lady of the land, who has played an important and great part in this drama of twenty-five years.

Her Majesty Queen Mary is undoubtedly the most gracious, the most dignified, and most important Queen reigning in the world today. She has endeared herself to the people of this country in no uncertain fashion. She is admired and esteemed, and there is no member of any royal household who takes the duties of royalty so seriously, or who works harder at what is perhaps the most exacting job in the world.

Queen Mary may be said to be a real Londoner. She was born on the stroke of midnight, May 26, 1867, in Kensington Palace, in a room which had been the nursery of Queen Victoria. She is descended from Adolphus, Duke of Cambridge, the seventh son of George III., who married the Princess Augusta, the daughter of the Landgrave of Hesse. The Queen's mother, the Princess Marie Adelaide, was the second daughter of the Duke of Cambridge, and therefore the cousin and a contemporary of

Queen Victoria, but some fourteen years her junior.

At her baptism by the Archbishop of Canterbury, she was given a garland of names—Victoria Mary Augusta Louisa Olga Pauline Claudine Agnes—only to have them all reduced to May, the name by which she was affectionately known long before she came to the Throne.

"A pretty child she was, with fair hair and blue eyes—very English looking," the Palace gatekeeper's wife said of her, remembering the child who was so inquisitive about the names of the flowers in the garden.

Princess May, as the future Queen Mary was known, had three brothers. At the time the Teck family were by no means wealthy. Because of a financial crisis they had to economise drastically. After a time Kensington Palace had to be given up, and then a period of exile in Italy was found necessary. For some eighteen months the Princess May studied in Florence under an Italian governess and had lessons from a painting master.

It was a time when women were emerging from their almost harem-like seclusion and acting and thinking for themselves. A quiet, sure revolution, with none of the hysterics and sensationalism which later was to be embodied in the Suffragette movement in Britain. Princess May was eager to develop her mental and intellectual qualities. She displayed an eager desire for knowledge. Helped by her Alsatian governess, Madame Bricka, she began a self-imposed task of six hours' serious reading each day. This decision was made in 1886, the year when she was seen on her appearance as a debutante.

Bricka, the Alsatian governess, was a

dominating character. She taught her young charge the importance of differentiating between the trivial and the important. The Empire owes much to that passionate, resolute, dark Alsatian woman, for Madame Bricka may be said to have moulded the character of our Queen.

Queen Mary has known what it is to be poor—really poor. When her father and mother lived at White Lodge, Richmond, they could not afford a carriage. Because it was the Victorian age and they were royalty, they had to have one. And so economies of the most stringent nature were absolutely necessary inside the house.

But Queen Victoria, with her passion for arranging the affairs of the House of Windsor, had already decided that Princess May should enter the royal circle. Under the watchful eye of the great Queen the young princess was encouraged to be studious, serious, and sedate. She was taught to read well and speak well.

Rumour said that she was shy and retiring, a contrast to the kindly, beloved, bustling Duchess of Teck, whom she often accompanied on philanthropic errands to the poor. She learnt the businesslike running of a household, getting a first-hand knowledge of that domestic art known as " making both ends meet."

Besides her course of serious reading, the future Queen studied music under Tosti, who found her an apt and amenable pupil. Her voice was a sweet but light soprano, which was unfortunately never heard outside the family circle.

But despite her life on the Continent and the opportunities she had of meeting many famous people, Princess May lived a life much different from that of the modern young woman on the Conti-

nent, drifting from Le Touquet to the Lido in a luxury cocktail tour. Her life was one of almost strict retirement.

This failure to extend her early circle of acquaintances may be due to the fact that all her life the Queen has not made friends easily. One of her best-informed biographers says: "In a less exalted circle, with fewer opportunities of coming into contact with every possible variety of temperament, she would probably have been a very lonely woman, but once she makes a friend, the friendship is a steadfast and enduring affection; she does not invite confidences, but in time of trouble she is a staunch and loyal supporter of those who have claims upon her."

Both Queen Victoria and the Princess of Wales (afterwards Queen Alexandra) developed a great affection and profound admiration for the reserved and beautiful daughter of the gay and debonair Duchess of Teck. She seemed marked out for greatness, and her engagement to the Duke of Clarence, the second in succession to the Throne, was received with no surprise, and, indeed, immense public enthusiasm.

This betrothal was announced in November, 1891. Then came the tragedy. The Duke died five weeks before the date of the wedding. Prince George, still convalescent from his own illness, became the heir-presumptive to the Throne.

The untimely death of the handsome young prince was looked upon as a national calamity. To Princess May it was a terrible blow. After the funeral she fled with her parents to White Lodge, Richmond, where she could think in quietness of the future and what it might have in store. Later she went to France with her mother to get over the blow. At the same time she did not forget the Princess of Wales, who was genuinely overcome with grief and sorrow over the death of her eldest son, for whom she had the deepest affection.

But, many months later, it was rumoured that Prince George was now paying court to the popular princess. There came the occasion when a family council was held at Windsor Castle to discuss the proposed marriage of Princess May and Prince George. Queen Victoria presided, and some shrewd comments were made by the subsequent King Edward VII.

Perhaps the preliminary tragedy of the death of the Duke of Clarence overshadowed and to some extent prevented the romantic courtship which the public delights upon in royal engagements. Nevertheless, when the future King asked her hand in marriage, Princess May replied: "I shall do my best to make you happy."

It cannot be said that she has failed. She has made herself the most dignified Queen in Europe, respected throughout the world. And her unswerving loyalty to England and its future has endeared her to all in the land.

There was genuine delight throughout the country when it was announced that the "Sailor Prince" had "made his own choice" and was to marry Princess May, a daughter of England. The engagement brought the congratulations of the Empire.

The Times expressed the popular feeling by saying: "We have the satisfaction of making the announcement for which the public will not be wholly unprepared. The understanding so long reported to exist between the Duke of York and Princess May has now taken

the form of a definite betrothal, which has received the ready sanction of Her Majesty the Queen. We are certain that this intelligence will be received with sincere gratification.

"In the peculiar circumstances attending such a union, there must perforce be present in every mind a certain conflict of emotions. But the predominant feeling, now that a sufficient interval has elapsed since the melancholy death of the Duke of Clarence, will be that this betrothal accords with the fitness of things, and, so far from offending any legitimate sentiment, is the most appropriate and delicate medicament for the wound, in its nature, never wholly ineffaceable. There is even ground for hoping that a union rooted in painful memories may prove happy beyond the common lot. The persons of both parties are such as to attract sympathy. On the one hand, the Duke of York enjoys not only the popularity attaching to the Navy, but also a personal good will, founded on his own frank and manly bearing on the occasions when he has come before the public. The Princess May is endeared to the public by her personal charm and her amiable disposition, by the memory of her bereavement, and still more by the devotion she displayed at that trying juncture. . . ."

King Edward took control of the wedding arrangements, though they had, of course, to be approved by Queen Victoria. King Edward was a first-rate hand at arranging big ceremonials and enjoyed it.

The wedding ceremony was a splendid affair at the Chapel Royal, St. James's. Queen Victoria attended in full state, and every nation in the world sent either its monarch or heir to the

DO YOU REMEMBER THESE FASHIONS FOR SPORTSWOMEN? *It is hard to believe that less than twenty-five years ago women competitors in the Olympic Games were hampered by such voluminous garments. Compare them with the modern sports styles in other parts of this volume.*

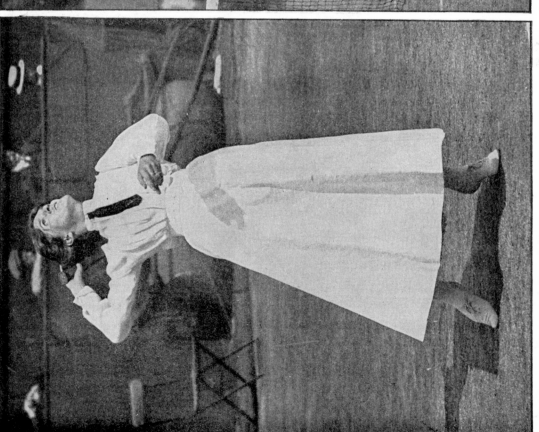

WHEN MRS. LAMBERT CHAMBERS *won the Ladies' Championship at Wimbledon before the war, her movements were hampered by prevailing fashions. Compare them with the simplicity and levity of the tennis girl's "shorts" in 1934. The player on the right is Mrs. Fearnley-Whittingstall, a pioneer of the new fashion.*

throne to do honour to the future King and Queen of England.

The Duke of Teck gave away his daughter. From the organ came the wedding march from *Lohengrin*. The Archbishop of Canterbury performed the ceremony, and Princess May had become the Duchess of York. At the end of it all a lone figure was seen leaning over a balcony railing in St. James's Palace, smoking a cigarette and looking rather forlorn. It was the Duke of Teck, father of the future Queen of England.

V

Once married, the Royal couple settled down to a life of quiet domesticity which, at the time, both desired, and which is still their desire to-day.

York House, in St. James's Palace, was a convenient and handsome residence in town, and York Cottage, if hardly a "stately domain," was sufficiently near to Sandringham House to be a welcome residence in Norfolk. It had served hitherto as an "overflow" annexe for those bachelor guests King Edward liked to have about him; but now it was to become rather a nursery than a guest house . . . so that, as Sir George Arthur has told us, our King ultimately was moved to exclaim: "I shall soon have a regiment, not a family."

The present Prince of Wales was born at White Lodge. The patron saints of England, Scotland, Ireland, and Wales were evoked at the baptism of the infant, who was destined to be the twentieth Prince of Wales, and for the first time in history a Queen Regnant held in her arms her descendant in the fourth generation.

It was little wonder that the birth of Edward Albert Christian George Andrew Patrick David was hailed with joy. Not since Tudor times, when Jane Seymour presented Henry VIII. with the sickly infant who was to become Edward VI., had an heir to the Throne been born in England of parents who gloried in their English birth.

The baptism was held in the Private Chapel at Windsor and was highly ceremonious. "Frock dress"—that is, knee-breeches and silk stockings, a uniform created by Prince Albert—was prescribed. The members of the Royal Family were gathered in force. Also many distinguished foreign guests. The Archbishop of Canterbury received the infant Prince, who, if carried by his nurse, was already attended by the Countess of Macclesfield. And a special choir broke into a chorale composed by the Prince Consort. "A trifle inappropriate," says Sir George Arthur, quoting the words:

In Life's gay morn, ere sprightly youth By vice and folly is enslaved.

Apropos this baptism, we have recently had the story given by Lord Esher, Constable of Windsor. Lord Esher once sat next the future King George at dinner on the Royal yacht.

"He (George) mentioned a queer prophecy which he made me promise I would not repeat to the King (Edward), who is rather influenced by these old women's tales. Someone, about forty years ago, said of the late Queen that she would have a long and glorious reign, the longest and most glorious of all the English sovereigns; that she would be succeeded by two Kings who would have short reigns, and by a third whose name would be David, and whose name would be as glorious as hers. One of Prince Edward's names is David!

"When Lady Waterford was dying she sent for the Prince of Wales and implored him to call his then unborn son David, as she had some fad about restoring the Jews to the Holy City. To humour her, he consented, and Prince Edward was given the names of the four patron saints of England, Scotland, Ireland, and Wales—*i.e.*, George, Andrew, Patrick, David."

And that prophecy was twenty years or more before the British themselves went to Palestine!

Other children arrived. Five of Queen Mary's six children were born at York Cottage. And the future Queen Mary soon revealed herself as a devoted mother. She did her utmost to implant in her children her own love of reading and serious interest in art and literature. The Duke of York, however, seems to be the only one of her children who developed the studious habits of his mother.

This younger generation of the House of Hanover, as it was then, interested Lord Esher. He wrote in his diary:

"I was amused to-day by taking the Wales children, two boys and a girl, to the Abbey. They climbed on to every tomb and got very dirty, but were thoroughly happy. . . . Prince Edward remarked of the Duke of Buckingham that he was a 'wicked man,' and when I asked why, he said he gave bad advice to Charles I. He knew that Buckingham had been murdered at Portsmouth by Felton. I think he must have been reading Dumas!"

"The girl," of course, was Princess Mary, now Countess of Harewood.

Lord Esher could not help comparing "the boys" with each other. "The second boy," he wrote, "is the sharpest"—a nice compliment to the Duke of York—"but there is something rather taking about Prince Edward. He wants a walking-stick with a horse's head on it for his birthday."

The end of the great Queen Victoria was near. She was 80, and tired of all the pomp and circumstance. She excused herself from meeting her ministers. They would argue with her, and she would say, "You know I cannot any longer argue." Even her secretaries were kept at a distance. Ladies-in-waiting read the papers to her and brought down messages from her room which led to "complications."

She made a brave fight of it. At Netley Hospital there were two wounded soldiers to be decorated with the Victoria Cross. They were "sitting in chairs," and when the Queen was wheeled in "they were ordered to rise." But the Queen said, "Most certainly not." Without help—"a very unusual thing"—she raised herself "and stood over them while she decorated them."

*　　*　　*　　*　　*

So we come to the final drama, which must be described in Lord Esher's own words. This historic passage is as follows:

"The dying scene was stately and dramatic. The Queen now and then recognised those about her and spoke their names. Her difficulty in breathing was the only painful symptom. Reid—the doctor—passed his arm around her and supported her.

"The King knelt at the side of the bed. The German Emperor stood silently at the head, near the Queen. The other children and grandchildren were there, all calling their names to her

THE HEART OF THE
BRITISH EMPIRE,
1910-1934.

*Piccadilly Circus has always been the heart of London, and is remembered with affection
throughout the Empire. But even the Circus has changed with the times. Practically the
only old landmark that remains is Eros, and even that has had a chequered career.*

REGENT STREET,
1910-1934.

Remarkable changes have taken place in London's main shopping street. It was almost entirely rebuilt soon after the war.

at intervals. She died quite peacefully. After the King had left for London the Emperor took charge of everything, so unlike what was expected of him.

"He refused to allow Banting's men (the undertakers) to measure the Queen for her shell. He turned them out of the room. He sent for Reid, and took all the measurements himself. He and the King and the Duke of Connaught lifted the Queen into her coffin.

"The day before her death, while the Prince of Wales was in the house, but not allowed to go near the Queen for fear of alarming her, she said: 'The Prince of Wales will be sorry to hear how ill I am. Do you think he ought to be told?' Another thing she said was: 'I don't want to die yet. There are several things I want to arrange.'"

So ended the greatest reign in English history, and for a time all was confusion. People who ought to have known had forgotten the precedents to be followed.

At Windsor, Esher would see the Indian attendants of the dead Queen no longer "statuesque," but "wandering about like uneasy spirits"—and, if we may add a few details to the picture, what a housecleaning there had to be! An Oriental trophy in the Waterloo Gallery was touched—out flew a cloud of moths, and the trophy had to be burned in the courtyard. Tons of ivory, delivered as tribute by an African chief, were rotting in an attic. Huge supplies of plates with royal portraits on them, which had been intended to be given away as presents, were quietly disposed of. An immense paraphernalia of illuminated addresses, silver trowels, and other gifts had to be quietly obliterated. Lord Esher felt the change from "the mystery and awe of the old court."

"Somehow," he wrote, "the sanctity of the Throne has disappeared." Dinner was served in the Edwardian style—not in the oak dining-room, but in a room all white—and "the quiet impressive entrance of the Queen into the corridor is as obsolete as Queen Elizabeth." Guests assembled in the green drawing-room and King Edward just walked in.

With King Edward's accession to the Throne a great change came to the household of Prince George and Mary. The real training of Prince George for the Kingship, which was to follow, now began.

Raised to the peerage as Duke of York, he was introduced in the House of Lords by his father. It was at that time he began the study of matters more closely related to the high office to which he was ultimately to be called—the working of the English Constitution and the various departments of public life—and he did it, as is his manner, with quiet, unostentatious, and thorough diligence.

During the ten years of the reign of King Edward, he was, as Prince of Wales, the companion and coadjutor of his father in the business of government. This was an experience which few Kings of England have had, although to-day the Prince of Wales does not hesitate to shoulder such burdens of State as come his way, and since the illness of King George, has relieved him of many tiring ceremonial duties.

The newly married couple, the Duke and Duchess of York, began an Empire tour soon after King Edward's accession to the Throne. The tour embraced India, Australia, New Zealand, South Africa, and Canada. They travelled over 50,000 miles, of which 38,000 were at sea.

Everywhere the Royal couple received a rapturous welcome. The moving experiences of a lifetime were packed into brief months. The Duke opened the first Parliament of Federated Australia at Melbourne; in New Zealand Maoris danced the War Poi-Poi dance before him and the Duchess; they ate the regulation lumberman's meal of soup, pork, beans, and hot, milkless tea, served in tin plates in a "combose" or lumberman's hut in Canada.

In a word, they entered thoroughly into almost every phase of Imperial life.

A pleasant musical incident occurred when the degree of LL.D. was conferred on the Duke at the Sydney University. The proceedings, as usual on these occasions, were uproarious, and the formalities preceding the presentation of degrees were more or less smothered by the singing of a special "anthem" composed for the occasion. It went to the tune of "A Life on the Ocean Wave," and the chorus ran thus:

> *Let every man with a voice*
> *His power of lung display;*
> *Yell loudly and rejoice,*
> *For the Jook is coming to-day;*
> *The Jook—the Jook—the Jook is coming*
> *to-day.*
> *The Jook—the Jook—the Jook is coming*
> *to-day.*

This breezy number amused the "Jook" very much.

During the *Ophir* tour the Duke shook hands with thirty-five thousand people, delivered nearly one hundred speeches, and distributed one hundred and forty titles. The brain reels at this endless procession of civic receptions, laying of foundation stones, opening of buildings, and other functions. But the Duke went through it all with a cheery smile and a kind word for everyone.

It was on his return home in March, 1902, that the Duke was made Prince of Wales. Speaking at a luncheon given at the Guildhall by the Lord Mayor and Corporation, he said:

"If I were asked to specify any particular impressions derived from our tour I should unhesitatingly place before all others those of loyalty to the Crown and attachment to the old country."

It was on this occasion that he delivered a memorable exhortation: "Wake up, England!" It was a call for settlers for the "boundless tracts of country yet unexplored, hidden mineral wealth calling for development; vast expanses of virgin soil ready to yield profitable crops."

But Destiny was hurrying on apace. Came that day in May, 1910, when King Edward realised that his reign was at an end. The eyes of the world, and particularly of England, were centred upon his son Prince George. And the future Queen Mary was with her husband in those dark hours which saw the end of one reign and the beginning of another.

And so they stood beside a dead king, these characters who were on the stage for twenty-five years of incredible and dramatic happenings. Not even the shrewd King Edward realised the cataclysm that these twenty-five years were to see upthrust. And even those who gathered about the death-bed of the King might well have quailed at the task before them if they had but known.

ENGLAND IN 1910

I

THE year 1910, twelve months before the official Coronation of King George V., opened ominously for royalty. There arrived on these shores the first of those royal exiles, the first king to lose his throne in an era that was to see half the thrones of Europe totter and fall.

Revolution had broken out in Portugal. As usual, the first act of the revolutionaries was to cut the cable between Lisbon and England, and for some days no news came through. Nobody could say what had happened to the young King Manoel, although it was rumoured he had escaped. Pessimists, however, recalled that two years previously King Carlos and the Crown Prince of Portugal had been shot while driving through the streets of Lisbon. It seemed certain that a similar fate awaited the young King Manoel at the hands of the desperate revolutionaries.

But in a few days the veil of silence was lifted. The special correspondents of the newspapers who had reached Lisbon began to send their dramatic messages. It was then learned that the secret, revolutionary societies had planned a *coup d'état* and been successful. King Manoel had escaped from the palace and been taken aboard a British warship.

By the time Manoel reached England it was obvious that Portugal intended to be a Republic. There was practically no chance of regaining the throne. Manoel accepted the situation philosophically. He settled down to the life of a country gentleman in England, with an income that caused him no immediate worries. He appeared in Mayfair, attended many public ceremonies, and in his later years was able to watch the debacle of the Great War sweeping over Europe and carrying with it many a royal throne.

But the new King of England was faced with a revolution which was taking place in the political world bounded by Westminster. It was the long constitutional battle between the House of Lords and the House of Commons, now coming to a head. The struggle had reached its intensity with the Budget of 1909. Mr. Asquith, as Prime Minister, warned the House of Lords that if the Budget was rejected he would demand Royal authority for a sufficient creation of peers to make the passing of Government Bills a certainty.

The death of King Edward had shaken the protagonists in this duel. Was there not then possibility of compromise? Men gossiped of what might well have happened if the King had lived and again called the leaders to conference. There was at any rate this ground for such speculation, that King

Edward was fairly well known to have used what influence he could within his marked discretion to prevent the precipitation, by the rejection of the Budget, of a struggle which he deplored as bad politics.

There was a distinct sigh of relief throughout the country when it was announced that a conference was to meet, composed of Mr. Asquith, Lord Crewe, Mr. Lloyd George, and Mr. Birrell on the one side, and Mr. Balfour, Lord Lansdowne, Lord Cawdor, and Mr. Austen Chamberlain on the other. It began its meetings in June.

At the same time there was a sudden demand throughout the country for prison reform. Critics of the system were suggesting that our prisons were still in the torturous atmosphere of the Middle Ages. Worst of all was the solitary confinement system.

This growing criticism was helped by the staging of a new play by John Galsworthy. The play, *Justice*, depicted a clerk condemned to solitary confinement. The wordless scene in which he is alone in his cell, pacing to and fro, and suddenly flings himself at the door, pounding madly with his fists, gave a thrill of horror to the well-dressed audience that filled the theatre nightly. The climax of the play, in which the convict on ticket-of-leave kills himself in sheer despair, added to the moral urgency of the theme.

Mr. Winston Churchill was Home Secretary at the time. He faced the clamour, and agreed that reform was necessary. He admitted, too, that Mr. Galsworthy's picture was not overdrawn, and that he had himself been moved by seeing the play. As a result, there began that series of reforms in prison life which have now reached a decent, humanitarian stage. Lectures and concerts were begun in prisons. The Borstal system was extended by the opening of a new institution at Feltham.

Wireless, too, came to the public notice in a sensational fashion. For some days police and Press had been indulging in a great manhunt for a missing Dr. Crippen, the murdered remains of whose wife had been discovered in the cellar of a house in Camden Town. This may be said to be the first occasion on which the Press entered upon a murder hunt in the full clamour of startling headlines and graphic, if gruesome, details.

But it was wireless that brought the hunted man to justice. The newspapers published the amazing news that the captain of a steamer on the way to Canada had sent a wireless message stating that he believed the missing man and his companion were on board. With their usual enterprise the *Daily Mail* began a series of wireless day-by-day stories with the captain of the ship, giving details of the daily life aboard of the couple. At the same time a Scotland Yard detective hurried by a faster steamer to Canada to head off the fugitives. Oblivious of the newspaper clamour and the cackling wireless above their heads, the couple believed themselves safe from detection.

Crippen was arrested and condemned to death. But the sordid details of the crime were lost in the public's dawning appreciation of the dramatic importance that wireless was going to play in their lives. For the moment broadcasting was unknown, although such brilliant brains as Marconi were toying with the idea. Wireless in 1910 was just a series of faint Morse messages between ships, likely to be useful in case of impending

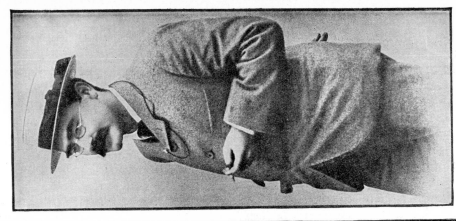

RUDYARD KIPLING *was the great literary figure of the day. His short stories and poems about the Empire appealed strongly to the Imperialists.*

LILY ELSIE *was at this time toasted as Britain's most beautiful actress.*

THE FIRST ALEXANDRA ROSE DAY, *inaugurated by Queen Alexandra, was held on June 21, 1912. This flag day is still maintained.*

disaster. It was a safety invention, with a dominant S.O.S. *motif*.

For the most part, however, England, and London in particular, found itself comfortable, rich, and secure. The Edwardian age had seen gay and frolicsome parties. They would continue into the reign of the new King. The world looked good to the middle-aged of those days. The Empire was prosperous. True, there were mutterings beneath the surface. The trades union movement was making itself felt, and entering the Law Courts to contest charges of illegality. A lean caballero in frock coat and top-hat, Mr. Cunninghame Graham stood on the plinth in Trafalgar Square and talked to workless men of the benefits of Socialism. And strange, strident women were appearing with an unreasonable demand for the vote. "Suffragettes" they were called, contemptuously.

But the solid Londoner ignored these storm mutterings. He was being driven with his family in one of the new-fangled taxicabs to His Majesty's Theatre in the Haymarket, where Sir Herbert Tree was displaying a lavish production of *Henry VIII*. But not "The Private Life of Henry VIII." It was Shakespeare's rather tame history made flamboyant and exciting by one of the most colourful theatrical figures that ever walked the London stage.

Musical comedy, too, essentially an English product, was at the height of its glory. *The Merry Widow* waltz and hat had swept the country, and the latest production of Oscar Strauss, *The Chocolate Soldier*, was then being performed for the first time.

It was the day of Lily Elsie and Gertie Millar. Their smiling faces stared at adoring youth from the glazed picture-postcards, the collection of which was the craze of the moment. When the English composer, Lionel Monckton, produced *The Quaker Girl* at the Adelphi with his wife, Gertie Millar, now the Countess of Dudley, in the leading part, the whole of London and the provinces flocked to hear the tuneful music and cheer the beauty of the Quaker Girl herself.

Daly's Theatre, the real home of musical comedy, countered with *The Dollar Princess*. Lily Elsie played the lead in this production, and began that series of tremendous successes which continued up to the days of the Great War.

For those who demanded even lighter entertainment there was a huge clown, with white face and pierrot's costume, one Pélissier, who presented his group known as "The Follies." They acted in farcical fashion a series of "Potted Plays." One first-night reception was hardly successful. The audience booed loudly at the fall of the curtain. But the curtain went up again to reveal the bulky Pélissier booing back at the audience.

And the first Russian ballets were exciting London. It was the time when Pavlova could be seen sinking gracefully to the stage, a lovely dying swan, to the music of Saint-Saëns. Mayfair, too, was being shocked in drawing-rooms by the dancing of Maud Allen, whose dramatic interpretation of *Salomé* raised a theatrical storm of the first order.

The cinema was practically unknown. Electricity was only just taking the place of gas for footlights. Eros, in Piccadilly Circus, stood on solid earth and not upon a series of lighted caves where electric trains rumbled. The West End was a luxury city. The clubs in Pall

Mall were the most exclusive in the world. To walk along Piccadilly was to feel oneself in the finest street of the greatest city in the world.

But the real home of entertainment for the people was the music-hall. It was, at the moment, freeing itself from that public-house atmosphere in which it really began. Its songs and people were racy and of the soil. It scorned the pretentiousness in life, and laughed at its own vulgarity, at its mothers-in-law, its West End drinks, its marital adventurers.

These were the days of giants in the music-hall. Cinquevalli, the greatest genius in balancing billiard balls and even billiard tables that the world has ever seen. It was the day of great tricksters on the stage. Chung Ling Soo, that almond-eyed, pigtailed conjurer who in reality hailed from Lancashire. The great Lafayette, the mammoth illusionist to whom, even in these days of mammoth shows, Mr. Bertram Mills might respectfully doff his hat. Twice nightly, and sometimes thrice nightly, these self-styled "artistes" amused the working world of England from Tyneside to Shoreditch.

It was the era of great comedians. George Formby, the consumptive lad from Lancashire. What a shout of laughter would rise as the sour-faced, rough-voiced comedian in the check suit too small for him staggered on the stage and nodded to "George" the conductor. And when he burst into that dry tremolo song:

"*I was standing at the corner of the street . . .*"

there would be thunderous applause at the finish.

Another northern comedian, Harry Weldon, had his own enthusiastic audience. Harry Weldon keeping goal! Stiffy, a football fool in a million. And Stiffy, the boxer, introduced by his comic manager, offering to fight " . . . any lady . . . any lady?" If a member of the audience showed a disposition to tackle the fighter on the stage, Stiffy would implore his manager to "tell 'em what I did to Colin Bell!" Thus, many a second encounter was avoided.

It was the day, too, when Harry Tate's moustache, twisting across his face, was becoming known to millions. The fishing episode, the motoring catastrophe— they rocked with laughter, those glittering halls, from the Five Towns to the sweaty atmosphere of Glasgow music-halls.

"Harry" was a generous name among comedians of that time. Harry Lauder was then emerging from his life as a miner to the top-liner in music-hall bills all over the Empire. But what the Empire in Leicester Square enjoyed to-day, the Empire beyond the sea would enjoy to-morrow. That crooked, knobby stick carried by the crooked, knobby figure of the man in tartan plaid, the raucous Scottish voice rolling forth:

"*Oh, stop yer ticklin', Jock!*"

even a wilderness of modern talkie films could not give the same zest as the audiences in those days received.

And the women of the music-halls! Can their like be found in the flat-chested sylphs of to-day's musical films? For the most part they were generous in figure, even if they only displayed legs as "principal boys" in Christmas pantomime. They had the hearts of millions of Englishmen before Mae West.

Chief among them was Marie Lloyd. Born at Hoxton, she staggered beneath the names of Matilda Alice Victoria. But to all the Cockney world until she died she was Marie Lloyd. Her two greatest songs, perhaps, which achieved world-wide renown for her are: "I'm One of the Ruins that Cromwell knocked abaht a Bit," and another whose chorus ran:

> "My old man
> Said 'Follow the van,
> Don't dilly-dally on the w'y!'
> Orf went the van
> With the old man in it;
> I walked behind
> With my old cock linnet.
> I dallied and dillied,
> And dillied and dallied,
> Lorst my w'y and don't know
>   where to roam,
> 'Cos you can't trust the speshuls
>   like the old-time coppers,
> When you can't find your way
>   home."

Marie Lloyd was at her zenith in these early Georgian days. At the time when the Oxford, London Pavilion, and Tivoli were the leading music-halls in London, Marie would be appearing at all three, booked for months on end. Her times would be:

Oxford	... ...	9.40
Pavilion	... ...	10.10
Tivoli	... ...	10.35

Her admirers used to go from one hall to the other to enjoy over and over again a performance which was frequently identical. These houses were one-show-a-night halls, and she used to fit in a suburban music-hall as well.

Marie Lloyd was three times married, "with varying unhappiness." During the Great War she sang again and again to wounded men, and brought some little brightness into those drab and tragic days.

Her own end was in itself a stage tragedy. She collapsed on the stage of the Edmonton Empire while singing her character song: "I'm One of the Ruins that Cromwell knocked abaht a Bit." When she swayed about on the stage in the song the audience thought she was realistically imitating a drunken woman; but actually she could have had little idea of what she was doing.

Perhaps the finest tribute to her art is that by Mr. James Agate, the famous dramatic critic.

"When in the Tottenham Court Road I saw, tucked under the newsboy's arm, the sheet which announced that Marie Lloyd was dead," he wrote, "everything around me became still. The street lost its hubbub, and for a space I was alone with a personal sorrow. . . .

"'Marie'—pronounced with the broad vowel beloved of the Cockney—was in everybody's mouth that day, in club and barrack-room, in bar parlour and in modest home. On the high seas 'Marie's dead' would be droned from ship to ship. Returning from Kempton a party of bookmakers fell to speaking of the dead artist. One said, with tears in his eyes, 'She had a heart, had Marie!' 'The size of Waterloo Station,' another rejoined.

"Her abounding generosity was a commonplace of the profession. She would go down to Hoxton, where she was born and make lavish distribution to the street-urchins of boots and shoes which she fitted with her own hands. She had numberless pensioners dependent upon her charity. She earned some two hundred thousand pounds and gave it all away. 'God rest her,' said the bookmaker who had first spoken, and

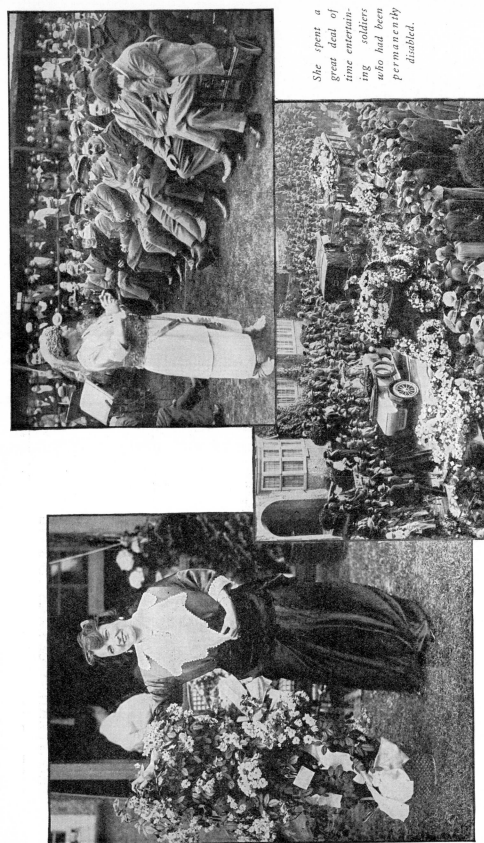

She spent a great deal of time entertaining soldiers who had been permanently disabled.

DEATH OF MARIE LLOYD.

The death of Marie Lloyd, the great Cockney comedienne, on October 7, 1922, came as a great shock to the English people. She was only 52, and had been appearing on the stage for 37 years. Her most famous songs were "Oh, Mr. Porter, Whatever Shall I do?" and "I Do Like to be Beside the Seaside." Thousands of Londoners were present at her funeral.

The companies agreed to call in all their old films and burn them. Then they began afresh on the present renting system. The photograph above shows a bonfire of Selig films.

Film producers in the early days had stock companies of actors. Films were made in the open, and the Essanay Company even had a special train for location purposes.

Photos: By courtesy of Will Day, Esq.

bared his head. That night, at Black-friars Ring, a bruiser with the marks of many fights declared: "We shan't none of us see the likes o' Marie again. She wur a great artist! . . ."

What a contrast to the Hollywood film stars of today! These artists of the old music-hall were flesh and blood, not creatures in a shadow-show or enticing covers to film fan magazines. They lived among the people, and made the people laugh and cry.

So one of the same group was Vesta Tilley, the first great female impersonator. In those days she was strutting the stage in male evening-dress, topper at the back of her close-cropped head, and singing about the Johnnies of the West End. There was Happy Fanny Fields, a Dutch girl in wooden clogs and with an infectious laugh.

The films, in fact, had hardly begun in those days. True, on the music-hall stage of the time was a little Cockney boy from Walworth, who sang with the Eight Lancashire Lads, and later on acted with the comedians who did acrobatic feats in Fred Karno's sketch, *The Mumming Birds*. His name was Charles Spencer Chaplin, and few people dreamed that in a few years he would be the most celebrated shadow comedian in the history of the world.

The only pictures which the public saw were those little boxes on pedestals in derelict shops. The box was called a mutoscope, and those who slipped a penny in the slot and looked through the slot could see a number of photographs whirled round so rapidly that the figures in the photographs appeared to be moving.

"The novelty of the mutoscope," writes Mr. St. John Ervine, "did not make it popular except among youths like myself, who, profoundly stirred by the information that if they dropped a penny in the slot they would see moving pictures of a young lady undressing, squandered large sums on disappointing exhibitions. For immediately after the lady had removed her blouse the light went out. Hollywood has learnt a lot since the days of the mutoscope."

Nevertheless, moving-pictures had definitely arrived. There were strange, shed-like contraptions fitted out like railway coaches. Seated inside the audience were given a photographic representation of a railway journey, and to add to the effect the coach was jolted slightly.

And, in the wilds of Twickenham, Chrissie White and Henry Edwards were already Britain's first film stars, producing a series of comedies which might to-day provoke mirth of another kind. But for the most part, no one paid attention to the queer people who were busy with moving-pictures, except, on occasions, to complain of their disastrous activities; for on January 11, 1908, there was a panic at a cinematograph exhibition in Barnsley, and sixteen children were killed, and two days later a cinematograph exploded at Boyestown, Pennsylvania, and more than 160 persons were killed.

The legitimate theatre was still triumphing, though a tremendous revolution was taking place there. The old theatrical stars who were content with any sort of play, providing that it gave them a good rousing theatrical speech and plenty of limelight, found themselves confronted by a group of playwrights with extraordinary ideas on what constituted a play.

It had all begun with a fellow named Ibsen, a Scandinavian who wrote most depressing plays. Modern playwrights were actually enthusiastic about Ibsen, and insisted upon writing plays in the same manner. Pinero, Henry Arthur Jones, Bernard Shaw, J. M. Barrie, John Galsworthy, and Harley Granville-Barker were calmly insisting that their plays were the plays of the future. Moreover, they were actually introducing bedsteads on to the stage, and not for farcical reasons either. Old "laddies" meeting at the Bodega shook their heads and declared that the theatre was "going to the dogs, old boy."

There was a night when a gentleman under the influence of liquor lurched into the Theatre Royal in Dublin during the performance of a play by Mr. Shaw. He sat, in some dismay, through three acts, and then, unable to bear the play any longer, cried out in a voice husky with drink and indignation, "D'you call this a play? Lasht time I was here I saw a fat fella and a tall, thin fella slapping him in the stummick wid a walkin' stick. That was a grand play. . . ."

None of these fierce critics and public protesters realised that somewhere in the sunshine wastes of California a group of men were getting together, who, with their cameras and their shadow artists, would completely transform the entertainment tastes of the world.

II

Another new era was opening, this time in the sky. Adventurous men in Norfolk jackets were attempting queer things in the air with glorified kites.

True, the public had heard of these things, but they were not taken too seriously. The Americans, Wilbur Wright and his brother, had been experimenting with their flying machines in France.

The Wrights were the real pioneers of flight. Their machine was, of course, made at Dayton, Ohio. It was a biplane with, in front, two small planes which served as elevator control, and two vertical planes behind for rudder. Its four-cylinder engine was of twenty-four horse-power, and was connected by chains to two wooden propellers.

It was not fashioned on wheels, as is the 'plane of to-day, but on skids like a sleigh, so that after each flight it had to be dragged back to an odd-looking device of spring-boards with a super catapult attachment. Then at the proper moment, with engine running, the 'plane all set and Wright aboard, the lever was pulled, the catapult did its job, and up went the 'plane.

But flying was already being discussed with enthusiasm by a little group in England. Very soon actual flights were being made. And, as seems natural in this country, the pioneer aviators started by breaking the law.

As recently as 1909 it was a punishable offence to fly, or rather to attempt to do so, except within certain hours. When in that year Mr. A. V. Roe, later Sir Alliott Roe, made his first flight he was followed ruthlessly by the police, who took his name and address. Before the case could come to court, however, the law was dramatically amended by M. Bleriot's flight across the Channel.

The twenty-fifth anniversary of this sensational flight was recently celebrated by the flight of a young Englishman across the Channel upside down. But Bleriot himself is still alive and the story of his flight is still an amazing adventure.

"One fine morning I took off from the village of Sangalle on the cliffs of Picardy at dawn," says Bleriot. "There

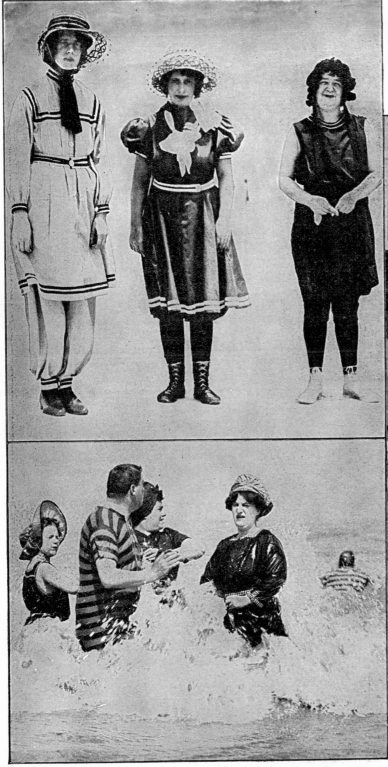

THE
LATEST STYLE.

*Bathing costumes are characteristic of the changed conditions. In 1910
you dressed to enter the sea. To-day costumes are designed to be as
brief as possible to make sun-bathing benefit the entire body.*

4

There has been little change in golfing fashions for women since 1910. The only difference until recently was styles. Now, however, trousers for women have invaded the golf course.

was hardly any wind. I had no compass, meteorology was not organised as is the case to-day, to supply aviators with essential information, and I had to steer by sight. The engine revolved regularly and without knocking. During the first minutes I saw behind me the white track of the torpedo-boat destroyer which Latham had lent me and which was trying to follow me in order to render assistance in case of need. But the boat went much less quickly than I, and I soon lost sight of her.

"Everything went smoothly, visibility was perfect and I had just caught sight of the cliffs of Dover when I was suddenly enveloped in fog. A most uncomfortable ten minutes followed. I was out of sight of the French coast and the English coast was still a long way off. If I should fall into the sea—which was extremely likely—I did not think I could get out again, as I was still a cripple as the result of a crash at Douai a few weeks before.

"In the fog I had drifted north of Dover, and had to fly in a wide circle to get back on my course. The morning mist dispersed; the sun shone brilliantly. Once more I saw the chalk cliffs flashing and the fields of the impregnable island. . . .

"Was victory assured?

"Three times I tried to land on the cliffs, and three times the machine refused to climb so high. I swung her round in desperation, happy to find that in spite of all that had been required of her she continued to throb regularly.

"At last I found a cliff near Dover lower than those which had defeated me before, and there I made an easy landing.

"The Channel was crossed."

The conquest of the English Channel by Bleriot brings us to the contentious subject with which I opened. Who was the first Englishman to fly? In 1908 an American, S. F. Cody, was making flights in England and soon A. V. Roe was doing likewise. In 1928 the Royal Aero Club tried to solve this problem. They appointed a committee to determine who was the first British subject to fly in a heavier-than-air machine in the British Isles.

After considering a variety of evidence, the committee decided that this distinction had been achieved by Lieut.-Col. J. T. C. Moore-Brabazon, at Leysdown, near Eastchurch in the Isle of Sheppey, between April 30 and May 2, 1909. On this occasion he flew a distance of between a quarter and half a mile at a height of from fifty to eighty feet.

The flights of A. V. Roe, made at Brooklands, were considered, but the committee decided that these were in the nature of hops and not official flights. Nevertheless, it was those early exploits of A. V. Roe that helped to build up the great industry of British aviation.

Among the other pioneers of those days in England were Handley-Page, Sopwith, de Havilland, Short and Blackburn. All of them helped in the development of British aviation and all have their machines flying the skyways of to-day.

It was the period, too, when the *Daily Mail*, under Lord Northcliffe's inspired guidance, began that series of gigantic money prizes for successful flights in this country. But for the most part the public were content to look up to the sky from the earth and not down at the earth from a machine. As an invention, the flying machine was considered too hazardous to be taken seriously.

There was the great race between London and Manchester, for the accomplishment of which within 24 hours the *Daily Mail* had offered £10,000. There were two serious competitors, Paulhan, a Frenchman, and our own Grahame-White.

There was a private agreement between the two airmen that they would give each other due notice when they were ready to start. But at six o'clock one evening Grahame-White learned that Paulhan had started from Hendon and got clear away with an hour's start.

Grahame-White determined to follow. Although the sun was setting and night flying in those days was an extremely hazardous business, the Englishman was not deterred. In a series of two exciting hops he reached the Midlands before midnight, his mother and sister following, desperately anxious, in a car. But at his second forced landing he learned that Paulhan had reached Manchester, and thereby won the £10,000 prize.

"The best man has won" was his sporting comment when the news came to him. Later Grahame-White with his aeroplanes was to make real history in the aviation world.

Not long after, these adventurous fellows of the air actually arranged an aviation meeting at Bournemouth in 1910. And the public shook its head sadly, but wisely, when the meeting was marred by the death of the Hon. C. S. Rolls, of the famous Rolls Royce car firm. This young man crashed in the sea.

The price paid by these early pioneers was high. There were thirty-three deaths during 1910, the total since the beginning of aviation being thus brought up to forty-two; sixty-five in 1911; ninety-five in 1912—the numbers mounted steadily. To the public, indeed, the progress of aeronautics was marked by a succession of spectacular feats of flight, punctuated by sudden death. To the inventor it was the gradual evolution of means to an end: the ultimate discovery of a machine which would combine all the requirements of an aerial conveyance with safety.

Flying over the sea at this time was considered a most daring feat; no one ever contemplated that the Atlantic could be flown. A fourth crossing of the Channel, this time by a Mr. Moisant, an American, and a flight by Robert Loraine, the actor, to Ireland in September, were enthusiastically described by the newspapers, as were also the facts that Loraine had flown on one occasion in a storm, and that another aviator had attained a speed in the air of some 75 to 95 miles an hour.

Airships, too, were still considered to be competing with aeroplanes for the future of flying. Mr. Willows flew a small dirigible from Cardiff to London, and later flew it round St. Paul's, by way of demonstrating its possibilities as a "one-man" rival to the 'plane.

In the meantime, an old man, by the name of Count Zeppelin, was experimenting in the construction of a rigid type of airship at Friedrichshafen on Lake Constance. Already four Zeppelins had been launched, the last perishing in flames as a result of being struck by lightning.

The disaster, in which happily no one was killed, seemed to have ended the experiments of the old inventor. To help him construct new airships subscriptions were raised all over the world. France, the United States, and Great

GRAHAME-WHITE *was one of Britain's pioneer airmen. He took part in the famous 1910 London to Manchester air race, which he lost, and later was to make history in the aviation world.*

Britain vied in generosity with his own country. Ironically, Britain did not realise that these same airships, over which the people were so enthusiastic, would in a few years be bombing London and the provincial towns.

But Count Zeppelin himself had fully realised the military value of his invention. He announced that he had placed his invention at the disposal of his own countrymen. The German Government presented him with a grant of half a million marks, and the subscriptions received from abroad were politely returned.

Further Zeppelins were built, each improved in various details and equipped with motors of greater power than its predecessor. So convincingly did they demonstrate the reliability of this type of aircraft that regular airship transport services were begun in Germany. At the time of the outbreak of the war in 1914 provincial airship travel was well established in that country.

But Britain was not entirely neglecting airships. Elongated balloons, not intended for long flights, but rather for surveying military operations, were being tested. The first British airship, built in 1907 at the Royal Aircraft Establishment at Farnborough, was of this type. Subsequently several other non-rigid airships were built or purchased by the Army authorities, but they were not very successful.

The *Beta*, a non-rigid airship of 35,000 cubic feet capacity, performed good work between 1910 and 1912 and on one of her flights flew from Farnborough to London and back.

The *Gamma* (capacity 75,000 cubic feet) had a speed of 28 miles an hour.

The *Delta,* also a non-rigid airship, with a capacity of 180,000 cubic feet, and a lifting force of 5½ tons, was completed in 1912. She was capable of a maximum speed of 45 miles an hour, with a range of 350 miles.

The *Delta* is notable for the fact that from it wireless telegraphy transmissions were successfully carried out, and on another occasion a parachute descent was safely accomplished.

The first rigid airship to be built in Great Britain was constructed in 1911 by Vickers, Ltd. It was built for the Admiralty, and was known variously as the *Mayfly*, and " Naval Airship No. 1." The *Mayfly* represented much thought and money, but its career was of short duration, for it was wrecked while being taken out of its hangar at Barrow-in-Furness.

And, as we shall see through the succeeding pages of this twenty-five years of history, ill-luck and terrible tragedy dogged all the British attempts in airship construction.

Nevertheless, in this year of 1910, men were beginning to lift their eyes to the skies; there were enthusiasts who envisaged the new air arm as the dominant factor in military and naval operations, while others saw the beginnings of air transport and passenger lines throughout the world. A great mechanical awakening, to which the pulses of men stirred.

But there was no doubt in the minds of the public regarding the great future of the motor-car. Although still a novelty on the English roads, supreme confidence had caused the building of Brooklands Track as early as 1906. Motor-racing was considered to be the great sport of the future.

It is strange to think that the familiar taxi-cab was not seen on the streets of London until 1904; and then there were only three of them, called motor-hansoms. Two had 12-horse-power Herald engines, and the third was a 6-horse-power single-cylinder De Dion. They were driven by cabmen specially trained for the work, and these men were required to bring in ten pounds a week. They sometimes made five pounds in a day. Officers going back to Aldershot were their special patrons.

The old hansom-drivers hated the new taxis. "Stinking steam-kettle" was the mildest term they used. The public, on the contrary, loved them, and they increased so rapidly that within four years there were two million pounds' worth of them running in London and another three hundred on order. Even so, London was still a long way behind Paris, where there were already 4,000 taxi-cabs.

The first London taxis charged eight-pence a mile, and relied on the old printed list of distances to calculate their fares. In 1906 the taximeter came into use, and for the first time the passenger knew exactly the legal fare for any distance.

The charge at the time was sixpence a mile. The change was a popular one, for the drivers who had previously paid ten shillings a day to the cab-owners were now entitled to keep one-third of the takings.

Arrangements were made to train a number of the old horse-cab drivers in the driving of motors. They received a month's training, during which they were paid a pound a week, and in return they signed a contract to work for the motor-cab company for two years.

By 1908 there were 758 taxi-cabs on the streets of London and 2,600 more on order. New drivers were coming in so rapidly that fifty-five certificates were issued each week. Within the next two years the number of motor-cabs had increased to 5,070. The taxis of those days had quite comfortable bodies, but the engines were small, usually only 8 to 10 horse-power. Their cost averaged £350 and the weekly takings of each cab about £16.

In this year of 1910 the last horse-drawn omnibus ran its final journey from London Bridge. London was to know no more that cheery, red-faced individual with a whip and a Cockney wit, both of which generously flashed. In his place came the mechanic at the wheel, the forerunner of that marvellous strategist of the London streets whom we know to-day.

The London General Omnibus Company had been early in the field applying the internal combustion engine to road transport. It began with a petrol-electric vehicle on the streets in 1903, and in 1904 the first horseless omnibus began to ply between Hammersmith and Piccadilly.

For some years a war raged between petrol, steam, and electric buses. They were all on the streets at once. The electro bus was by far the quieter and more pleasant vehicle in which to travel, but the weight of the accumulators killed it as a paying proposition. These weighed from thirteen to twenty hundredweight as compared with a hundred pounds' weight of petrol for a petrol-driven vehicle of similar carrying power.

Eventually the petrol bus triumphed, and the L.G.O.C. devoted its energies to constantly improving its rapidly increasing service. Between 1910 and 1911 its drivers and conductors were provided with a uniform, and motor-omnibus services began to run to the country on Sundays and Bank Holidays. Epping Forest was the first resort to be visited by bus, and thousands of Londoners took advantage of the cheap fares to get out of the streets into the country. These new outings proved so popular that by 1912 services were running to Windsor, St. Albans, Watford, Farnborough, and Sidcup, and in the following year to Reigate, Caterham, and Dorking. There were as yet no motor coaches. These were a post-war development.

The transformation of London's tramways from horse-drawn to electrically-driven vehicles was also complete. They were extending their wires and rails even further into the suburbs. The running of the tramway along the Embankment in 1906, and the opening of the tram subway under Kingsway in 1908, at last linked up the systems serving north and south London. The tramways of the provinces emulated those of the capital in their adoption of electricity as motive power.

The old and dirty "Tuppenny Tube" had also gone. The Underground Electric Railways Company had been formed, and they proceeded to electrify and extend their services. The Piccadilly tube, between Hammersmith and Finsbury Park, had been completed in 1906. The year following Mr. Lloyd George, then President of the Board of Trade, opened the Hampstead, Highgate, and Charing Cross tube. Passengers were carried free on the opening day, and some 127,500 availed themselves of this privilege. London, it will be observed, was beginning to sprawl into that huge cosmopolis that we know to-day.

This, too, was the era of the turbine and the monster liner. In 1907 the *Lusitania* and the *Mauretania*, sister ships, unprecedented floating towns of 31,500 tons apiece, were launched. Even bigger ships for the Atlantic route were demanded. The challenge of the Cunard Company was countered by the White Star Line in 1910 by the launching of the *Olympic*. And a few feet away, in the same shipyard, the ill-fated *Titanic* was being constructed.

Both the *Lusitania* and the *Titanic* were to become symbols of great international tragedy—the one bringing the United States alongside Britain in the war against Germany, the other producing a common bond of sorrow between the relatives of the drowned in this country and America.

But of all these great liners that marked British shipbuilding at its best, the *Mauretania*, only just withdrawn from the Atlantic ferry, has the outstanding record of service.

Built in 1907, she was, before the Great War, a wonder of the western ocean. To cross in this fast ship was rightly regarded as a remarkable experience. During the war she was of great value to the nation, and she was called upon to render, in turn, various vital services. After the war she returned to her regular routes of peace-time and she continued to make the fastest passage across the ocean.

The work which she has performed over a long period is a tribute to the designers and builders of the ship and her engines. To steam across the North Atlantic in all weathers at high speed involves a strain on hull and machinery which, in the course of time, must tell, and only a very finely built ship could have lasted as she has done, and have seemed for years to possess the qualities of youth.

DO YOU REMEMBER *the old omnibuses before the war? They rattled through London at a few miles an hour. Compare them with the speed and comfort of the modern omnibus.*

Photos: London Transport.

TRAMS *have not changed so much as omnibuses, but even they have been improved and made more comfortable. The latest tendency is to displace trams by trolley-buses.*

Photos: London Transport.

A catch phrase was dominating the construction of battleships in Britain. "We want eight and we won't wait!" was the slogan that began the building of those super-dreadnoughts, the marvels of modern naval construction. In 1909 the *Colossus* was launched on the Clyde, and the *Orion* at Portsmouth, more than 40,000 people witnessing the latter ceremony. The year after three super-dreadnoughts, including the *Thunderer*, at which the wife of the Archbishop of Canterbury officiated, were launched.

The gigantic race in naval armaments with Germany had begun. Naval experts believed, triumphantly, that the dreadnought was the last word in supremacy of the seas. They did not foresee—neither did the Germans for that matter—that these floating steel fortresses would really reduce war at sea to a stalemate, just as the increasing mechanisation of armies would make a mobile war almost impossible. During the Great War these super-dreadnoughts revealed themselves as being at the mercy of any chance floating mine or the undersea torpedo launched by a submarine.

But as they slid down the stocks in the year 1910 and were launched in a furore of excitement, everybody sincerely believed that Britannia really ruled the waves.

III

Not only was this the period of limelight stars of whom we are told "the like will never be seen again," but it was also the age of literary giants.

Bernard Shaw, H. G. Wells, Arnold Bennett, James Barrie, George Moore, and Thomas Hardy—they had each helped to place England on the literary map of the world.

It was the era, too, of the new journalism. Pearson, Newnes, and Harmsworth were a trinity of men who were achieving astounding success with periodicals that frankly catered for the million.

And the writers of those days enjoyed the full tide of that popular journalism, with its high prices and good reading. It is doubtful whether the short story, as one example, has ever risen to the heights maintained by the writers of those days.

Still firmly established at the head of this school was Rudyard Kipling. His jingling verse, with its imperialistic theme, appealed strongly to a country that had come through the Boer War victorious, but slightly ashamed of itself.

The short stories of Kipling, with their insistence upon the romance of "the day's work," were read widely from Sydney to Grimsby, from Cape Town to Hong Kong, and from Toronto to Calcutta. Heroes in mechanics' overalls; swearing, blasphemous, but heroic figures in khaki; sun-stewed men of the tropics; salt-stained men of the seven seas—these were the characters who stamped and tramped their way through the pages of Rudyard Kipling, and even the Little Englander of those days was shaken from his beliefs by these sagas of the men who had taken up "the white man's burden."

About the same time, Mr. Arnold Bennett was religiously writing in that famous diary:

"*After several days' delay, owing to indisposition, I began to write 'Hilda Lessways' yesterday afternoon; only 400 words. To-day 1,100 words. It seems to be a goodish beginning. . . . The*

'Chronicle' asked me to resume my articles at five guineas a col. I asked for six."

A most remarkable character, Arnold Bennett. Quite the equal in audacity and success to his own creation, "The Card." He was born a child of the people, the eldest of a family of six, amidst the flame, smoke, mud, and din of the Midland manufacturing district they call " The Potteries "—those grimy, linked up Five Towns which have provided the main reservoir of his literary inspiration.

Beginning with a job in a lawyer's office—he made an excellent lawyer's clerk—he was soon writing in his spare time. Then, by "influence," he obtained a post on a woman's magazine and soon was editor.

Ironically enough, it was a book which Bennett did not believe would bring him in five pounds—and his publishers were inclined to agree—which established him. From it his fortunes, financial and otherwise, began their steep upward rise. This was *The Old Wives' Tale,* which he wrote when he was forty-one.

He had, against the advice of his friends, given up his salaried editorial job and gone to live first in the country and then in Paris. His livelihood depended upon a prolific output of magazine short stories and articles of literary, dramatic, and musical criticisms. He had published a dozen books, none of which had made a great hit. Also he had married a dark, serious, good-looking young Parisienne he had met in the circle of poets, artists, composers, and writers in which he moved.

For years he had wanted to write this story which he called *The Old Wives' Tale,* but it looked a formidable and financially unprofitable task, and at the critical point he had always turned away to lighter and smaller enterprises.

Now, settled at Fontainebleau, he tackled it. It took him eight months. He wrote it with sweat and anguish, and in printed characters. He felt it was good, he knew it was the best thing he had ever done; and he was certain it would never be understood. There he underestimated the artistic penetration and appreciation of his fellow human beings.

The book began to sell slowly, but it went on selling and it is still selling. It made Bennett's name, fame, and fortune. It established him on an unshakable pillar as a serious artist.

Then there was the creator of *Peter Pan*—James Barrie, a young Scot who had come south from the grim, wild barren kingdom north of the Tweed, determined to follow his predecessors and conquer England by peaceful penetration.

Barrie was encouraged to go to London and free-lance by getting several articles taken by a couple of editors who liked his Auld Licht sketches. He lived in a boarding-house in Bloomsbury, amid piles of papers which he went through for ideas for articles, keeping himself so busy that he seldom went out.

Was he happy? Thirty-five years later he told an audience of students that " the greatest glory that has ever come to me was to be swallowed up in London, not knowing a soul. . . .

"Now I am going to tell you about the most romantic fact of my life," he went on. "When my train ran into St. Pancras in the early morning my eye alighted on the most beautiful sight in London. It was the evening bill of the previous night's *St. James's Gazette,* and in large letters on it were the lovely lines 'The Rooks Begin to Build.' That was an article I had sent up to the *St. James's Gazette* a few days before, and so I knew that before I had been a day in London I had earned two guineas. I sat down on my box and gazed on that placard. Even now, I will not listen to one word against rooks."

Barrie came at a good time. Editors were tired of heavy-handed Victorians. They welcomed anyone with a light touch, who could give a comic twist to ordinary things. Barrie, made more and more aware of the demand, supplied it quite deliberately, just as later on, becoming aware that the theatre is the big gold-mine, he turned to plays instead of to books, and cast his fantasies into dramatic form.

At the same time a serious writer, John Galsworthy, was sitting down to work in the same room as a rover of the seas, Joseph Conrad. Galsworthy was beginning that great Forsyte Saga which was to reveal the cracking of the old Victorian order, the sense of property, the insistence of class, the instincts of gentlemen, and the suspicion of the mob.

The Forsytes represent the end of the Edwardian period and the beginning of that disruption of property by taxation which has proceeded into our present period of history.

Joseph Conrad, a Pole by birth, was struggling with the intricacies of the English language. At one time, in despair, he almost abandoned writing in English and turned to French.

But with the help of Galsworthy and a few friends who recognised the genius of this sea-captain turned writer, he persisted and began that series of novels, including *Lord Jim, Chance,* and

Nostromo, that marked him as a writer concerned with the loneliness of the human soul against the overwhelming odds of Fate.

Conrad, as a writer, lived in dire poverty, and success and fame came to him only after the war, when he was too tired and ill to enjoy it.

Thomas Hardy also was one of the great pillars of English literature at this time. The storm of criticism aroused by his novel *Jude the Obscure*—decidedly tame in its so-called immorality when compared with the frank writings of to-day—induced Thomas Hardy to turn his back upon the novel as a form of literature and write only verse.

That verse, dour and bleak like the Dorset downs in winter, its insistence upon the mortality of man and the overpowering will of Fate, has, nevertheless, the stuff of genius in it. Without a popular appeal, it yet persisted, nagged the minds of the discerning. There was no doubt that Thomas Hardy was already taking his place among the immortals when our history begins.

And there was that "enfant terrible" of letters, George Moore. Determined in the beginning to write French novels in English, and, later, Greek romances in Anglo-Saxon prose, he had settled in Ebury Street—a chasm among the houses of London, very long, very dingy, very old-fashioned.

In the morning the street echoed to the clatter of milk cans, and ash cans; in the evening the children from the poor quarter clamorously played about its worn pavements; and over it hung always the remote but persuasive rumble of the sprawling railway terminus of Victoria.

At No. 121 George Moore lived and wrote his books in perfect prose, undisturbed by the atmosphere without his room. From it came the volume of the inimitable *Conversations*. But then, the room in which George Moore wrote was entirely different to the rowdy, blowsy world of Ebury Street without. It was a quiet, cosy, curtained room, enshrining the memories of its inhabitant's Bohemian youth spent in Paris with post-impressionist painters and Parnassian poets.

The walls of his long dining-room and the little drawing-room over it were hung with paintings by Manet, Monet, Berthe, Morisot, and many another man whose studio and company he used to frequent. From the walls of his study one could take portraits and sketches and make a straight-line record of the long life of George Moore, from the early, funny, faded tintypes of little George to the quaint sketches of young George made by pioneer impressionists, and the odd, cramped-up portrait done by his friend Orpen. A man deeply, enormously interested in himself.

And he wrote chiefly about himself. Those books were his most successful. It was at thirty, inspired by Zola and Flaubert, that he began that series of books, *A Modern Lover, A Drama in Muslin,* and *Confessions of a Young Man,* which made people talk and shocked a good many But it was *Esther Waters,* published when he had passed forty, that made his name.

One must not forget H. G. Wells, the boy who began as a draper's assistant and reached the proud position of imaginative schoolmaster to adults. His *Outline of History* became the popular textbook of the age.

But in his literary beginnings he produced a series of scientific romances, *The War of the Worlds, The Food of the Gods, The Invisible Man,* and *The Island of Dr. Moreau,* which marked him out as the Jules Verne, and a better Jules Verne, of his age.

Soon, he abandoned these romances for those great Cockney novels, *Kipps, The History of Mr. Polly,* and *Tono Bungay,* where the wealth of humour and characterisation were worthy of Dickens at his best.

But the sociological and scientific itch in the writer sent him, to the despair of his literary friends, into the realms of sociological writings. In *The New Machiavelli,* which appeared in 1911, he showed the dubious atmosphere of party politics.

For a time Mr. Wells flirted with Fabianism, an intellectualised brand of Socialism, but then found the pressure of social forces too much for his literary imagination. He abandoned story telling for semi-scientific glimpses at modern civilisation.

But these were the giants, the aloof, literary gods. What of the popular writers, the creators of the " thriller," the inspirers of the modern detective school of fiction?

Sherlock Holmes, the great creation of Conan Doyle, had made his appearance to the British public. He was already a great national hero. When Conan Doyle, a young medical man with few patients and a good deal of time on his hands, sat down to write of the adventures of an expert in criminology, he did not realise that he was creating not only a character who would be known throughout the world, but would inspire a whole school of literature of its own.

Those stories, hesitantly submitted to the editor of the *Strand,* Mr. Greenhough Smith, were soon the most excitedly awaited stories of the age.

SHERLOCK HOLMES, WORLD'S GREATEST DETECTIVE. *When Sir Arthur Conan Doyle created this character in a short story written for the "Strand Magazine," he little realised that Holmes would become a national hero.*

These illustrations appeared with "A Scandal in Bohemia," the first Holmes story to appear in the "Strand Magazine."

Conan Doyle, with Sherlock Holmes, created a character whom all readers felt they knew, and, by a real stroke of genius, he created a second person, Dr. Watson, who not only made a foil against which the flash of the super-detective mind stood out, but also a relationship that could go on for ever.

When Conan Doyle rashly killed Holmes at the villainous hands of Dr. Moriarty, he had thereafter to be continually finding papers the hero had left to supply the continuous demand for more stories. Finally, he had to resurrect Holmes, and bring him back to Baker Street after a miraculous escape in the Swiss Alps.

In the year 1910 Sherlock Holmes was well established as the favourite hero of all thrillers. A play, *The Speckled Band*, was being performed in London to crowded audiences every night. Mr. H. A. Saintsbury was acting the rôle of Holmes, and young people were thrilled by that final act where the great detective kills the snake in a girl's bedroom.

Mr. Greenhough Smith has described the literary birth of Sherlock Holmes.

" . . . It was in 1891 that, as editor of the *Strand Magazine*, I received the first of those stories which were destined to become famous over all the world as 'The Adventures of Sherlock Holmes.'

"I have cause to remember the occasion well. The *Strand Magazine* was in its infancy in those days; good story-writers were scarce, and here to an editor, jaded with wading through reams of impossible stuff, comes a gift from Heaven, a godsend in the shape of a story that brought a gleam of happiness into the despairing life of this weary editor. Here was a new and gifted story writer; there was no mistaking the ingenuity of the plot, the limpid clearness

of style, the perfect art of telling a story. I saw the great possibilities of a fine series, and said so to Sir Arthur. . . ."

Conan Doyle himself has told us that the redoubtable Sherlock had a prototype in real life. Here is the account of this person as written by Sir Arthur, relating his student days in Edinburgh:

" . . . But the most notable of the characters whom I met was one Joseph Bell, surgeon at the Edinburgh Infirmary. Bell was a very remarkable man in body and mind. He was thin, wiry, dark, with a high-nosed, acute face, penetrating grey eyes, angular shoulders, and a jerky way of walking. His voice was high and discordant. He was a very skilful surgeon, but his strong point was diagnosis, not only of disease, but of occupation and character.

"For some reason which I have never understood, he singled me out from the drove of students who frequented his wards and made me his out-patient clerk, which meant that I had to array his out-patients, make simple notes of their cases, and then show them in, one by one, to the large room in which Bell sat in state, surrounded by his dressers and students. Then I had ample chance of studying his methods and in noticing that he often learned more of the patient by a few quick glances than I had done by my questions.

"Occasionally the results were very dramatic, though there were times when he blundered. In one of his best cases, he said to a civilian patient: 'Well, my man, you've served in the Army?'

"'Aye, sir.'

"'Not long discharged?'

"'No, sir.'

"'A Highland regiment?'

"'Aye, sir.'

"'A non-com. officer?'

" ' Aye, sir.'

" ' Stationed at Barbadoes?'

" ' Aye, sir.'

" ' You see, gentlemen,' he would explain, ' the man was a respectful man, but did not remove his hat. They do not in the Army, but he would have learned civilian ways had he long been discharged. He has an air of authority and he is obviously Scottish. As to Barbadoes, his complaint is elephantiasis, which is West Indian and not British.' . . ."

And so we must leave the earliest and still the best of English detective thrillers. It only remains to add that he nearly came into the world with a different name. A leaf exists from an early notebook on which the author had written "Sherinford Holmes." One somehow feels that "Sherinford" would never have achieved the world fame of ' Sherlock."

There must not be forgotten that other writer of thrillers whose real fame was to come after the war—Edgar Wallace. He was partly newspaper-reporter and partly novelist at this time. *The Four Just Men* had received a great vogue from the news that it was the thriller Dr. Crippen had been reading aboard the S.S. *Montrose* when he was escaping from Europe.

Later, Edgar Wallace was to make use of his African experiences in the famous *Sanders of the River* stories which, to many people, still remain the finest things he has written.

Altogether, the "thriller" was entering into its own. Magazine and newspaper editors were just discovering that twentieth-century individual "The Tired Business Man." And for the years to come writers and editors set out to amuse this particular individual.

One great literary career came to an end in 1910. The world learned of Tolstoy's death in November. The chafing of long years against the inconsistencies of the life he had to live as a Russian landowner, with the creed of simplicity he preached so passionately in his books, had torn him at last from his family ties and driven him into the world, alone and penniless. Too weak of body to shake off the family attentions he longed to repudiate, he died in the waiting-room of a railway station not far from his home.

His was a simple, Christian communist creed. He felt it was the gospel which the simple, Christian peasant of Russia needed. He did not realise as he lay dying in that waiting-room that somewhere in London was a bearded Russian, Lenin, devouring the books of Marx in the British Museum reading-room, who would ultimately bring to Russia the creed of Bolshevism and a revolution more complete than that of the French Revolution.

Most of the writers of this time were story-tellers, content to let their imagination roam in romantic cloud worlds. Only at the end of the year did a book appear that, with remorseless logic, shocked a good many people into a realisation of the horror to which the world was swinging rapidly.

The publication of Mr. Norman Angell's *The Great Illusion*, with its thesis that war among great modern communities was financially unthinkable, seemed only another indication of how near everybody was coming to thinking about it.

5

CHAPTER III

GUNMEN IN LONDON

The Sidney Street siege—German Emperor's last visit to London—Pre-war literary favourites—The King's Coronation—Glittering ceremony in Westminster Abbey—Investiture of the Prince of Wales at Carnarvon Castle—Suffragette Movement—Tragedy at the Derby—Big railway strike—The King and Queen visit India—The Delhi Durbar.

I

THE New Year of 1911 was ushered in by a sensational affair in the East End of London. It was to suggest Chicago during the reign of the gangsters after the war.

This was the period when the political exile, the refugee criminal or assassin from the Continent had unrestricted entry into England. The East End of London provided a home for much of the riff-raff of Europe in those days. It was a bunch of characters out of this riff-raff who provided the country with a sensation known as the Siege of Sidney Street.

It is still difficult to believe that the Scots Guards were called out with loaded rifles in the centre of London, that Royal Horse Artillery were rushed to the scene with field-guns, that several hundred armed police were present, and that the Home Secretary, Mr. Winston Churchill, was himself on the spot, all to capture two armed murderers who had taken refuge in No. 100, Sidney Street.

A fortnight earlier a gang of men, interrupted in a burglary in Houndsditch, had fired on the police, killing three of them. Two men believed to be of the gang, whose names, "Fritz" and "Peter the Painter," were now to be on everyone's tongue, had been traced to a house in Sidney Street. The police quietly cleared other people out of the house in the small hours of January 3 and began operations.

At half-past seven, just as dawn was breaking, Inspector Wensley, Inspector Hallam, Sergeant Leeson, and other officers went into the roadway and threw a number of stones at the first floor window. The reply was as sudden as it was dramatic. A perfect fusillade of shots came from the room. Sergeant Leeson staggered back into the arms of Wensley with a bullet in his chest.

"Mr. Wensley, I am dying," he gasped. "They have shot me through the heart. Good-bye. Give my love to the children."

Although severely wounded, so severely that he was afterwards invalided out of the force on a pension, Sergeant Leeson had missed death by a miracle. It was a difficult problem to get him away to hospital, for the whole street was under the range of the murderous Mausers. The doctor who was sent for, in fact, had to climb over a roof and down ladders to get to the wounded man.

66

THE FAMOUS SIEGE OF SIDNEY STREET, *January*, 1911. *Gunmen, resisting arrest, had barricaded themselves in* 100, *Sidney Street, and opened fire on the police. A detachment of Scots Guards and several hundred armed police were called out to capture them. Mr. Winston Churchill, the Home Secretary, seen in the photograph above, directed operations.*

No. 100, SIDNEY STREET, *after the siege. The two gunmen were killed, and several policemen were wounded. The ringleader of the gang, Peter the Painter, is believed to have escaped*

As soon as he saw him, the doctor ordered the sergeant to be removed to hospital. But to carry out that order was not an easy matter.

The wounded man had not only to be placed on a stretcher, but had to be carried up a ladder and over a roof to safety. Just as he was being carried over the roof another fusillade of shots came from the house in Sidney Street. It was only by a miracle that no one was killed.

To show how heavy was the firing it may be mentioned that after Inspector Wensley had seen the wounded sergeant into safety, and all those who had helped, he was forced to remain on the roof for the next half-hour, sheltering as best he could. It was not until the two besieged murderers were compelled to turn their attention away from the roof that the inspector was able to make his way down again.

In his book, *Detective Days,* Inspector Wensley gives a graphic description of the hours that followed:

"As morning wore on it became more and more evident that the weapons of the police were outmatched. Appeal was made to the officer commanding the Scots Guards at the Tower of London, and a detachment of eighteen marksmen with service rifles was sent out to our aid.

"Later, I believe, additional men were sent. Some of these were stationed in the buildings at front and rear of the besieged house, and others lay at each end of the street on boards intended for the display of newspaper posters that had been borrowed from newsagents.

"The wisdom of having a large number of police at hand was demonstrated as news of the siege gained ground and thousands of people crowded the adjacent streets, eager to view the happenings. With the powerful weapons that were then being used it was a mercy that none of the spectators was injured by ricochetting bullets.

"Sir Edward Henry, the Commissioner of the Metropolitan Police, was out of London and Major (later Sir Frederick) Wodehouse, the Deputy Commissioner, came down between nine and ten to take charge of the operations. Other high administrative officials also arrived, and later in the day Mr. Winston Churchill, the then Home Secretary.

"There was a great deal of confusion and it would have been utterly impossible for any one man to have exercised effective control of the proceedings. For those at the front of the house to communicate with those at the back, for instance, meant a long and intricate detour through houses, back-yards, and over walls, and to find any particular person was a long job. We were dealing, too, with an utterly unprecedented situation which could not have been foreseen.

"Soldiers and police kept up an unremitting fire, which was vigorously returned from the windows of the besieged house. Very nearly every pane of glass had been shattered and the broken fragments littered the sidewalks. The men within fired from behind the fluttering curtains and it was hard to detect their movements.

"A burst of firing would come first from one floor and then from another. In the house immediately opposite, bedding and other household furniture was piled near the windows as some sort of cover for the besiegers. Various devices, including the exhibition of dummies in police uniform, were tried to induce the cornered men to expose themselves, but they never did.

"The last act of the drama opened at about one o'clock. A thin whiff of smoke showed at one of the top windows. As it grew in volume, its significance was realised. The house was afire. A fresh burst of firing came from the lower windows and was fiercely answered by the besiegers.

"There were a few minutes of tension, and scores of rifles and pistols were levelled at the street door, which at any instant might have been flung open by those within, whose only remote chance was now to make a wild despairing rush. Personally, I have always held as a probable surmise that they deliberately set fire to the place, intending to create a distraction with a view to an attempt at escape. If so they abandoned the idea.

"The smoke grew thicker and fire-engines dashed to the edges of the police cordon, where, in spite of the protests of the firemen, they were halted. Spasmodic firing was still coming from the burning house. There could be no point in useless sacrifice of valuable lives. The end, in any event, was close at hand.

"As the fire worked downwards shots came at more infrequent intervals from the lower floors. The slackening in the defence was due, as we afterwards learned, to the fact that one of the assassins—'Joseph'—had been killed by a rifle bullet and that Fritz continued the fight alone.

"Towards two o'clock the house was a mass of flames, and it seemed impossible that anyone could remain in it alive. So far as I could observe—and I was fairly close—all attempts at resistance had finished some time before the firemen were allowed to get to work, although there was a statement that shots were fired afterwards. Another rumour that gained currency was that the men had broken through a wall into one of the adjoining houses, but, in fact, there were ample men there to deal with them.

"As soon as the fire had been got under control I was foolish enough to follow at the heels of the firemen when they entered the still-smoking building.

"Luck must have been with me that day, for again I escaped without a scratch when within an inch of death. An immense mass of stone coping suddenly crashed just in front of me, overwhelming some of the firemen. One poor fellow lost his life and three or four were badly hurt. Apart from Leeson, these were the main casualties throughout the day. One or two people received comparatively trivial injuries and there were several narrow escapes. From that point of view the proceedings had ended better than they might have done.

"In the debris two charred bodies were found. One of them had been shot through the head and the other had apparently died of suffocation. At the subsequent inquest a verdict of Justifiable Homicide was returned. So ended the siege of Sidney Street."

Did Peter the Painter, the ringleader of this famous gang in the Sidney Street battle, really die?

Ex-Detective-sergeant Leeson, who was badly wounded in the first attack on the stronghold, has since written a book, *Lost London*, in which he declares he saw Peter the Painter once again.

"He fled to Australia," writes the ex-detective-sergeant. "There I was to meet him."

Mr. Leeson went on a health voyage

to Australia to recover from the wounds received during the battle.

Describing a trip from Sydney to the Blue Mountains, he says:

"On the day of my departure who should I see in the booking-hall of the Central Station but 'Peter the Painter' himself! I knew the 'Painter' well by sight. . . . You can imagine my surprise and discomfiture when the door of my compartment opened, and in walked Peter.

"He could not, of course, guess that I was not in Australia on any official mission or that my connection with the force had been severed through my wound.

"He could not know that there was no jot of evidence to prove his participation in the Sidney Street affair, however gravely the finger of suspicion pointed towards him.

"It was a tense moment. He wondering when I was going to show my hand, I asking myself how soon I should be looking down the barrel of a revolver. But nothing happened.

"At my destination I stepped out on to the platform, leaving Peter to travel —who knows where?

"That was the last of him so far as I was concerned, until I received a letter from his brother saying that he had died in America in 1914."

Mr. Leeson introduces another famous figure into the case.

"The crime itself," he says, "was organised by Stalin, now head of the Soviet Government."

Naturally, the affair led to a clamour for more stringent regulations regarding the entry of foreigners into Britain. And this clamour was emphasised by another crime in which an alien was involved, which occurred in the same period.

A Frenchman had been found murdered on Clapham Common, with the letter S slashed into both his cheeks, and another foreigner, Stinie Morrison, was soon under arrest. Morrison protested his innocence and despite the fact that he produced some evidence of an alibi was condemned to death. He made an appeal, but even this failed. Finally, at the eleventh hour, he was reprieved.

II

However, crime and the growing bitterness in politics were soon forgotten in the preparations for the Coronation of King George. The whole of the nation prepared to celebrate this occasion in a fine, patriotic spirit.

The curtain on this Royal cavalcade rose in May, when the preliminary spectacle of the unveiling of the Queen Victoria Memorial opposite Buckingham Palace and the opening of the new Mall and the Admiralty Arch was witnessed by thousands of people.

The personages at this great ceremony little dreamed of how Fate would play with them like wilful puppets. It was to be the last occasion on which the German Emperor was to show himself to a London crowd. Wearing a British field-marshal's uniform, the Kaiser had a definite military bearing. With the Emperor of Germany came the Empress and their only daughter.

Just a year previously, in May, 1910, the Kaiser had come to England for the funeral of King Edward VII., to lay a wreath on the coffin of the man whom he had declared to be "A Satan—you cannot imagine what a Satan. . . ." He had also, with the other crowned heads and envoys extraordinary, sat at the

State dinner given at Buckingham Palace on that occasion.

Ex-President Roosevelt was also at that dinner, and he has described how he listened to the tearful plaints and cares of the King of Greece. He was then buttonholed by the Tsar of Bulgaria, but the Kaiser promptly contrived to tear the American away from this confabulation, whispering to Roosevelt that Ferdinand was quite unworthy to know him. " In your place I should not speak to him. He is a miserable creature. . . ."

On this second occasion, at the unveiling of the Queen Victoria Memorial, the Kaiser found himself once again at a dinner party and State ball, given at Buckingham Palace. Again and again the Kaiser sought to ingratiate himself with Lord Kitchener, but in vain. Maybe it was a case of iron men meeting. Kitchener, as usual, had nothing to say.

The unveiling itself took place on May 16. As Sir George Arthur has pointed out, this gigantic piece of statuary has met with no fewer critics than champions, and there have been many to suggest that Queen Victoria was appropriately represented as turning her back on the Palace which, through fifty years, she was always so reluctant to enter and so eager to leave.

The King and Queen, with their Imperial visitors and the Kaiser, walked from the Palace to the foot of the memorial to take part in a brief dedicatory service conducted by the Archbishop of Canterbury, of which the music was finely rendered by the choirs of the Royal Chapels of Westminster Abbey and St. Paul's Cathedral.

The Kaiser deposited a gigantic wreath before the memorial; the sculptor, Mr. Brock, was presented to the King, who called him back, asked for a sword, and knighted him.

In his reply to an address read by the Chairman of the Memorial Committee, the King paid a finely worded tribute to the greatness of England's greatest Queen, and then passed on to lay emphasis on the presence of the Kaiser and on the " strong and living ties of kinship and friendship " between the thrones and persons of the two sovereigns; it was hoped that the visit—with the cordial reception which had admittedly delighted the Kaiser—would initiate a definite improvement in Anglo-German relations.

The Kaiser himself must have realised that these hopes were premature. He had not failed to observe that England was in the throes of a big naval campaign, and that the naval estimates for that year had already been increased by nearly £4,000,000. And the North Sea was definitely regarded as the scene of a future conflict between the two great Sea Powers.

Within a year the ties of kinship were to wither into dust, and the ties of friendship were to be irreparably broken. And the next occasion when a visit of the Kaiser to England was suggested was to be made by Mr. Lloyd George, at the election after the Armistice. Then it was boldly proposed that the man responsible for the war and all its miseries should be brought to England as a prisoner and tried for his life by some great tribunal.

As the Kaiser left London for the last time he little realised that some years hence the hoardings would be pasted with slogans: " Hang the Kaiser!"

And now the actual day of the Coronation approached. London was invaded by vast crowds of people, and it was estimated that altogether some 3,000,000 visitors came to the great city.

Vast wooden stands were fixed up along the route of the procession and troops were brought into the city to line the streets.

On the eve of the great day, June 22, there appeared a huge list of Coronation honours containing upwards of 550 names, peerages, baronetcies, knighthoods, and privy councillorships, although this was a period when the struggle between the House of Lords and the House of Commons had reached a climax.

The great ceremony itself was held at Westminster Abbey. The Duke of Norfolk, as hereditary Earl Marshal, stage managed the show. It was estimated that a congregation of some 8,000 people was waiting in the Abbey when the King's procession entered.

Immediately before the Queen, whose train was borne by four duchesses, there was the Archbishop of York and the Archbishop of Canterbury.

The King himself, in his crimson Robes of State and with his train upheld by pages of honour, was followed by the great military and naval officers and personages of his household. The rear was brought up by the Yeomen of the Guard.

The great doors of the Abbey were then closed. Their Majesties went to the Chairs of State near the High Altar and the King then came forward in full view of the congregation to be presented by the Archbishop of Canterbury.

For the first time since 1689, the Coronation Oath was shorn of a paragraph which had given a certain amount of offence to the Roman Catholics of Britain.

Under this amended Coronation Oath, King George was enabled to signify his adherence to the Protestant religion and pledge himself to secure the Protestant succession in the simple terms: "I do solemnly and sincerely in the presence of God profess, testify and declare that I am a faithful member of the Protestant Reformed Church by law established in England, and I will, according to the true intent of the enactment which secures the Protestant succession to the Throne of my Realm, uphold and maintain the said enactment to the best of my powers according to Law."

Following upon this, divested of his Robes of State, the King sat on the chair containing the Coronation Stone, with a pall held over his head by four peers who were alike highly placed and familiar friends, while the Primate solemnly anointed his head, breast, and hands.

Then the Royal Robes having been assumed, the Archbishop presented the Orb, with the admonition, "When you see the Orb set under the Cross remember that the whole world is subject to the power and empire of Christ our Redeemer."

The ring and the two sceptres were then handed to the King.

Finally, after Queen Mary had been anointed and crowned and had made her obeisance as the first subject of the Empire to the King Emperor, Westminster Abbey was hushed from east to west and the Holy Sacrament was administered to a kneeling King and Queen in all their gorgeous array.

Not until two o'clock in the afternoon did the King and Queen leave the Abbey to drive along the very circuitous route and receive the plaudits of the great crowds that gathered.

Some 60,000 troops were lining the

KING GEORGE'S CORONATION, June, 1911. London had never seen before such glittering pageantry as attended their new King's Coronation. 3,000,000 people visited London for the celebrations, and 60,000 troops lined the streets. This photograph shows the impressive scene in Westminster Abbey during the Coronation.

THEIR MAJESTIES KING GEORGE AND QUEEN MARY *in their State Robes after the*
Coronation ceremony.

streets, and all these men and the arrangements had been in the hands of the General Officer Commanding for the occasion, Lord Kitchener. Despite the gigantic scale of these celebrations, it is recorded that there was not a single incident or casualty throughout the whole period.

The third day of the Coronation was celebrated by a review at Spithead of the most formidable fleet that has ever been assembled.

It consisted of no fewer than 165 warships formed in even columns each nearly five miles in length. There were also present some 18 foreign warships.

The King and Queen, with Princess Mary, the Prince of Wales, and the Duke of York, together with the many Royal guests, travelled by special train to Portsmouth, then embarked in the Royal yacht, *Victoria and Albert,* which steamed along the line.

That night all the ships were illuminated, searchlights scattered the sky, and the Solent was a blaze of light.

Other celebrations included a special State performance at His Majesty's Theatre, and garden parties at Buckingham Palace. Almost every Empire and foreign figure of note was present at these occasions, and London had never seen such a galaxy of figures before.

The illuminations in London made it the brightest city in Europe. Huge crowds drifted about the streets, and observers noted that here was a city at the zenith of its success. Perhaps never again was London to appear so prosperous and happy.

It was during these celebrations that the Prince of Wales came into the public eye. Naturally shy and diffident, and still being fairly young, he had up to this moment kept rather in the background.

Now he mentally shouldered the burdens of ceremonial and State duties which devolved upon him. His dignified appearance in Westminster Abbey during the Coronation of his father was remarked by all. On that occasion the Prince wore his picturesque garter, robes and hat. His train was carried by Lord Ashley and his crown borne by Lord Revelstoke.

Immediately after the King was crowned by the Archbishop of Canterbury, the Prince was the first to do homage to the Sovereign. Taking off his crown and kneeling before His Majesty, the Prince said: "I, Prince of Wales, do become your liege man of life and limb and of earthly worship; and faith and truth I will bear unto you, to live and die, against all manner of folks. So help me God."

Having thus rendered homage, the young Prince touched the crown so newly placed on the King's head and kissed the King on his left cheek. The King with outstretched arms drew the Prince towards him and kissed him on the right cheek.

But soon after the Coronation ordeal an even greater welcome awaited the Prince of Wales. This was the Investiture at the historic castle of Carnarvon in Wales.

This was the scene where, many years ago, the infant Edward of Carnarvon was traditionally believed to have been accepted by the people of Wales as their first English Prince.

This was indeed a remarkable celebration, made particularly brilliant by the manner in which the Welsh people set themselves out to make the affair one of great patriotism and national enthusiasm.

On a splendid sunshine day in June

the little town of Carnarvon was packed with loyal Welshmen and people from every part of the King's dominion.

The Prince of Wales, wearing his midshipman's uniform, arrived by train and drove to the castle, where his first duty was to receive an address from the Corporation of the borough of Carnarvon.

The Prince's reply—the first speech in which a Prince of Wales had used the Welsh language—is worth quoting:

"I thank you most sincerely for your kind welcome and address. It gives me great pleasure to visit your historic town. I have read how, as Segontium, it was famous in the days of the Romans, and your noble castle has especial interest for me. I have already heard some of your far-famed singing, of which I have been told so much. It gives me great delight. It touches all who hear it, coming as it does from the heart as well as from the head. As we say, 'Mor o gan yw Cymru i gyd" ('All Wales is a sea of song').

"When I think of the many links which bind me to our beautiful country, the title I bear seems more real to me than ever. You greet me on behalf of all in your ancient mother tongue with 'Croesaw' ('Welcome'), and let me end by saying 'Diolch o waelod fy nghalon i hen wlad fu nhadau' ('Thanks from the bottom of my heart to the old land of my fathers')."

The King had also to receive an address from the Corporation, and in his reply used words which will long be remembered in Wales. His Majesty said:

"I believe that the occasion will serve a still deeper purpose in assembling in union and power around the Prince's person all the forces of Welsh national life which preserve the fame and achievements of your historic ancestors, and will sustain in the world of modern times the virtues of the British race and the glories of the British Empire."

The procession which conducted the Prince to the Chamberlain's Tower, where he was robed for the ceremony, recalled the ancient pageantry of a people who have preserved their national customs and national privileges in a manner which is beyond all praise.

Heralds, the Arch Druid and Druids matched the surroundings of the medieval castle, whilst the martial glories of Wales were recalled by the presence of the Welch Regiment and other national military formations.

The King and Queen wore none of the panoplies of their exalted rank on this occasion.

The King was merely an Admiral of the great Service to which his son belonged, and the Queen was only a beautiful and gracious lady proudly attending a ceremony in which her firstborn was playing the leading part.

The Prince's sister added to the family character of the ceremony. She wore a pretty white frock and hat, and her girlish simplicity and charming appearance won all hearts.

Mr. Lloyd George, as Constable of the Castle, received Their Majesties, and handed the King the great key of the Castle, which His Majesty received and handed back to his Constable.

The King and Queen seated themselves on two thrones, with a vacant throne on the King's right hand, and His Majesty then summoned the Prince to the Presence through the Earl Marshal.

The Prince soon appeared, preceded by heralds and pursuivants and great nobles bearing his Insignia.

THE INVESTITURE OF THE PRINCE OF WALES AT CARNARVON CASTLE,
*July 13, 1911. He delighted the Welsh people by being the first Prince of Wales ever to
make a speech in the Welsh language.*

He was followed by the officers of his household. His youth was marked by the presence of his tutor amongst these gallant gentlemen.

The Prince wore a picturesque kit consisting of a short purple surcoat, white knee-breeches, and white stockings. He had no head-dress, as hats belong to a later period than his medieval uniform. He kneeled at the King's feet whilst the Home Secretary read the Letters Patent of his appointment, and then did homage in the ancient formula which he had already repeated at the King's Coronation.

Rising, he was kissed by the King and placed on the vacant throne by the King's side.

An eloquent address was then delivered by Sir John Rhys, to which the Prince replied:

"I thank you with all my heart for your cordial welcome, and with you I wish that this may be the first of many visits to our beautiful country. As your address reminds me, the many links of the past, my Tudor descent, the great title that I bear, as well as my name David, all bind me to Wales, and to-day I can safely say that I am in "hen wlad fy nhadau' ('the old land of my fathers').

"I assure you that I shall never forget to-day as long as I live, and I hope sincerely that it will always mark a happy day in the Principality as one which brought you a new friend. He is, it is true, a young friend—I am very young—but I have great examples before me. I have my dear father and my dear mother and good friends to help me, and so, bearing in mind our ancient and beautiful saying, 'Heb Dduw, heb ddim; Duw a digon' ('Without God, without anything; God is enough') I hope to do my duty to my King, to Wales, and to you all."

The use of the Welsh language by the young Prince a second time aroused immense enthusiasm, and after a short religious service conducted by not only the bishops of the Welsh dioceses, but representatives of the Free Churches of Wales, the King presented their Prince to his people.

Four times the Prince appeared to the waiting throngs outside the castle and four times he was greeted with a musical welcome which only Welsh people could give.

When at last the Sovereign led the Prince to the King's Gate for the last presentation, the final welcome must have touched the heart of the most hardened cynic.

The singing of the "Land of my Fathers" and of the "Old Hundredth" by the assembled multitude produced a volume of stirring melody which could not have been achieved anywhere except in the land which the Prince had claimed as a "Sea of Song."

It was a wonderful and unforgettable pageant, but must have been a trying experience for a youth of seventeen.

Yet no sooner had these national celebrations ended than the clouds began to gather over Europe. Various startling incidents revealed that the world was rapidly drifting towards that war which already men were talking about, thinking about, and fearing in their own hearts.

As usual, it was an incident in an out-of-the-way part of the world which provoked the Powers into threatening each other. It was in Morocco, where France was rapidly extending her empire and had almost completely taken possession of that country.

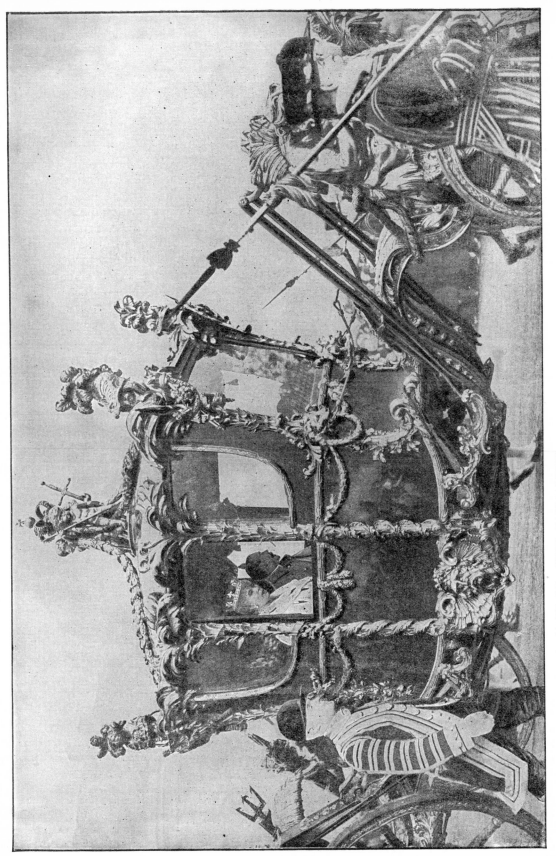

THE KING AND QUEEN GO IN STATE TO OPEN PARLIAMENT.

Germany, feeling that she had been left out of that African Empire, this great scramble for a continent which had been going on for some years, ordered the German gunboat *Panther* to sail to the port of Agadir in Morocco.

It was really a definite gesture against France, and, in order that France might continue her occupation of Morocco, Germany in return demanded the whole of the Congo as the price of her good-will, or non-interference. Britain, although apparently not concerned in this dispute, did not hesitate to warn Germany of the consequences of her action.

Mr. Lloyd George, who might be said to have been the least imperial-istic of all the Cabinet Ministers in Britain, made a startling speech at the Mansion House, which conveyed a note of warning to Germany. He even spoke of "Teutonic bullying."

Three days later there were rumours of orders for the British Fleet to stand by, although Mr. Asquith, then Prime Minister, promptly made a statement that there was no question of interven-tion at Agadir by Britain.

Although this affair began to blow over, it was obvious to acute observers that the World Powers were jostling each other for position. The war seemed in-evitable. Only Germany realised that the time was not quite ripe.

At the same time many of the European nations were scrambling for the loot which followed on the break-up of the Turkish Empire. Italy seized Tripoli and the twelve Ægean Islands off the Asia Minor coast. Germany, never noted for shrewd diplomacy, stood by baffled while this loot was being seized

III

But a war was in full blast on the home front of Britain. The Women's Suffrage Movement was conducting its greatest offensive. During the reign of King Edward VII., the Women's Suf-frage Movement, the demand that all women should have votes, had been in the nature of a constitutional and rather stationary movement. But now, with Mr. Asquith as Prime Minister, himself a confessed opponent to any form of suf-frage for women, the movement had taken on a more aggressive form. The chief leader of this militant section was Emmeline Pankhurst; for more than twenty years she had been working for Women's Suffrage, but the fact that the constitutional movement had gained no ground decided her to adopt more aggressive methods.

Mrs. Pankhurst, an autocratic but violently appealing speaker, soon proved herself a born leader. She gathered round her a group of women, many young, some middle-aged, a few old, who desired with fanatical intensity to achieve the vote, and all it stood for. Among her ablest lieutenants were her handsome, electric daughter Christabel; her gentle, passionate daughter Sylvia; and Annie Kenny, mill-hand, an odd representative of the aspirations of her fellow-workers.

By 1908 the Women's Social and Political Union, as this body called themselves, had worked out a tech-nique of propaganda. They organised a procession to march to the House of Commons.

This was dispersed by the police in a rather harsh method about a mile from Westminster. Nevertheless, a young woman actually managed to reach the

House of Commons and dashed on to the floor of the assembly, shouting in the face of the members that they were denying rights.

Needless to say the House of Commons was profoundly shocked with this interruption, but it was only the beginning of a long and desperate campaign.

On the occasion of this march on the House of Commons, fifty-six women and two men were arrested. They were fined from ten shillings to forty shillings each, with short terms of imprisonment as the alternative. Most of them decided to go to prison.

The women, in fact, soon discovered that by going to prison they became heroines of the cause. On one occasion several Suffragettes chained and padlocked themselves to the area railings of No. 10, Downing Street, after the Prime Minister had refused to receive them.

Then three Suffragettes managed to chain themselves to statues in the central hall of the Houses of Parliament.

Once, while a group drove up to the Strangers' Entrance to Parliament, concealed in a furniture van from which they alighted and proceeded to hold a meeting, others drove round Parliament Square in cabs, shouting Suffrage battle cries through a megaphone.

The House of Commons, in fact, became a sort of besieged castle which the Suffragettes were determined to enter and capture. There was the occasion when the placards demanding "Votes for Women" were thrust through the grille in the Ladies' Gallery and feminine voices called on members to give justice to women.

Two of the interrupters having chained themselves to the grille, some of its rails had to be removed with them. While they were being arrested, a man threw a bundle of leaflets into the House from the Strangers' Gallery, shouting at the same time "Justice for Women!"

As a result of this exploit, the Gallery of the House of Commons was closed to strangers for six months. No Cabinet Minister could address a political meeting without Suffragettes interrupting him and creating fierce disturbances. "Are you prepared to give votes for women?" was the cry raised at every meeting.

The authorities decided to take severe action against the women disturbers. They began to inflict terms of imprisonment on all those who were brought before the magistrates for creating scenes in the streets. Holloway gaol began to be filled with many martyrs to the cause.

But here again the women proved that they were more than a match for the authorities. They began to break every prison rule they could find. They refused to work. They refused to parade. They refused to obey orders. Finally these women adopted the policy of the hunger strike.

This was perhaps the most powerful weapon they used. All the tempting meals which were placed before them were refused. Days were passed in complete starvation.

Finally the authorities decided to adopt the method of forcible feeding. Stomach pumps and other barbarous instruments were used. Naturally this caused a great outcry in public.

The Suffragettes made the most of it On their political platforms they brought these women who had been forcibly fed in prison and who were able to tell the stories of the indignities heaped upon them, and thus gained public sympathy.

Christabel Pankhurst herself was one

6

of the martyrs in Holloway prison. Very soon the Suffragettes had enlisted a large body of men to help them fight their cause.

Public processions and street corner meetings were organised. Over 3,000 women marched in their first procession from the Embankment to the Albert Hall, over 15,000 in the second.

Indoor meetings, advertised by notices chalked up on the pavements, multiplied from year to year. There were thousands of applications for membership, enquiries for pamphlets, some literature for the cause. Large sums of money also came in from various sources. Apparently there was no lack of sympathisers with the women in their desperate cause.

Released from prison, the campaign of these determined women became wilder than ever. They had got beyond the stage of smacking faces of Cabinet Ministers. Now they indulged in window smashing, which was extended to include the windows of the big West End shops.

Telegraph wires were cut; empty houses, sports pavilions, and racecourse offices were burned. Even pictures in famous galleries were slashed.

Finally came the incident in June, 1913, which was regarded by the women as the greatest martyrdom of all.

Miss Emily Davison, who for some days had been brooding on the wrongs of women, attended the famous Derby on Epsom Downs. When the horses came thundering round Tattenham Corner she deliberately slipped beneath the rails, and flung herself under the King's horse.

The horse and jockey crashed to the ground. The crowds shrieked their alarm. The King's horse—Anmer—was injured, as also was the jockey riding. Miss Davison herself was very badly injured, and died four days later.

Her funeral procession through London, on June 14, was the most solemn and impressive pageant ever organised by the Suffrage Movement. They were determined to make the most of the occasion.

Even so the Government refused to be moved. The Prime Minister, Mr. Asquith, became almost as fanatical in his determination not to grant the vote for women as the women themselves were fanatical in their determination to achieve it.

In order, therefore, to prevent the women escaping from prison by the process of starvation and hunger striking, a new Act was instituted, which promptly became known as the Cat and Mouse Act.

The idea of the Act was that when a woman prisoner was in danger of death from hunger striking, she could be released. As soon as her health was restored she was to be rearrested, sent back to prison and complete serving the sentence.

Mrs. Pankhurst, sentenced in 1913 to three years' penal servitude, had, a year later, served but thirty days of her sentence. During the same year, 182 other Suffrage prisoners came under the effects of the Act.

In May, 1914, a deputation of women tried to reach Buckingham Palace, in order to present a petition to the King against forcible feeding. Some sixty women and two men were arrested. In June of that year a lady fell on her knees before the King and Queen at Court and cried, "Your Majesties, won't you stop torturing women?" Her cry unheeded, she was removed.

SUFFRAGETTE INTERFERES WITH THE DERBY. *Miss Emily Davison threw herself in front of the King's horse Anmer during the 1913 Derby, just as the horses were rounding Tattenham Corner. The woman died from her injuries four days later. Both the horse and jockey were injured.*

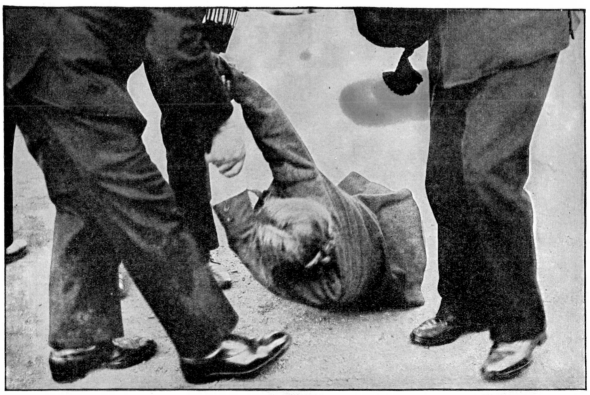

SUFFRAGETTES' CAMPAIGN. *Demonstrations were held almost daily by women claiming equal rights with men. When arrested for breaking the law, many of them went on hunger strike. Their campaign continued until the outbreak of war.*

The fierceness with which this controversy between men and women was carried on at the time is exemplified by the demand of Lord Robert Cecil for the deportation of the women militant leaders.

It was the coming of the Great War, however, which really ended the Suffragette Movement. It changed all these political and militant leaders into women war workers. Perhaps sufficient credit has not been given to the Suffragette leaders for the manner in which they did fling themselves wholeheartedly into the work of providing for the soldiers who had left for France.

Eventually the women gained all and more than they demanded. The time came when the different political parties were only too willing to obtain the sympathy of women by promising votes to the largest possible majority that democracy could provide.

But there were also many other changes and upheavals in Britain which kept the people of this country from paying too much attention to the foreign scene.

There was, for example, the growing strength of the Labour Movement and a series of strikes. Seamen came out in various ports in June. This was followed by a sympathetic strike of carters and vanmen, who refused to handle goods for the shipping line. In July the London dockers came out. Each of these strikes was attended by violence. At Hull and Cardiff, at Manchester, which had to call for a strong force of London police and the Scots Greys from a York garrison, there had been fighting in the streets.

Then the railwaymen began to reveal that they were seething with unrest. There were violent scenes in Liverpool.

Two men were shot dead and two people injured.

At Llanelly, where again two were shot and four killed by the explosion of a petrol tank, the whole railway system was suddenly threatened.

On August 15 twenty-four hours' notice was given for a general railway strike. For the first time the various trade unions were acting in concert.

This railway strike revealed that the Amalgamated Society of Railway Servants, the Locomotive Engineers and Firemen, and the General Railway Workers could sink their personal differences and combine in one general strike.

Although this railway strike threatened to disorganise the transport system of Britain, it did, in fact, come to an end with surprising suddenness. It began on August 17, and yet on August 19 it was over.

The men resumed work on the promise of an immediate special commission to investigate their grievances. Ultimately it was discovered that the strike was too big even for the unions to organise thoroughly. There were times when work was in progress on railway lines which were supposed to be on strike.

Nevertheless, this succession of railway strikes revealed that the Labour Party itself and particularly the trade unions were advancing to a dominant position in English society. Politically, Labour was more powerful than ever. The time was coming when it would even be accepted as the governing party.

The prominent leaders of this time were Mr. Lansbury, Mr. Snowden, and Mr. Will Thorne. They were all powerful speakers and understood the men's cause. They agitated, risked imprisonment, and questioned the Government at every turn.

It seemed that the spirit of perversion and militancy seized upon various sections of society. Even medical men suddenly found themselves in conflict with the Government of that day.

Mr. Lloyd George had just introduced his Insurance Bill. It was the time of that great slogan "Ninepence for Fourpence!"

The Bill was intended to insure vast numbers of wage-earners. Employers and labourers were expected to contribute sums, and the Government themselves added to those sums.

It is strange to-day to read of the protests that broke out in various quarters about this Bill. Some newspapers, making discoveries that housewives would actually have to stamp cards for domestic servants, worked up a wild campaign against the indignity of "stamplicking," and filled the Albert Hall with society ladies and others who were determined that they would not be cajoled into such undignified action.

But the strongest opposition came from the British Medical Association, which definitely demanded a revision of the scale to their satisfaction, the fixing of a limit of income for panel patients and more medical representation on the local committees under the Bill.

Even the medical men were stampeded into holding an Albert Hall meeting of refusal to work the Bill when passed.

These symptoms of a growing unrest among the peoples of Britain were seized upon by the pacifists.

This was the year in which the new Dean of St. Paul's, Dr. Inge, earned for himself the title of "The Gloomy Dean." He had not hesitated to lament the "Dehumanised Industrialism" which was dragging England to a fall and on marked tendencies towards an "unnatural and bloody horror of taking life." On this dismal note of unrest and despair the year was closing.

IV

Throughout the Coronation festivities King George conceived an idea which in its bearing and originality was to be of the utmost importance to India, the great empire of which he had been crowned Emperor.

He had decided that the Oriental splendours of the great city of Delhi, once the seat of the Mogul emperors, should be restored again. Since the British occupation of India, Calcutta had been the seat of Government. Now King George was to revive the importance of long neglected Delhi.

In November the King and Queen sailed for India. Already as Prince of Wales he had visited India in 1905 and revealed himself as a great sportsman, and a big game hunter of no mean ability.

But he had not neglected to study the Indian political situation, as was shown in his own words at the conclusion of that early visit:

"I cannot help thinking, the more I have heard and seen, that the task of governing India will be mainly easier if we, on our part, infuse into it a wider element of sympathy. I will venture to predict that to such sympathy there will be an ever abundant and genuine response."

In this State visit to India, for the magnificent Durbar to be held at Delhi, the King Emperor was to reveal that those early words of his had a meaning.

THE KING *rode into Delhi for the Durbar in December,* 1911, *amid scenes of great rejoicing. It was announced by the King at the Durbar that the capital of India was to be Delhi and not Calcutta.*

THEIR MAJESTIES *wore their crowns and Coronation robes, and were surrounded by the leading princes of India.*

The Royal voyage to India was made in the *Medina,* a new ship of the P. and O. line, a great company which has maintained regular connection between England and the East for half a century.

For the time being the *Medina* became a King's ship, and a third mast was stepped to enable His Majesty to fly all three flags, which indicate the presence of the Sovereign—the Royal Standard at the main, the Admiralty flag at the fore, and the Union Jack at the mizzen.

A tremendous reception was held when the King and Queen arrived, but very soon they were proceeding up country for the great Durbar to be held at Delhi.

Months of work had created a great imperial camp in Delhi. Splendid new roads, lighted with powerful lamps, were constructed, a polo ground was created, and gardens resplendent with flowers sprang into being. Few people could realise that a short year before, the site had been brown desert land.

The days and nights preceding the Durbar were crowded with events. There were receptions of ruling chiefs. India believes in pageantry, as also in the mysteriousness and aloofness of its emperors.

King George, as Emperor of India, decided that his arrival in Delhi should be impressive as well as mysterious. He arranged to enter the great fortress of Delhi and come forth and show himself to the multitude as had the Mogul emperors in other days.

The day when the King rode forth from the Delhi gates to the great camp and amphitheatre that had been prepared in his honour was, indeed, a memorable occasion to the Indian people.

The road itself was one along which the old Mogul emperors had passed in ceremonial procession with palanquins, elephants, and glittering trappings of all kinds. Tens of thousands of Indians comprising the various tribes of this great empire were lining the routes. They had been crowding into the city for weeks beforehand. Many of them had slept and eaten and lived along the line of the route.

One holy man was said to have trekked four months without ceasing in order to be present on this great occasion. After having seen the Emperor pass he started on his return journey, happy in having beheld " The Shadow of God on Earth."

The windows of the crazy Oriental houses were crowded with spectators, veiled women peeped from lattice windows, coloured turbans of every description were seen.

Thousands of troops paraded the two miles route. British and Indian cavalry trotted to and fro, the pennants of their lances fluttering in the slight breeze.

Besides the British Army in full ceremonial uniform, there was also the whole pageantry of Indian military display. It included Baluchis in cherry and green uniforms, Sikhs and Pathans in khaki. There was the North-west Frontier Regiment in blue and grey. Several Gurkha regiments were parading, and also the Camel Corps riding on their huge brown beasts. Altogether some 50,000 troops took part in this procession from the gates of Delhi.

The King Emperor himself had an escort of the leading princes of India. These princes wore glistening coats of mail and steel armour which caught the bright sunshine and glittered against the eyes of the watching multitudes.

The Governors of the various provinces of India led the procession. Then came Lord Kitchener in full uniform, a striking figure as Commander-in-Chief to the Emperor.

He was followed by a glittering group of Imperial Heralds, with trumpets. Then came the senior corps of the Indian Army, the Governor-General's bodyguard raised in 1777 by Warren Hastings, a superbly mounted contingent drawn from the pick of the fighting races of India.

It was separated from the Emperor by an escort of His Majesty's Life Guards and Royal Horse Guards, which had fittingly accompanied the Sovereign. Their glittering breastplates and plumed helmets gave them a special appeal, even in that dazzling array of gorgeous uniforms.

Finally came the King Emperor himself, in the dress of a field-marshal and bestriding a magnificent dark brown Australian charger.

The one disappointment of the big, eager-eyed multitude was that the King Emperor was wearing a sun helmet, which, to some extent, shaded his familiar features from the crowd.

Many of the natives also expected the Emperor to be riding in a howdah on top of a huge elephant. The fact that he was astride a horse and wearing a uniform which seemed to them rather like that of any British general was to some extent a disappointment. Many of the natives missed him altogether. Seeing the Queen alone in a carriage, regal in bearing and marked out by the gorgeous fan and umbrella, the multitude murmured that the King was not in the procession at all.

However, the Durbar left no doubt in their minds. Here was a King Emperor indeed, seated on a throne and wearing the Royal crown.

The Durbar was held on December 12 in the large amphitheatre which had been specially prepared. Some 10,000 spectators, including all the great officials of India, filled the semi-circular stand. In the very centre of this huge semi-circle was the Royal dais under a gorgeous canopy.

Their Majesties wore their crowns and Coronation robes and sat on special thrones, while the heralds read the Royal proclamation in English and Urdu, ending with a fanfare of trumpets and rolling of drums.

The arena itself was occupied by 20,000 troops of all arms, and, outside the amphitheatre, a mound had been built up to accommodate 50,000 natives.

Standing stiffly to attention at one corner of the pavilion beneath which sat Their Majesties was a solitary and striking figure. It was a British Grenadier, wearing the bearskin familiar in Europe, but never seen in India before. Despite the tropical sunshine, this superb figure never flinched, and at the end of his long period of duty was found to be none the worse.

The Emperor and his Consort then received the homage of India. Procession after procession passed. Thunder after thunder of artillery roared its salute.

Finally, when the last salute had been sounded and the Viceroy by the King Emperor's order had read a proclamation of boons to be conferred in honour of the day, the chief herald stood up to his full height in his stirrups and, doffing his helmet, called for three cheers for the King Emperor, and three more for the Queen Empress.

A final fanfare from the trumpeters, and then, in a clear voice, the King read from a slip of paper news which startled even the Viceroy himself.

DELHI DURBAR, 1911. 80,000 *troops and civilians were present at this great pageant. A remarkable incident followed the ceremony, when 200,000 people filed past the throne on which the King Emperor had sat.*

The capital of India was to be transferred from Calcutta to Delhi.

The announcement was received with tremendous enthusiasm, cheering, shouting, weeping, by the many multitudes of India present.

Later, Their Majesties moved to another pavilion, where they received the homage first of the Viceroy and then of the Indian princes.

It was a scene of unforgettable splendour. The princes wore magnificent robes and priceless jewels, and the ceremony of doing homage to their Emperor was an education in Indian customs. One prince, carrying a cane and finely dressed, would only bow, whilst another would lay his sword or white scarf at the feet of Their Majesties. This caused some misunderstanding in one place, and an Indian prince had to explain away an act of apparent discourtesy.

But that this great Durbar had aroused India to a fever of imperial patriotism was revealed by an incident which occurred at the end. It is described by Col. R. J. Blackman.

The thousands of people who had been watching from the mound outside suddenly surged across the vacant arena like a huge oncoming wave, which swelled up to the steps of the pavilion, the place where the Sovereign had been sitting.

This sudden and unexpected flood of people at first caused some alarm to the military guard of Highlanders which was stationed round the vacant throne.

The people were impelled by an irresistible impulse to approach the sacred places where the Emperor had been. They swarmed up the pavilion on every side, and men of all races and religions prostrated themselves before the empty throne, or strained over one another's heads to touch with just the tips of their fingers the fringe of the carpet on which Their Majesties had stood.

This extraordinary scene, which will remain deeply rooted in the memory of those who witnessed it, was most impressively touching, a striking manifestation of the great spiritual idea underlying the respect and affection of Eastern people for their Sovereign.

Eventually, with some difficulty, a regular queue was formed, the people passing up one side and down the other. It was estimated that over 200,000 persons thus passed before the throne, to say nothing of the many more who followed on the succeeding days.

The following day saw a great national festival, filled with all the displays and shows in which the Indian revels. It was the people's day, with musical rides, daring displays of horsemanship, groups of jugglers, and other variety entertainment.

Suddenly on a balcony of the old fortress overlooking this joyous scene appeared the King and Queen, unheralded by any trumpets. In an instant they were seen and recognised by the great crowd. There was an upward surge of dark arms in salute and a great shout of acclaim rent the air.

From the balcony Their Majesties passed to two thrones on the ramparts in order to come more entirely within view. And for hours the people filed past them, unrestrained by police or military, until with the sunset King George and his Queen returned to camp.

Then came the great review of the troops who had been gathered together in Delhi for these celebrations. To the number of 40,000 they paraded, British and Indian, horse, foot, and guns, going through the many complicated movements of a pre-war review.

Then came the charge of cavalry, frenzied dashing, clattering masses of clans, each trying to beat the other in the speed by which they galloped across the plains.

One of the great moments was when the boy Maharajah of Bahawal, a tiny figure on a great war camel, leading his own regiment of bearded warriors, passed the King Emperor, his baby arm touching the toy sword outstretched in perfect salute.

The final scene of that glittering Durbar was the investiture held by the King Emperor in the gardens of Delhi Park, which had once seen the magnificence of the Moguls.

Many orders and decorations were bestowed. The first to enter was the Queen Empress, who, dressed in pale blue, a colour which for so many years she has specially affected, knelt before the King to receive the Star of India.

It was a touching scene when Her Majesty kissed the hand of her Sovereign.

After these many ceremonies the King left Delhi and journeyed to Nepal to enjoy ten days' big game shooting. Many fine tigers were bagged on this great hunt.

This visit of the King Emperor and Queen Empress to India has never been forgotten. It is still remembered as the glittering pageant by the multitudes of India. It has done more perhaps, during the persistent attempts of unrest engineered by agitators in the East, to hold the patriotism of the people and retain their unswerving loyalty.

The time was swiftly coming when the King Emperor was to call upon the millions in India to join in the World War, which was even then rumbling on the great horizon.

At noon on January 8 the King and Queen left Calcutta for Bombay under a final salute of 101 guns from the ramparts of Fort William. Tears streamed down the face of the Maharajah of Scindia, and Sir Pertab Singh, toughened warrior though he was, could only stammer that he was growing an old man, for he, too, broke down under stress of emotion.

On the 10th the shores of India faded in the *Medina's* wake as the King left the empire which had spread itself at his feet.

CHAPTER IV

A YEAR OF TRAGEDY

Captain Scott's Antarctic expedition—It reaches the South Pole—Amundsen has preceded him—The journey back—Scott's death—The "Titanic's" maiden voyage—1,490 drowned when vessel is wrecked—Home Rule for Ireland—Warning of war—The Boy Scouts.

I

THE eyes of the world were suddenly centred upon the South Pole. Arctic and Antarctic exploration, its hardships, struggles, and desperate endeavours of a few solitary individuals, had always seized the imagination of the public. England, in particular, had played the leading part in the penetration of the white wastes. The achievements of her explorers had done much to map these trackless regions of snow and ice.

But now it seemed that other nations were to reap the benefits and the plaudits of the world sown by these pioneer English efforts.

A year before King George had come to the throne, Commander Peary, an American, had achieved the distinction of being the first man to reach the North Pole.

There had been an absurd and sensational claim by another American, Dr. Cook, who returned from the Arctic regions with dubious reports of having reached the North Pole. His claim had been equally sensationally exposed following upon an interview by Philip Gibbs, then special correspondent to the *Daily Chronicle.*

Now, on March 7, 1912, the news came that the Scandinavian, Roald Amundsen, had reached the South Pole.

It was twelve months since the ship of Captain Scott's expedition, back at Hobart from landing the British expedition on the ice barrier, had awakened the world to the fact that Amundsen was then making his dash. It added all the excitement of a contest to the dangerous enterprise.

Now there could be little doubt that Amundsen must have the glory of being the first to reach the Pole. However, until news came from Captain Scott, it was believed that there were laurels still to be won by the British.

When the news did come through, it was to reveal a tragedy of gallant gentlemen who died in a welter of loneliness and yet achieved an epic of adventure that remained a shining example of endeavour.

Captain Robert Falcon Scott held rank in the British Navy. He made two expeditions to discover the South Pole. On the second and last he took with him forty-five men from the Navy, two of whom accompanied him in the final dash; fifteen scientists, including Dr. E. A. Wilson; and one Army officer, Captain Lawrence E. G. Oates, of the 6th Inniskilling Dragoons.

Scott's plan of exploration included some novel features. Instead of relying on dogs alone for transportation, he intended to cross the six hundred and twenty miles of ice called the Great

CAPTAIN SCOTT'S ILL-FATED EXPEDITION. *Sixty-one men accompanied Captain Robert Scott on his expedition to the Antarctic. They sailed from England in the Terra Nova. Ill-luck dogged the expedition. Scott found that Amundsen had reached the South Pole before him, and on the return journey he and his companions perished.*

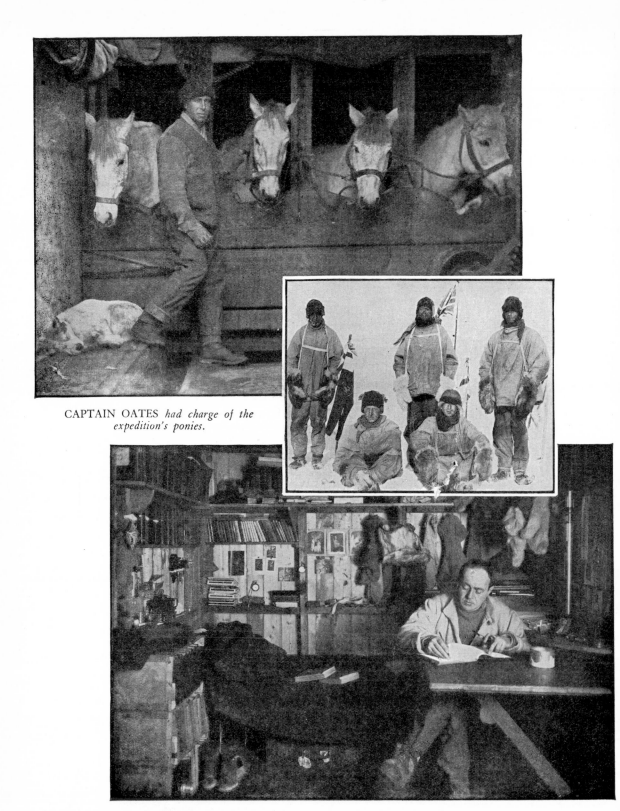

CAPTAIN OATES *had charge of the expedition's ponies.*

CAPTAIN SCOTT'S ILL-FATED EXPEDITION. *The centre photograph was taken at the South Pole. It shows Captain Oates, Captain Scott, and Petty-Officer Evans. Sitting: Lieutenant Bowers and Dr. Wilson. Lieutenant Bowers took the photograph by pulling a thread. Below: Captain Scott writing up his diary.*

From "The Great White South," by H. G. Ponting.

Barrier with two motor sledges and numerous ponies. As they advanced southward the ponies would be killed and fed to the dogs. But none of these animals was to be driven all the way.

His party left England in the *Terra Nova*, a wooden vessel especially equipped for polar exploration, and made final preparations in New Zealand. Early in January, 1911, they anchored in the Ross Sea, and made preliminary trips until the end of October. On November 1, at the opening of Antarctic spring, Scott and his group set out after the motor sledges.

Scott left a magnificent record of the tense days that followed. Every night in his tent he set down the events of that day. Those hasty notes, unrevised by their author and never written into a connected narrative, form an unsurpassed chronicle of hardship and sportsmanship.

From the first bad luck dogged the expedition. The motor sledges broke down early in the game. The ponies found it hard going in the snow, and the weaker held back the stronger. At the end of the thirty-first day's march all that remained had to be shot. From the moment the party reached the Beardmore Glacier they were dependent on dog power and their own marching and pulling strength.

Bad weather battled them along the glacier. When they undertook the summit climb they had already been going six weeks on polar rations. They let out a bit on Christmas Day and had a four-course supper, beginning with pemmican mixed with horse meat and ending with caramels and ginger. Scott wrote: "We have slept splendidly and feel thoroughly warm—such is the effect of full feeding." It is easy enough to guess that full feeding and feeling warm were already the exception.

On December 20 Scott sent back the last group to the main base. There remained with him only four: Dr. Wilson, head of the scientific staff; Lieutenant Bowers, who had charge of the rations; Captain Oates, who originally had charge of the ponies; and Petty Officer Edgar Evans, a Welshman of great physical strength and capacity for work, who attended to the packing, the skis, and the repairing of sledges.

The second party had followed for a short distance in case of accidents to the main party. Then they turned back, and the five adventurers were alone, with the South Pole before them.

It was very bad going most of the time. At an altitude of over nine thousand feet, over fields of corrugated ice, the explorers had to walk on their skis and pull their sledges. With perpetually lightening rations they kept their spirits light as well.

They were sure they would reach the Pole, or at worst come very near to it. Each admired the spirit with which his comrades withstood the hardship. Scott's diary speaks again and again of their courage, cheerfulness, comradeship.

Only one dreadful doubt would keep rearing its head. Amundsen, the Norwegian explorer, was also on his way to the South Pole. Would he get there first?

But on January 16 the weather was fair for a change and the goal only twenty-seven miles distant. Two long marches would get them there. They left a last depôt with nine days' provisions. Scott's entry for the day concludes: "We *ought* to do it now."

And the next day's entry begins: "The worst has happened, or nearly the worst." Amundsen had forestalled him. Scott had achieved his great ambition and reached the South Pole, only to find himself beaten in the race and the Norwegian flag already planted.

Even Scott's record of his disappointment is generous: "It is a terrible disappointment, and I am very sorry for my loyal companions."

Yet he cannot disguise his own chagrin: "All the day dreams must go; it will be a wearisome return." He plants his "poor slighted Union Jack," gives credit to Amundsen for a perfect achievement and tries to console himself: "Well, it is something to have got there."

Yet on the very first march toward home he is driven to write: "I'm not sure that we don't feel the cold more when we stop and camp than we did on the outward march." They had no difficulty in picking up their own tracks. They found their food caches. But they were on scant rations, toiling fearfully at a high altitude. And then there is all the difference between hopeful men and men defeated.

Then they struck bad weather. Blizzard after blizzard fell upon them, and blizzards were their terror. The temperature was on an average 20° lower than it had been a few days before in these same places.

Wilson, Scott, and Evans were all injured in falls on the ice. Scott's injury was to his shoulder. Wilson had hurt his leg, which was bad enough for a man who had to walk back to safety over hundreds of miles of rough ice with the thermometer as low as 70° below zero! But the indomitable Evans had fallen on his head, and, although his comrades did not realise it at the time, he tramped over the rugged ice day after day suffering from a concussion of the brain.

They were getting hungrier at each meal, but with their slow progress did not dare to increase their rations. Scott writes: "There is no getting away from the fact that we are not pulling strong."

Yet they held to even the minor objects of their quest. They collected geological specimens and pulled behind them on their sledges about seventy pounds of interesting rocks! What that extra weight must have meant under those circumstances to men in their condition staggers the imagination. But geological specimens were one thing they came for. Seventy pounds of rare specimens stayed with them to the end!

On February 15 they again reduced rations. On the 16th Evans seemed very ill. But he rose the next morning and set out with the others. Soon he fell behind the sledges, but caught up presently and apologised. Again he fell behind, and this time they had to turn and look for him. They found him on his knees in the snow, quite bewildered. He had marched and pulled a sledge for thirteen days while suffering from a concussion of the brain. He died that same night.

This dreadful experience unnerved the others. But after they had buried their comrade in the snow the other four pushed on. Snow caked on the runners and they could not get rid of it. Fuel ran short. Oates froze his feet—the worst misfortune that can happen to a polar explorer. And the thermometer fell to 40° below.

"Amongst ourselves," records Scott, "we are unendingly cheerful, but what each man feels in his heart I can only guess."

Forty below zero: cold pemmican for

meals: Oates limping along, unable to help with the pulling now, barely able to keep up. And the record runs: "We mean to see the game through with a proper spirit."

It was on March 2 that Oates' feet failed. For a few days he hoped for improvement. But the bitter cold continued, and thanks to their shortage of fuel none of them was ever warm.

Oates began to see that he was holding back his comrades. If they were freed of the drag he put upon them they might be able to battle through to the depôt, and find there food and warmth.

On the 15th, after nearly two weeks of desperate effort, Oates decided it was time to end this infliction. He asked his comrades to go on and leave him in his sleeping bag. They refused, and he made one last afternoon march with them.

The next morning when he awoke it was to another blizzard. He said to his companions, "I am just going outside and may be some time." Then he deliberately walked off into the storm and lost himself. They never saw him again.

But the lives for which he gave his life were worth only a few days' purchase. On March 21 they were caught by another blizzard which was still raging on the 29th, when Captain Scott made the last entry in his diary. Only eleven miles from shelter and safety, the three men were quite unable to leave their tent.

With Dr. Wilson's drugs they could have shortened the agony of what was now only hopeless endurance. That was not the way they did things. Quite legibly Scott writes on the last page of his journal: "We shall stick it out to the end, but we are getting weaker of course and the end cannot be far.

"It seems a pity, but I do not think I can write more. R. Scott."

And then scrawled at the bottom, tragically, if ironically, in letters that stagger at last: "Last entry. For God's sake look after our people."

When Surgeon Atkinson found the tent, eight months later, Wilson and Bowers were seen to have died in their sleep, with the flaps of their sleeping bags closed against the cold. Scott had flung back the flaps of his sleeping bag and opened his coat as if for air. The little wallet containing his journal was under his shoulders, and his arm was flung across the body of his friend Wilson.

Something else was found in the tent. Scott, although dying, had found strength to write to Wilson's wife and Bowers' mother; a letter to the public explaining that the failure of the expedition was not due to bad management; letters to his superiors in the Navy and the men who backed his expedition; letters to his mother, his wife and his boy, far away back in England.

We quote one paragraph from the letter to his wife:

"What lots and lots I could tell you of this journey. How much better it has been than lounging in too great comfort at home. What tales you would have for the boy. But what a price to pay!"

And he had just written to one of his backers in England: "We very nearly came through and it's a pity to have missed it, but lately I have felt that we have overshot the mark. No one is to blame and I hope no attempt will be made to suggest that we have lacked support."

II

News of a much bigger and more appalling disaster, and yet one that brought out some splendid heroism, also reached the public in 1912. On April 15 came the terrible news of the loss of the White Star liner *Titanic*.

At her launch in the previous June she had been described as by far the biggest liner in the world. It had been said that she was so huge that the sea, so far from endangering her, could scarcely even disturb the comfort of life aboard her; passengers need not know, if they did not want to, that they were even at sea.

And now, the sea, calling up its terrors, had drifted an iceberg across her track in the night and engulfed her. At first the curt radio messages gave the world to understand that the giant liner was limping into port. But later the real extent of the disaster became known. It was possible from the stories of survivors to piece together the greatest sea tragedy of our times.

The *Titanic* sailed from Southampton on her maiden voyage to New York on April 10, 1912. Many distinguished British and American people, attracted by the experience of making the first voyage in the vaunted liner, were passengers. There were a score of millionaires, and any number of celebrities. Down in the cabins of the steerage class were 706 immigrants bound for the land of promise. Altogether there were 2,201 persons aboard.

Of those fatal last hours at sea, many graphic stories have been written. Perhaps the best is by the American writer, Mr. Hanson W. Baldwin. Let him tell of the tragedy hour by hour.

* * * * *

Sunday in mid-Atlantic dawned fair and clear. The purser held services in the saloon in the morning. At 9 a.m. a message from the steamer *Caronia* sputtered into the wireless cabin:

Captain, *Titanic*: Westbound steamers report bergs growlers and field ice in 42 degrees N. from 49 to 51 degrees W. Compliments.—BARR.

In the afternoon Marconi Operator Bride, ear-phones clamped on his head, was figuring accounts; he did not stop to answer when he heard a nearby liner, the *Californian*, calling the *Titanic*.

The *Californian* had some message about three icebergs; he didn't bother to take it down. About 1.42 p.m. the rasping spark of those days spoke again across the water. It was the *Baltic* warning the *Titanic* of ice on the steamer track. Bride sent the message up to the bridge.

The bearded master of the *Titanic*, Captain E. C. Smith, read the message as he was walking on the promenade deck and handed it to Mr. Ismay without comment. Ismay read it, stuffed it in his pocket, told two ladies about the icebergs and resumed his walk. Later, about 7.15 p.m., the Captain requested the return of the message in order to post it in the chart-room for the information of officers.

Dinner that night in the Jacobean dining-room was gay. It was bitter on deck, but the night was calm and fine. After dinner some of the second-class passengers gathered in the saloon for a "hymn sing-song." It was almost ten o'clock as the group sang:

"*O hear us when we cry to Thee*
For those in peril on the sea."

TITANIC DISASTER. *The* Titanic *sailed from Southampton on her maiden voyage to New York on April 10, 1912. Four days later she struck an iceberg, and sank. Only 711 of the 2,201 people aboard were saved. The photographs above show the* Carpathian, *the ship which rescued the passengers, and the survivors.*

ONE OF THE LIFEBOATS, *filled with survivors, being picked up.*

TITANIC DISASTER.   *The captain of the ship, Captain E. C. Smith.*

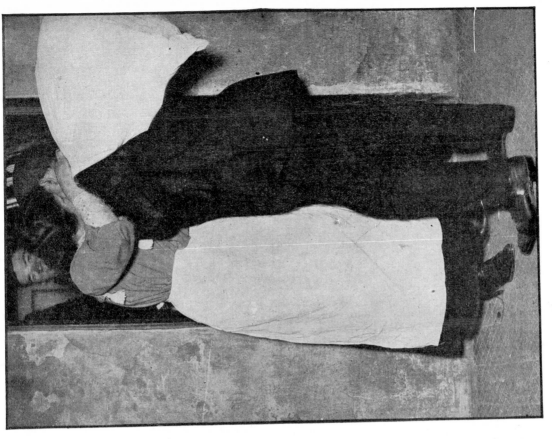

TITANIC DISASTER. *Survivors from the Titanic's crew arrive in Southampton. The centre figure in the photograph on the left, Mr. E. Brown, was unable to swim, but kept afloat for an hour by clinging to a lifebelt.*

On the bridge Second Officer Light-oller was relieved at ten o'clock by First Officer Murdock. At least five wireless ice warnings had reached the ship; look-outs had been cautioned to be alert; officers expected to reach the field at any time after 9.30 p.m. At 22 knots, its speed unslackened, the *Titanic* ploughed on through the night. In the crow's nest, Lookout Fleet and his partner, Leigh, gazed down at the water, still and unruffled in the dim, starlit dark-ness.

In the wireless room, where Phillips, first operator, had relieved Bride, the buzz of the *Californian's* set again crackled:

Californian: "Say, old man, we are stuck here, surrounded by ice."

Titanic: "Shut up, shut up; keep out. I am talking to Cape Race; you are jam-ming my signals."

Then, a few minutes later—about 11.40. . . .

Out of the dark she came, a vast, dim, white, monstrous shape, directly in the *Titanic's* path. For a moment Fleet doubted his eyes. But she was a deadly reality. Frantically he telephoned the bridge:

"Iceberg. Right ahead!"

Bells clanged the first warning in the engine-room. Danger! The indicators on the dial faces swung round to "Stop!" Then "Full speed astern!"

There was a slight shock, a brief scraping, a small list to port; shell ice—slabs and chunks of it—fell on the fore-deck. Slowly the *Titanic* stopped.

Captain Smith hurried out of his cabin. "What has the ship struck?"

Murdock answered, "An iceberg, sir. I have closed the watertight doors."

A few lights switched on in the first and second cabins; sleepy passengers peered through porthole glass; some casually asked the stewards:

"Why have we stopped?"

"I don't know, sir, but I don't sup-pose it is anything much."

In the smoking-room a quorum of gamblers were still sitting round a poker table. They had felt the slight jar of the collision and had seen an 80-foot ice mountain glide by the smoking-room windows, but the *Titanic* was "unsink-able"; they hadn't bothered to go on deck.

But far below, in the forward holds and boiler-rooms, men could see that the *Titanic's* hurt was mortal. All six com-partments forward of No. 4 were open to the sea; in ten seconds the iceberg's jagged claw had ripped a 300-foot slash in the bottom of the great *Titanic*.

On deck, in corridor and stateroom, life flowed again. Men, women, and children awoke and questioned; orders were given to uncover the lifeboats; water rose into the firemen's quarters; half-dressed stokers streamed up on deck.

But the passengers—most of them—did not know that the *Titanic* was sink-ing. The shock of the collision had been so slight that some were not awakened by it. The *Titanic* was un-sinkable; the night was too calm, too beautiful to think of death at sea.

In the radio cabin the blue spark danced, calling for assistance: "CQD—CQD—CQD——"

The sea was surging into the *Titanic's* hold. At 12.20 the water burst into the seamen's quarters through a collapsed bulkhead. Pumps strained in the engine-rooms—men and machinery making a futile fight against the sea. Steadily the water rose.

The boats were swung out—slowly;

for the deckhands were late in reaching their stations; there had been no boat drill, and many of the crew did not know to what boats they were assigned.

12.30 a.m. The word is passed: "Women and children in the boats." Stewards finish waking their passengers below. Life-preservers are tied on. Some men smile at the precaution. "The *Titanic* is unsinkable."

The *Mt. Temple* starts for the *Titanic*. The *Carpathia* radios "Coming hard." The CQD changes the course of many ships—but not of one. The operator of the *Californian,* a dozen miles away, has just put down his ear-phones and turned in.

12.45 a.m. Murdock, eyes tragic, but calm and cool, orders Boat No. 7 lowered. The women hang back; they want no boat ride on an ice-strewn sea; the *Titanic* is unsinkable. The men encourage them, explain that this is just a precautionary measure. "We'll see you again at breakfast." There is little confusion; passengers stream slowly to the boat deck. In the steerage the immigrants chatter excitedly.

A sudden sharp hiss—a streaked flare against the night. A rocket explodes and a parachute of white star lights up the icy sea. "God! Rockets!" The band plays ragtime. No. 6 goes over the side. There are only 28 people in a lifeboat with a capacity of 65.

1.0 a.m. Slowly the water creeps higher; the fore ports of the *Titanic* are dipping into the sea. Rope squeaks through blocks; lifeboats drop jerkily seaward. Through the shouting on the decks comes the sound of the band playing ragtime.

The "Millionaires' Special" leaves the ship—No. 1, with a capacity of 40 people, carries only Sir Cosmo and Lady Duff Gordon and ten others. Aft, the frightened immigrants jostle and rush for a boat. An officer's fist flies out; three shots are fired in the air, and the panic is quelled. . . . Four Chinese sneak unseen into a boat and hide in its bottom.

The rockets fling their splendour towards the stars. The boats are more heavily loaded now, for the passengers know the *Titanic* is sinking. Women cling and sob. The great screws aft are rising clear of the sea. Half-filled boats are ordered to come alongside the cargo ports and take on more passengers, but the ports are never opened—and the boats are never filled. The water rises and the band plays ragtime.

1.30 a.m. As one boat is lowered into the sea a boat officer fires his gun along the ship's side to stop a rush from the lower decks. A woman tries to take her Great Dane into a boat with her; she is refused and steps out of the boat to die with her dog.

Benjamin Guggenheim, in evening clothes, smiles and says: "We've dressed up in our best and are prepared to go down like gentlemen." Major Butts helps women into the last boats and waves goodbye to them. Mrs. Straus puts her foot on the gunwale of a lifeboat, then she draws back and goes to her husband: "We've been together many years; where you go I will go."

Colonel John Jacob Astor puts his young wife in a lifeboat, steps back, taps cigarette on fingernail: "Goodbye, dear; I'll see you later."

1.45 a.m. The foredeck is under water, the great stern is lifted high towards the bright stars. Below in the stokeholds the sweaty firemen keep steam up for the flaring lights and the dancing spark. Stokers slice and shovel as water laps about their ankles. Safety valves pop as the stokers retreat aft, and the watertight doors clang shut behind them.

There are about 660 people in the boats and 1,500 still on the sinking *Titanic*.

On top of the officers' quarters men work frantically to get over the side the two collapsibles stowed there. In the radio cabin Bride has slipped a life-jacket about Phillips as the first operator sits hunched over his key. A stoker, grimed with coal, mad with fear, steals into the shack and reaches for the life-jacket on Phillips' back. Bride wheels about and brains him with a wrench. The band still plays—but not ragtime:

> "*Nearer, my God, to Thee,*
> *Nearer to Thee . . .*"

A few men take up the refrain; others kneel on the slanting decks and pray. People are leaping from the decks into the nearby water—the icy water. A woman cries, "Oh, save me, save me!" A man answers, "Good lady, save yourself. Only God can save you now."

The water creeps over the bridge where the *Titanic's* master stands; heavily he steps out to meet it.

2.17 a.m. "CQ——" The *Virginian* hears a ragged, blurted "CQ——," then an abrupt stop. The blue spark dances no more. The lights on the ship flicker out.

2.18 a.m. Men run about blackened decks; leap into the night; are swept into the sea by the curling wave which licks up the *Titanic's* length.

The great stern rises like a squat levi-athan. The forward funnel snaps and crashes into the sea; its steel tons hammer out of existence swimmers struggling in the freezing water.

The *Titanic* stands on end, poised briefly for the plunge. Slowly she slides to her grave.

2.20 a.m. The greatest ship in the world has sunk. From the calm, dark waters, where the floating lifeboats move, there goes up in the white wake of her passing "one long continuous moan."

*   *   ·   *   *

The boats that the *Titanic* had launched pulled safely away from the slight suction of the sinking ship. There were only a few boats that were heavily loaded; most of those that were half empty made but perfunctory efforts to pick up the moaning swimmers, their officers and crews fearing they would endanger the living if they pulled back into the midst of the dying.

Some boats beat off the freezing victims; fear-crazed men and women struck with oars at the heads of swimmers. One woman drove her fist into the face of a half-dead man as he tried feebly to climb over the gunwale. Two other women helped him in and staunched the flow of blood from ring-cuts on his face.

It was 2.40 when the *Carpathia* first sighted the green light from No. 2 boat; it was 4.10 when she picked up the first boat and learned that the *Titanic* had foundered. The last of the moaning cries had just died away then. It was soon afterward, when her radio operator put on his earphones, that the *Californian*, the ship that had been within sight when the *Titanic* was sinking, first learned of the disaster.

And it was then, in all its white-green majesty, that the *Titanic's* survivors saw the iceberg, tinted with the sunrise, floating idly on the blue breast of the sea.

MR. ASQUITH *was Prime Minister in these eventful pre-war days, and he had the task of preparing Britain for the European conflict which everyone feared.*

DEATH OF GENERAL BOOTH. *In* 1912 *General William Booth, founder of the Salvation Army and one of Britain's greatest Evangelists, died. He was blind in his later years, but he still retained his power over the remarkable organisation he had built.*

A GREAT NAVAL REVIEW *was held just before the war, and was attended by H.M. the King and the Prince of Wales.*

On Thursday night, when the *Carpathia* reached her dock in New York 30,000 people jammed the streets; ambulances and stretchers stood on the pier; coroners and physicians waited, and relatives of the 711 survivors, relatives of the missing—hoping against hope. The dense throngs stood quiet as the first survivor—a woman—half staggered down the gangway. A "low wailing" moan came from the crowd, grew in volume, and dropped again.

The British Board of Trade's investigation was tersely damning. The *Titanic* had carried boats enough for 1,178 persons, only one-third of her capacity. Her sixteen boats and four collapsibles had saved only 711 persons; 400 had needlessly lost their lives. The *Californian* also was damned. She had seen the *Titanic's* rockets, and she had not received the "CQD" because her radio operator was asleep.

"When she first saw the rockets," said the report, "the *Californian* could have pushed through the ice to the open water without any serious risk and so have come to the assistance of the *Titanic*. Had she done so she might have saved many if not all of the lives that were lost."

III

In the meantime King George and Queen Mary had returned from their tour of India. For the next few months they were travelling about Britain opening new buildings, visiting housing estates, and generally getting acquainted with their people.

Everywhere they were received in the greatest fervour and patriotism. One of their first public duties was the laying of the foundation stones of the new London County Hall on the south bank of the river, opposite Westminster.

But throughout this Royal progress of Britain the real trouble was centring itself in Ireland. Politically, Ireland had been troublesome to Parliament for a good many years. Now the Irish Nationalist Party held the balance of power in the House of Commons.

During the conflict in the House of Lords, Home Rule for Ireland had been relegated to the background. Now, under the leadership of John Redmond, the Irish Party were insisting on their long neglected demands being met.

Very soon passions were running high. On April 11, 1912, the Home Rule Bill was introduced into the House of Commons. It gave Ireland a Senate and a House of Commons, reserving certain subjects of legislation and taxation to the Imperial Parliament, but making provision for a possible larger transference of power later on.

The Conservatives, who opposed this Bill, had as their leaders two extraordinarily virile and able men. One of them was Sir Edward Carson, and the other Mr. F. E. Smith, a master of invective at that time. The latter was later to become Lord Birkenhead, while the former, who is still alive, is Lord Carson.

Another Nationalist Bill was proceeding through the House of Commons at the same time. This was the Welsh Disestablishment Bill.

Again strong feelings were roused. When the Bill achieved its third reading in the House of Commons the extraordinary scene was witnessed of Welsh members singing "Land of my Fathers" in the Lobbies of the House of Commons. The Home Rule Bill for Ireland was also passed about the same time.

HIGH NECKS *and small waists were features of the styles
of 1910, and hats were much befeathered.*

A SHORT TRAIN *adds grace to a 1913 fashion; the bodice
has a draped line on the shoulders.*

CONTRASTS IN HAIR-DRESSING STYLES *throughout the years, showing the Eton Crop and the Bob, two popular styles, with the more elaborate coiffures favoured for evenings.*

HATS FROM 1910-1934. *The trend of fashion for shallow crowns has reached a stage when, in* 1934, *a crown is almost non-existent, as seen in the model felt* (left centre) *with the split brim.*

Needless to say, both Bills were immediately rejected by the House of Lords.

At this time Mr. Lloyd George seemed to be the centre of all these political troubles. Not only was he in the midst of his own great Insurance Act, which was arousing much opposition, but he was also championing the cause of the Welsh countrymen and indulging in a great deal of his well-known invective on the passing of the Home Rule Bill for Ireland.

It seemed to the outside world, and particularly Germany, that the whole of the British Isles was breaking up under these national complexes. The whole of Northern Ireland was well organised and blatantly rebellious under the leadership of Sir Edward Carson and F. E. Smith (Galloper Smith, as he was known in those days).

Conditions in Ulster were such that the Governor was being seriously asked whether it was not his duty to put Sir Edward Carson under arrest.

Two seizures of arms had been made in Ireland, large forces were drilling steadily in Ulster, and the whole organisation of an army—signal corps, army service corps, and so on—was in being. But not only were gun-running and preparations for civil war going on in Ireland. There were industrial troubles, too. For some years two men had been busily organising labour in Ireland.

James Larkin, breaking away in 1908 from English trade unionism, had founded the Irish Transport Workers' Union, which soon became a strong militant body.

In 1910 he was joined by James Connolley, who had spent the previous seven years in the United States, and been deeply imbued with the fighting spirit of the industrial workers of the world.

These two firebrands began a regular campaign of the most direct action type. Strikes were launched without any notice to employers. They believed in swift, very definite action.

In August, 1912, the whole of Dublin was disorganised by a series of strikes engineered by these two leaders.

The employers in Dublin did their best to smash the strikes. They began by dismissing members of the Transport Workers' Union from their employment. Larkin retaliated by calling a general strike.

Then the employers capped it with something like a general lock-out. Larkin came to England to obtain help for his cause. He travelled the country, making speeches of a violent character. He warned the British public that civil war and class war were about to break out throughout the whole of Ireland.

The Government could not stand aside while these flamboyant speeches were being made. In October Larkin was arrested and sentenced to seven months' imprisonment for using seditious language.

But the critics of the Government's Home Rule policy seized upon this arrest to point out its absurdities. If Larkin could be arrested, why not Sir Edward Carson? Both, the critics claimed, had been using seditious language.

The Government succumbed to these criticisms. Larkin had hardly served a fortnight of his sentence when he was released.

But the situation in Northern Ireland was becoming definitely ugly. Ulster Day, on September 28, saw the immense signing of the Ulster Covenant to

8

obey no laws and to pay no taxes imposed by a Parliament at Dublin. This was followed by inspections and reviews of forces. They were armed, as yet, in the open, only with dummy rifles. But it was known that the extensive gun-running which had been going on had provided these forces with real weapons of a deadly character.

As an indication of the passions that had been roused, there was the great Unionist demonstration in Belfast when, after a march past of 80,000 men, Sir Edward Carson bade the meeting repeat after him: "We will never, in any circumstances, submit to Home Rule."

Then the south of Ireland began gun-running of rifles and machine guns in reply to the policy already adopted by the north.

Even the staidest of politicians began to be alarmed. Mr. Bonar Law made a speech at Bristol in which he warned the country that it was "rapidly drifting to civil war." The Archbishop of York preached a sermon in which he begged for peace.

By this time the Irish conflict had swept into the fatal year of 1914. The Home Rule Bill began to be a regular discussion in the House of Commons. But the speeches of the members became more and more violent in character. As Prime Minister, Mr. Asquith tried to arrange a compromise so that Ulster could vote itself out of any Home Rule schemes which were produced for Ireland. But even the Unionists themselves would not accept this compromise. Sir Edward Carson called it: "A sentence of death with stay of execution for six years."

No sooner had this compromise been announced than it was swept aside by startling reports, ten days later, that officers of the Colour were resigning their commission rather than risk having to march against Ulster.

Sir Edward Carson in the House of Commons made a sensational assertion in his speech that the War Office had been discussing mobilisation for active service in Ireland. Then, in an ostentatious manner, Sir Edward Carson and eight other Unionists walked out of the House. The public were demanding news of what had really happened at the Curragh, that great military barracks outside Dublin. Eventually the facts came forth.

After interviews with General Sir Arthur Paget, commanding in Ireland, most of the officers of the cavalry brigade at the Curragh—fifty-seven out of seventy—and the Brigadier himself, General Gough, had intimated that they preferred dismissal to obeying orders for service in Ulster.

This arose out of an action by the Government in which they had decided on March 14 to take steps to protect military stores and munitions in the disaffected parts of Ireland.

General Paget, following a quite usual course in the moving of troops, arranged meetings at the Curragh, first with General Gough to work out details, and then with the other officers of the brigade to make the details clear.

Thinking it prudent to make sure of his ground with the senior officers, he had intimated that if any of them were not prepared to obey orders they should absent themselves from the conference. The result was that some of the officers did so.

It also came out that General Gough had received a document from the War Office signed by Colonel Seeley, General French, chief of the General Staff, and

Sir J. S. Ewart, Adjutant-General. After a couple of short paragraphs stating the duties of troops in keeping civil order and the right of the Government to their services, this document went on to say that the Government had "no intention whatever of using this right in order to crush political opposition to the policy or principles of the Home Rule Bill."

It was also heard that, during the Cabinet discussion of this document, which had contained only the two paragraphs on the duties of troops, Colonel Seeley had had to leave for an audience of the King. The discussion being over when he returned, he had on his own responsibility added the intimation about the Government intention.

The Prime Minister stated that all the three signatories of the document had tendered their resignations, but these had not been accepted.

There was a tremendous outcry and vehement speeches from all sides of the House of Commons on this document. It dragged on for a few days, with even more violent speeches.

Eventually, on March 30, the Prime Minister announced that Colonel Seeley, General French, and General Ewart had persisted in their resignations. A breathless fortnight ensued. All eyes were turned towards the West. It was seen that most protagonists in Ireland were ready to engage in a desperate conflict.

What the observers did not do was to turn their eyes towards the Continent, where bigger and more mighty war clouds were gathering.

IV

There were, however, in Europe a few men who realised the European cataclysm which was coming and which would almost overwhelm these islands.

First and foremost was Lord Roberts, that hero of the Boer War, who had preached the necessity of military service for the youth of this country.

He did not hesitate to point to Germany as the most aggressive nation in the world. He also pointed to our defencelessness in the face of all this armed aggression. Ridiculed and criticised, jeered at by crowds, this little man with the great spirit nevertheless persisted in his warnings to the public.

Another figure who also realised the dangers creeping upon us was that Socialist writer, Robert Blatchford. He himself had been a serving soldier in the Buffs regiment, and the military outlook which had been stamped upon him was very unpalatable to many of his Socialist adherents.

Nevertheless, in that simple, direct prose which had made him one of the leading journalists of the day, he began a series of articles in the *Daily Mail* on the North Sea danger.

He insisted that this grey, misty, shallow sea which divided England and Germany and which the Germans themselves persisted in calling the German Ocean, would undoubtedly be the scene of the great conflict of the future.

His articles aroused immense interest and a certain amount of conviction. But it had to be admitted that the majority of people were indifferent to these warnings. As has been said before, their eyes were fixed on Ireland, rather than on Europe in general.

There was, however, a man of extraordinary foresight, a hidden genius of the War Office in those days. This was the extraordinary Scots lawyer, Haldane. Haldane was a fine logical thinker, and deeply immersed in German literature. Germany was, he once said quite truly, his spiritual home.

Appointed War Minister in the Liberal Government, he went to the War Office, called the staff round him, and asked them to teach him. He mastered what they could tell, prepared a scheme, which, so far as they could understand, incorporated their wishes, and then went down to the House of Commons and read off the elaborate instrument to a House still less able to follow him.

But War Office and Commons both felt that he knew his job and could both learn and teach, organise and inform and supply. Haldane also reorganised the Territorial force, that great body of patriotic and efficiently drilled men that rendered such remarkable service in the early days of the war.

As for the Regular Army, small though it was, Haldane made it easily the best in Europe, as was proved when it was used. He made an Expeditionary Force, with a Liberal Government in power, which was far more effective than any Army which a Conservative Government had ever had or even attempted to have.

As Mr. Gerald Heard has said, he equipped the party of peace with a first-rate weapon of offence.

Neither must be forgotten the enthusiasm among youth for the Boy Scout Movement organised by Sir Robert Baden Powell.

This movement was a novel advance on anything that had been tried in Europe before, and is the real forerunner of those extraordinary Youth Movements which are now sweeping the countries of Europe in various directions.

But the Boy Scout Movement in Britain had no direct military bearing. It was merely a romantic, healthy idea which appealed to the youth of the country.

Sir Robert Baden Powell, by his picturesque defence of Mafeking in 1899 and by his reputation for craft in game tracking, had become a kind of hero to boyhood all over the country. By a stroke of real genius he turned all this into a channel which was to give to thousands of boys in dreary towns and dull industrial quarters of mean streets a vivid interest in their lives, a pride in handy usefulness, and hours—days and weeks with luck—of fresh air, a countryside and camping.

He knew exactly how to hit the imagination of the boys with his organisation of patrols and totems, the uniform of loose shirt and shorts with just the light romantic touches of broad-brimmed hat and jack knife slung at the belt, and with badges for efficiency in all the arts of camp life.

Not the least part of it was that in classes and practice so much scout life could go on in winter and keep boys keen. The Movement spread very rapidly and managed to keep its influence for self-respect and friendliness and health from becoming boring.

In time girls grew so envious of it that they had to form the Girl Guides.

Finally, of those men who were at the head of affairs during these months when Europe was rapidly organising itself into an armed camp for a great war, mention must be made of Prince Louis of Battenburg, who was in charge of the Navy.

Mr. Winston Churchill, as First Lord of the Admiralty, has already paid many tributes to the efficiency and foresightedness of Prince Louis in bringing the British Navy to a pitch of efficiency so that on the outbreak of war it was prepared for worldwide action within a few minutes of the declaration.

But for the most part the British public was blind to the gathering forces that were soon to sweep them into the great conflict. They were much more concerned with the sporting and entertaining trivialities of the times.

There was that great hero of the boxing world, Bombardier Billy Wells, a tall, handsome youth, who became the adored idol of thousands, particularly women. Early in December, 1913, a big fight was staged between Bombardier Billy Wells and Georges Carpentier, the French champion.

One of the biggest and most fashionable crowds ever attending a fight in this country gathered to see this conflict. Actually it lasted for precisely seventy-seven seconds. Carpentier, with lightning rapidity, knocked out Bombardier Billy Wells in that time.

The summer of 1914 showed Britain, despite its internal conflicts, trouble in Ireland and elsewhere, bent on pleasure. People were arranging their summer holidays, money was being spent freely, prosperity seemed everywhere in the streets of London.

When the news came that an Archduke, one of the Austrian Hapsburgs, had been murdered in a place called Sarajevo, somewhere in the Balkans, few people realised that the curtain was rising on the greatest drama of modern time.

CHAPTER V

EUROPE AT WAR

Assassination at Sarajevo—Austria's ultimatum to Servia—Alarming messages from Russia—Austria declares war—King George's appeal to the Czar—Russia and Germany at war—Britain's ultimatum—Britain at war—Scenes at the Foreign Office—How Britain receives the news—Lord Kitchener is appointed War Secretary—An appeal for recruits—British cruiser is sunk —Battle of Mons—" The Angel of Mons" controversy—The British Army in retreat—Battle of the Marne—British Fleet sinks three German cruisers off Heligoland.

I

THE drama of Sarajevo has been told again and again. But by its apparent insignificance to the peoples beyond the Balkans it has an ironic fatality which makes its retelling a necessity in the true history of these twenty-five years of the British people.

The scene of that shot that began the Great War was Sarajevo, a city in the provinces of Bosnia-Herzegovina, a Balkan country which had been incorporated within the boundaries of Austria-Hungary.

The peoples of those newly acquired territories were thought to be hostile to the rule of the old Emperor Francis Josef, and for that reason it was considered wise to arrange a Royal demonstration and procession in the streets of Sarajevo itself.

The Royal figure chosen for this demonstration of the might of Austria-Hungary was the heir to the throne himself, Franz Ferdinand, Archduke of Austria.

Accompanied by his wife, Sophie Chotek, Duchess of Hohenburg, he decided to make a formal entry into the town of Sarajevo on Sunday, June 28,

1914. Incidentally, that day was also the anniversary of his wedding.

The Archduke and his wife were staying at Ilidzhe, a watering-place a few miles from Sarajevo, from which Franz Ferdinand had just directed the military manœuvres.

In his entry to the town of Sarajevo he was to pass along a wide street, on one side of which was a wall and the River Milyatsa. There were three bridges across the river, one of which he was to cross. Five assassins were waiting for him near the first bridge; one, a boy, Princip, at the second; and one more at the third.

A little after ten o'clock on that fateful morning the Royal party arrived from Ilidzhe in four cars. As they drove rather swiftly along the street near the first bridge one of the conspirators threw a bomb. It bounced off the Archduke's car and wounded several spectators as well as a lieutenant-colonel in the Archducal suite.

But the cars drove on to the Hotel de Ville. There the party were received by the Mayor of Sarajevo, who, not knowing what had happened, began an address of loyal welcome on behalf of the citizens. Franz Ferdinand inter-

BRITAIN IS AT WAR. *Thousands gathered outside Buckingham Palace when war was declared to demonstrate their loyalty to their Sovereign. Within a few hours Sir John French had assumed control of the Army, and Sir John Jellicoe of the Navy, and the nation began a war that was to last over four years. Yet in August, 1914, most people expected it to be over by Christmas.*

LORD KITCHENER *was appointed Minister for War immediately war was declared. Historians and politicians have criticised him severely, but it was public affection for him which made it so easy for the British Army to secure recruits, and he had great influence among Britain's Allies. His death at sea while on a mystery visit to Russia was a shock to the nation.*

CROWDS *reading the Proclamation of War in Whitehall, August,* 1914.

Within a few hours of war being declared thousands were offering themselves at recruiting offices.

WOMEN RECRUITERS FOR THE ARMY.

RECRUITS BEING SWORN IN.

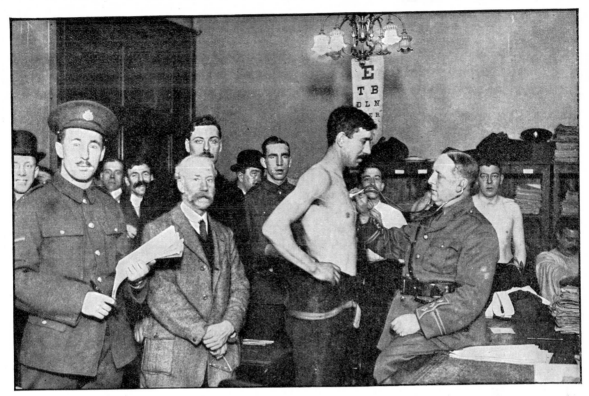

MEDICAL EXAMINATION.

DRILLING RECRUITS IN HYDE PARK.

"YOUR COUNTRY NEEDS YOU"

DO YOU REMEMBER *this famous poster? It stood out on every hoarding in the country, and induced thousands of men to join Kitchener's Army. The artist, Alfred Leete, was also famous for his war cartoons.*

rupted him and said there was not much loyalty in bombs. A few minutes later an officer announced that they had arrested the man who threw the bomb.

"Better hurry and hang him," said the Archduke laconically, "or they will be sending him a decoration from Vienna."

Then the Archduke decided to visit his wounded aide-de-camp at the hospital and the Duchess declared that she would go with him. They set off again —but the driver of the car made a mistake. Instead of driving straight over the bridge he made a turn to the right. Seeing his mistake, he backed the car to turn.

This was the moment for Princip, standing there in the crowd. He jumped forward and fired with his revolver. He hit the Archduke first. He then fired at Potiorek, the military governor, but hit instead the Duchess, who had flung herself forward to protect her husband. They were hurried at once to the Konak, or official residence. The Duchess was dead before they reached there, and Franz Ferdinand died in about ten minutes. It was just eleven o'clock in the morning.

Immediately the telegraph was buzzing with the news across Europe. In Servia itself the news was received with great excitement. In Belgrade, the capital of Servia, the Government, fearing lest in the heat of the excitement aroused by the patriotic rejoicings which were taking place the chauvinist element might lend an anti-Austrian colour to the demonstrations, issued an order to the effect that, as a sign of mourning, all places of entertainment, including cafés, should turn out lights and close at ten o'clock.

Three days later, on July 2, the bodies of the Archduke and his consort reached Vienna. There was no special military display to receive them, though the Archduke was head of the Army. Next day they lay in state in the Hofburg Chapel.

At four o'clock in the afternoon a funeral service was held at which only a few diplomats were present, and some of the courtiers.

It lasted for a quarter of an hour only out of regard for the old Emperor. There was no opportunity for the public to pay their respects to the dead.

A great part of the Vienna garrison followed the bodies in the evening to the Western Railway station. At the last moment a large contingent of Vienna notables, who had received no invitations to the funeral, followed the procession on foot as a mark of respect.

At eleven o'clock in the evening the train left for Pochlarn, which it reached about one in the morning of July 14.

A terrible storm burst and the coffins were hurried into the tiny waiting-room of the village station. In the early dawn the hearse was put on a ferry to go over the Danube. Lightning and thunder made the horses shy and they almost precipitated the hearse into the river. The roads at Artstetten were impassable, and the mourners had to wade in the river.

Finally the bodies were borne up the hill to the vault. "The ceremony at the Chapel of Artstetten," says the Archduke's physician, "was simple but dignified." At a sharp turn at the entrance to the vault the bearers knocked the coffin against an edge of the wall, breaking loose a piece. "I saw the picture of the Archduke rise before my eyes, as, upon viewing the vault which was being completed, he jokingly said to me, 'Then I shall turn in my grave.'"

Although the news of this assassination set the windows of the Foreign Office in Wilhelmstrasse at Berlin and in St. Petersburg to be lighted night after night whilst couriers dashed about with important messages, it seemed that the diplomatic world in general was not unduly perturbed.

The Kaiser himself was on his Royal yacht refreshing himself in the cool Scandinavian fjords.

A few weeks previously, as Admiral of the Fleet, he had been host at Kiel to a squadron of British warships, H.M.S. *King George*, H.M.S. *Ajax*, H.M.S. *Audacious*, and H.M.S. *Centurion*. They were ranged alongside the fine dreadnoughts of Germany's High Fleet.

British and German officers as well as the ordinary seamen and marines had fraternised as good comrades. One of the German commanders noted a toast drunk privately between the German and the British Admirals, "To the White Nations." None of them at that time realised that they would later be meeting in the greatest sea fight of history off Jutland.

At the same time, by the irony of circumstance, the Light Squadron of Admiral Sir Christopher Craddock cruised companionably in Mexican waters with the German ships of Admiral Graf von Spee. At that time Coronel and the Falkland Islands were merely names on the charts carried in the chart-room of each of the ships.

Even in the Wilhelmstrasse the ministers of the German Foreign Office were enjoying their summer holidays. Von Moltke was taking a cure. A certain Colonel Ludendorff, zealous officer of the General Staff, on duty at Strasburg, was taking a few days' leave in the Bavarian hills.

A retired general of blameless and unexciting career, Von Hindenburg, stalked about his Pomeranian country place in gaiters and a shooting jacket.

And even in England, despite the Irish situation, there was little to disturb the serenity of affairs. There was a great naval review off Spithead, King George's ships coming up in columns from the misty sea, to thunder their salutes before the King.

Officers and men of the ships were looking forward to the leave which was to follow this review. Lord Kitchener, who had just been appointed to a command in Egypt, had booked his passage. Only Mr. Winston Churchill, studying plans and charts, and particularly the rather alarming messages coming from diplomats in various European countries, sat in the Admiralty awaiting events.

Even in Paris nobody seemed to realise that the hour had struck. Paris was as gay as ever, and M. Poincaré, as French President, was giving a series of brilliant receptions. Only a month previously King George and Queen Mary had visited Paris, and there had been scenes of enthusiasm and brilliance which revealed that the *entente cordiale* was still on the same firm base that his father, King Edward VII., had placed it.

St. Petersburg, a capital which now no longer exists, was still the scene of romance, mystery, and luxury. Russian princes and grand dukes, with their ladies, were spread about Europe, enjoying themselves in the playgrounds of the rich. Few people paid attention to the fact that in Ekaterinburg, a garrison

KING ALBERT OF THE BELGIANS AT THE FRONT. *When his country was invaded by the Germans, he fought with his subjects in the trenches.*

KAISER WILHELM OF GERMANY INSPECTS THE WAR ZONE. *He had never been a popular figure in England, and he was hated by everyone during the war. There was great indignation in the early days of the war at the rumour that he had boasted he would be "eating his next Christmas dinner in Buckingham Palace."*

OFF TO THE FRONT!

THE BRITISH ARMY *was drafted to the Continent in the early part of August to help to stem the German advance. "Tommy's" marching song was "Tipperary," which was made famous by George Curnock (above) in his despatches to the "Daily Mail."*

THE GREAT GERMAN INVASION. *German battalions swept across France and Belgium.
They received a momentary check at Mons, where thousands were mowed down by
British bullets. But the "Old Contemptibles" had to retreat to avoid annihilation, and
only a miracle saved Paris from falling into German hands. Then began the Battle of the
Marne, and the German hordes were forced back.*

LIFE ON THE WESTERN FRONT.

A QUIET GAME OF CARDS *on captured German equipment.*

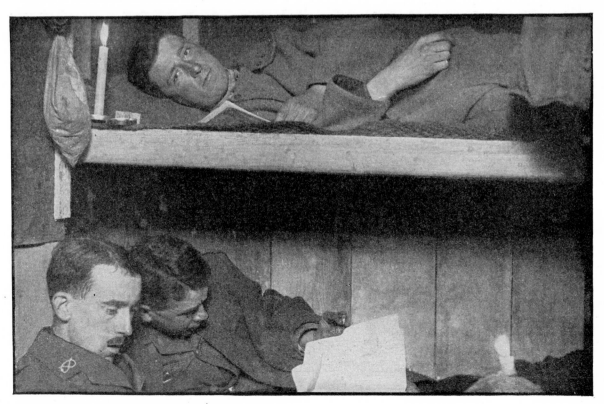

A " DUG-OUT " *somewhere on the Western Front.*

A NIGHT RAID.

"ALL QUIET ON THE WESTERN FRONT."

town just beyond the Urals, a man named Stalin was well guarded in a political prison on the far side of Siberia. At the same time an obscure agitator, Nikolai Lenin, had settled in Switzerland.

And even in Vienna itself there did not seem to be undue excitement over this assassination. The Emperor Franz Josef had known many sorrows in his long life, and he bore this one with more than Christian fortitude. The late Archduke had been a man of liberal tendencies and independent mind, unusual and unbecoming to a Hapsburg. Furthermore, the old Emperor had never approved the marriage with the Countess Chotek.

The next in line was the young Archduke Karl, more amenable and more conscious of the great considerations hedging about the oldest throne in Europe.

Many of these diplomats and others looked back upon a Europe that had been at peace for more than forty years. It did not seem conceivable that war would come now.

The only thing that seemed to be agitating New York was the fact that a very ordinary painting entitled "September Morn" had been suppressed. Some critics had said that the little lady, shivering without a bathing suit in the cold water of sunrise, was lewd and lascivious. Other art critics objected equally as strongly to the ban. Subsequently the ban was removed, and, as was only to be expected, copies of the painting were sold everywhere.

Nevertheless, the assassination of an Archduke could not be ignored by Austria-Hungary. An official investigation had been ordered by the Austro-Hungarian Government into the circumstances leading to the murder of the Archduke.

As a result of this enquiry it was revealed that, although there were indications that the plot to assassinate the Archduke had been concocted in Servia itself, there was nothing to prove or even lead one to suspect the complicity of the Servian Government in the suggestion or preparation of the crime or the providing of the weapons.

Before drawing up their ultimatum to Servia, however, the Emperor Franz Josef and his advisers made diplomatic enquiries in Germany as to whether that country and the Kaiser would support them in the event of war with Russia.

Apparently the Kaiser gave every assurance that Germany would stand by Austro-Hungary.

On July 21, therefore, Austria presented an ultimatum to Servia. Two days later, on a Saturday, the Prime Minister of Servia brought the Servian reply to the ultimatum to Baron Giesl, the Austro-Hungarian Minister in Belgrade. The Prime Minister of Servia said, "We have accepted part of your demand. For the rest we rely upon your loyalty and chivalry. We have always been quite satisfied with you."

Baron Giesl took up the reply of the Servian Government and studied the note for a few moments. Then he turned and looked at the Prime Minister. "The term fixed in the note," he said, "having expired without a satisfactory reply, I have the honour to inform you that I am leaving Belgrade this evening with the staff of my Legation."

And that evening Baron Giesl left the Embassy en route for Vienna. War was now declared between Austria and Servia.

In the meantime the diplomatic excitement had not passed unnoticed in Russia. The Crown Prince of Servia, seeking desperately for help, had applied personally to the Czar.

The Czar did not hesitate to reply quickly. "When your Royal Highness applied to me at a time of especial stress," he telegraphed, "you were not mistaken in the sentiments which I entertain for you or in my cordial sympathy with the Servian people. So long as the slightest hope exists of avoiding bloodshed all our efforts must be directed to that end. But if in spite of our earnest wish we are not successful your Highness may rest assured that Russia will in no case disinterest herself in the fate of Servia."

When the Russian Minister in Belgrade read the Czar's reply to the Prime Minister of Servia, the Prime Minister embraced the Russian Minister and exclaimed, "The Czar is great and merciful."

The British Minister in St. Petersburg at the time was Sir George Buchanan. He was in constant touch with Sir Edward Grey at the Foreign Office. On July 25 he telegraphed to Sir Edward Grey as follows: "On my expressing earnest hope that Russia would not precipitate war by mobilising until you (Grey) have time to use your influence in favour of peace, His Excellency assured me that Russia had no aggressive intentions and she would take no action until it was forced on her.

"M. Cazanov added that Austria's action was in reality directed against Russia. He did not believe that Germany really wanted war, but her attitude was decided by ours. If we took our stand firmly with France and Russia there would be no war. If we failed them, new rivers of blood would flow and we would, in the end, be dragged into war."

Nevertheless, while the diplomats were talking throughout Europe, forces seemed to be driving towards the inevitability of war. Russia began mobilisation of her army. On July 29 the Czar sent an urgent message to the Kaiser, which read as follows:

"Am glad you're back. In this most serious moment I appeal to you to help me to try and avoid such a calamity as a European War; I beg you, in the name of our old friendship, to stop your allies from going too far. Signed, Nicky."

Reading this telegram at his desk, the Kaiser scrawled across it, "A confession of his own weakness, and an attempt to put the responsibility on my shoulders."

On another document the Kaiser was writing: "I have no doubt left. England, France, and Russia have agreed among themselves to have the Austro-Servian conflict for an excuse for waging a war of extermination against us. Edward VII. is stronger after death than I who am still alive, and there have been people who believe that England could still be won over or pacified by this or that puny measure!"

On the night of July 24 Mr. Asquith, the Prime Minister, was writing this in his diary: "At 3.15 we had a Cabinet—the real interest was Grey's statement of the European situation, which is about as bad as it can possibly be. Austria has sent a bullying and humiliating ultimatum and demands an answer in forty-eight hours, failing which, she will march. This means almost inevitably that Russia will come on the scene, and, if so, it is difficult for both Germany and France to refrain from lending a hand.

So that we are in measurable distance of a real Armageddon."

In the meantime France was offering her support to Russia, although all the ministers and diplomats in France seemed to be quite in the dark as to the attitude Britain would take in this rapidly approaching conflict.

Sir George Buchanan from St. Petersburg was sending more and more alarming messages. On one of these which he received Sir Edward Grey made the following annotation:

"Mr. Churchill told me to-day that the Fleet can be mobilised in twenty-four hours, but I think it is premature to make any statement to France and Russia yet."

Sunday, July 26, was an important day for the British Fleet. This is how Prince Louis of Battenburg, then First Sea Lord, describes it:

"The Fleet reassembled at Portsmouth was on the point of dispersing for demobilisation. The political outlook took an alarming turn by Austria's ultimatum to Servia. On the Sunday the Admiralty, as a precautionary measure, ordered the ships to remain where they were until further orders. For the moment Austria-Hungary, which had really provoked the diplomatic tangle by presenting Servia with an ultimatum and refusing to consider the acceptance in part of the Servian nation, seemed to be hesitating. No actual military move had yet been made."

On July 28 a formal declaration of war was sent by telegraph to the Servian Minister of Foreign Affairs from Vienna. It read: "The Royal Servian Government not having answered in a satisfactory manner the note of July 23 presented by the Austro-Hungarian Minister at Belgrade, the Imperial and Royal Government are themselves compelled to see to the safeguarding of their rights and interests, and with this object to have recourse to force of arms. Austria-Hungary consequently considers herself henceforward in a state of war with Servia."

Slowly, but surely and inevitably, Russia was proceeding with the mobilisation of her enormous army. The German Chief of Staff, Moltke, late on the night of the 30th, telegraphed to Conrad, the Austro-Hungarian Chief of Staff:

"Stand fast against Russian mobilisation. Austria-Hungary must be preserved. Mobilise at once against Russia. Germany will mobilise."

At about eight o'clock in the morning of July 23 mobilisation of the whole Austro-Hungarian Army was decided upon. The old Emperor Franz Josef signed the decree just after noon.

He telegraphed an hour later to the German Emperor: "In the consciousness of my grave obligation towards the future of my Empire I have ordered the mobilisation of my entire armed forces. I am aware of the full meaning and extent of my decision, at which I arrived with confidence in the justice of God, combined with the certainty that the strength of your defence will, with unflinching fidelity, furnish security for my Empire and for the Triple Alliance."

The German Emperor promptly replied:

"The preliminary mobilisation of my entire Army and Navy ordered by me to-day will be followed within the shortest period of time by actual mobilisation. I am reckoning on August 2 as the first day of mobilisation, and I am ready in fulfilment of the obligations of my alliance to commence war at once against Russia and France."

It now appeared that forces had been set in motion which nobody could stop. Despite the alarming reports of mobilisation everywhere in Europe, Sir Edward Grey was undoubtedly trying to save the situation. It was equally obvious that it had gone too far for it to stop.

France fully recognised that they were on the eve of a great conflict. The French Prime Minister had informed both St. Petersburg and London that "France is resolved to fulfil all the obligations of her alliance."

Sir Edward Grey asked the German Ambassador in London, Prince Lichnowsky, to call upon him. He told Prince Lichnowsky that if Germany could get any reasonable proposal put forward which made it clear that Germany and Austria were striving to preserve European peace, and that Russia and France would be unreasonable if they rejected it, he, Sir Edward Grey, would support it at St. Petersburg and Paris. He would also go to the length of saying that if Russia and France would not accept it, His Majesty's Government would have nothing more to do with the consequences. Otherwise Sir Edward Grey told the German Ambassador that, if France became involved, Britain would inevitably be drawn in.

A few hours later His Majesty King George V. sent a last appeal to the Czar of Russia. Mr. Asquith describes this appeal in his diary.

It reads as follows: " A long message from Berlin to the effect that the German Ambassador's efforts for peace have been suddenly arrested and frustrated by the Czar's decree for a complete Russian mobilisation. We all set to work to draft a personal appeal from the King to the Czar. When we had settled it, I called a taxi and, in company with Tyrrell, drove to Buckingham Palace by about 1.30 a.m. The King was hauled out of his bed, and one of my strangest experiences was sitting with him, clad in a dressing gown, while I read the message from Berlin and the proposed answer. The text was as follows: ' I cannot help thinking that some misunderstanding has produced this deadlock. I am most anxious not to miss any possibility of avoiding the terrible calamity which at present threatens the whole world. I therefore make a personal appeal to you.' "

The Czar promptly replied:

"I would gladly have accepted your proposal had not the German Ambassador this afternoon presented a note to my Government declaring war."

So Russia and Germany were definitely at war on the night of August 1. Germany had not waited for Russia's answer. At five o'clock that afternoon the Emperor Wilhelm had signed a decree mobilising the German Army. He signed it on a table made from the wood of the *Victory,* Nelson's flagship at Trafalgar. That night the Kaiser spoke thus to his people from the balcony of his Berlin castle:

"A fateful hour has fallen for Germany. Envious people everywhere are compelling us to our just defence. A sword has been forced into our hands. I hope that if my efforts at the last hour do not succeed in bringing our opponents to see eye to eye with us, and in maintaining peace, we shall, with God's help, so wield the sword that we shall restore it to its sheath again with honour.

NURSE CAVELL. *The execution of Nurse Cavell in 1915 for helping Allied soldiers to escape from the Germans aroused the horror of the world. Her body now lies in Norwich Cathedral.*

SIR ROGER CASEMENT, *hanged as a traitor in* 1916. *He was an Irishman who conspired with the Germans to start a rebellion in Southern Ireland. He sailed to Ireland in a German submarine, which was accompanied by a vessel loaded with arms. This was captured by a patrol boat. Casement landed in a collapsible boat, was captured, and tried for treason. He was sentenced to death, and on the following day he was deprived of his knighthood.*

THE SINKING OF THE BLÜCHER. This is one of the most dramatic photographs ever taken, showing the German battleship Blücher just as she was sinking. The crew can be seen clinging to the vessel or jumping into the sea. The ship was sunk by the British Fleet, commanded by Vice-Admiral Sir David Beatty, in an engagement in the North Sea, January 24, 1915. Only 123 members of the crew, out of 885, were saved.

BATTLE OF JUTLAND. *The German battle-cruiser Seydlitz ablaze. Shortly afterwards it sank.*

"War will demand of us enormous sacrifices in property and life, but we will show our enemies what it means to provoke Germany. And now I commend you to God. Go to church and kneel before God and pray for His help and for our gallant Army."

II

So far, the attitude of the British Government was still uncertain. There had been Cabinet meetings presided over by Mr. Asquith, in which the question of the neutrality of Belgium had been discussed. Britain was one of the signatories to that Treaty guaranteeing the independence of the country.

France had already declared to Britain that they would respect the neutrality of Belgium, and only in the event of some other Power violating the neutrality would France, in order to ensure defence of her own security, act otherwise.

It seemed certain, too, that France was about to be involved in this great conflict. France, in accordance with her Treaty obligations with Russia, began mobilising at 3.55 p.m. on August 1.

On August 2, very early, German troops began marching into Luxemburg. France was desperately anxious to know if Britain was going to stand by her. A Cabinet meeting had been held in Downing Street on the morning of Sunday, August 2, and a letter was read from Bonar Law, leader of the Conservative Opposition, agreeing to back up the Government in any measure they might take for the support of France and Russia.

That afternoon Sir Edward Grey received the French Ambassador and said: "I am authorised to give an assurance that if the German Fleet comes into the Channel or through the North Sea to undertake hostile operations against French coasts or shipping, the British Fleet will give all the protection in its power. This assurance is, of course, subject to the policy of His Majesty's Government receiving the support of Parliament, and must not be taken as binding."

The Cabinet again met in the evening, and came to a decision that if Belgian neutrality was violated, this country would declare war on Germany.

At 3 o'clock in the afternoon of Monday, August 3, Sir Edward Grey made a speech in a crowded House of Commons.

In a hushed and tense atmosphere he began his speech: "To-day events move so rapidly that it is exceedingly difficult to state with technical accuracy the actual state of affairs, but it is clear that the peace of Europe cannot be preserved. Russia and Germany at any rate have declared war upon each other.

"I now come to what we think the situation requires of us. For many years we have had a long-standing friendship with France. But how far that friendship entails obligation, let every man look into his own heart and his own feelings and construe the extent of the obligation for himself. I construe it myself as I feel it, but I do not wish to urge upon anyone else more than their feelings dictate as to what they should feel about the obligation.

"The House individually and collectively may judge for itself. I speak my personal view and I have given the House my own feeling in the matter. The French Fleet is now in the Mediterranean, and the northern and western coasts of France are absolutely undefended. The French Fleet being concentrated in the Mediterranean, the situation is very different from that it used to be, because the friendship which has grown up between the two countries has given them a sense of security that there was nothing to be feared from us.

"My own feeling is that if a foreign fleet, engaged in a war which France has not sought and in which she has not been the aggressor, came down the English Channel and bombarded and battered the undefended coasts of France, we could not stand aside.

"I believe that would be the feeling of this country. We feel strongly that France is entitled to know—and to know at once—whether or not in the event of an attack upon her unprotected northern and western coasts, she could depend upon British support."

Sir Edward Grey then read the telegram from King Albert to King George. "Remembering the numerous proofs of your Majesty's friendship and that of your predecessor," telegraphed King Albert, "and the friendly attitude of England in 1870, and the proof of friendship you have just given us again, I make a supreme appeal to the diplomatic intervention of your Majesty's Government to safeguard the integrity of Belgium."

Then Sir Edward Grey added: "If in a crisis, a time like this, we run away from these obligations of honour and interest as regards the Belgian Treaty, I doubt whether, whatever material force we might have at the end, it would be of very much value in place of the respect which we should have lost."

Just after Sir Edward Grey sat down he received a message from the Belgian Minister. Promptly he read it out:

"Germany sent yesterday evening at seven o'clock a note proposing to Belgium friendly neutrality covering free passage on Belgian territory, and promising maintenance of independence of the kingdom and possession at the conclusion of peace, and threatening in case of refusal to treat Belgium as an enemy. A time limit of twelve hours is fixed for the reply.

"The Belgians have answered that an attack on their neutrality would be a flagrant violation of the rights of nations and that to accept the German proposal would be to sacrifice the honour of a nation. Conscious of its duty, Belgium is firmly resolved to repel aggression by all possible means. Of course I can only say that the Government are prepared to take into grave consideration the information which it has received. I make no further comment upon it."

III

A dramatic scene ensued at the Foreign Office, in Whitehall. Night after night throughout this crisis lighted windows and hurrying couriers told of the excitement that raged within. Long despatches in code were being received from diplomats abroad.

Ministers in search of information were constantly on the telephone and interviewing the then Permanent Under-Secretary, Sir Arthur Nicolson.

The very small spy service then under control of the Foreign Office were sending their valuable reports. There is no doubt that the officials of the Foreign Office were fully aware of the trend of opinions in the various European countries, all of which showed a strong disposition for war.

While Sir Edward Grey was making his important speech in the House of

Commons a group waited tensely to hear the result of that speech. At five o'clock in the evening Sir Arthur Nicolson was waiting in his room at the Foreign Office. A clerk burst in. He had been listening to the speech in the House of Commons.

"He has had a tremendous reception, sir," the clerk said. "The whole House was with him."

Sir Arthur Nicolson, weary with nights of vigil, rose from his chair.

"Thank God," he said. "Now the coast is clear. But it will be a terrible business."

Immediately the whole organisation of the Foreign Office began drafting out messages to be sent to the various Dominions and outposts of the Empire warning them that the British Empire was at war with Germany. Typewriters clattered, clerks scurried to and fro, codes were brought out from pigeon holes, and those plans prepared well in advance for the use of our Consuls and Embassies abroad were immediately prepared in code for despatch abroad.

As this tremendous machinery was being set in motion Sir Edward Grey himself came into the room, and Sir Arthur Nicolson congratulated him on the success of his speech.

Sir Edward did not answer. He moved into the centre of the room and raised his clenched fists above his head. Then he brought his fist down with a crash upon the table.

"I hate war," he muttered. "I hate war."

At 8.30 that same evening Sir Edward Grey was still in the Foreign Office, conning the various despatches that were coming in from all over Europe. Twilight was sweeping across the whole of London. Sir Edward walked to the window and looked out.

"The lamps are going out all over Europe," he said. "We shall not see them lit again in our lifetime."

The Foreign Office received confirmation of the news that the Germans had entered Belgium and had announced that, if necessary, they would push their way through by force of arms.

These telegrams were rushed over to Downing Street, where Mr. Asquith was sitting with a Cabinet. After grave consideration of the reports, an ultimatum was drawn up by the British Cabinet and sent to the Germans, requesting them to give an assurance that they would respect Belgian neutrality. Otherwise the ultimatum would expire at midnight and the two countries would be at war.

Midnight in Germany meant 11 p.m. in England. So that only a few hours were left to know whether Germany and Britain would be at peace or at war.

Meantime the Foreign Office was working at full pressure. Countless electric lights blazed in every room. The great diplomatic plans for the event of the British Empire being at war were being put into operation. It necessitated immediate notification to all British representatives abroad, high and low, and for automatic telegraphic instructions regarding such necessities as the destruction of ciphers, the handing over of the protection of British subjects and interests to a neutral power, the departure of British officials from enemy countries, and other such matters.

The procedure to be followed had been most carefully worked out, elaborately enshrined in a sort of bible and entrusted for its execution to particularly efficient members of the staff. It seemed that should war break out this machinery must work like clockwork.

And so, in fact, it did. Only the clock was fast, and here the Foreign Office made their one great mistake. Into a crowd of Foreign Office officials gathered in the corridors dashed a private secretary saying that Germany had declared war on England. This was not what was expected. Already a message had been typed and prepared which was to be sent to Prince Lichnowsky, the German Ambassador in London, at eleven o'clock that evening, announcing that the British Government had declared war on Germany.

In view of the report of the private secretary, this message was now altered. It was amended to "The German Empire having declared war upon Great Britain." This message was at once sent to Lichnowsky with his passport.

The Foreign Office messenger returned about 10.15. A few minutes later an urgent telegram arrived from Sir Edward Goschen at Berlin. It reported that the Chancellor had informed him by telephone that Germany would not reply to the ultimatum, and that therefore, to his infinite regret, a state of war would arise by midnight. Germany had, in fact, not declared war.

The Foreign Office realised that the mistake had been made, and that they had handed to Prince Lichnowsky an incorrect declaration of war. It was decided that at any cost this document must be retrieved and the right one substituted.

The youngest member of the Foreign Office staff was selected for this queer mission. It was Harold Nicolson, son of the Permanent Under-Secretary.

He walked across the Horse Guards Parade to the side door of the Embassy, at the bottom of the Duke of York's steps. After much ringing a footman appeared.

He stated that Prince Lichnowsky had gone to bed. The Foreign Office clerk stated that he was the bearer of a communication of the utmost importance from Sir Edward Grey. He was conducted to a room. There was a screen behind the door and behind the screen a vast bedstead, upon which the Ambassador was reclining in pyjamas.

The Foreign Office clerk stated that there had been a slight error in the document previously delivered, and that he had come to substitute for it another and more correct version.

Prince Lichnowsky indicated the writing-table in the window.

"You will find it there," he said.

A receipt had to be demanded and signed. A blotting pad was brought across to the bed, and the pen dipped in the ink. Whilst the Ambassador was signing, the sound of shouting came up from The Mall below, and the strains of the Marseillaise. The crowds were streaming back from Buckingham Palace.

The Great World War had begun. The wireless from the Admiralty was already cackling its warning messages to the British Fleet scattered over the seven seas.

IV

The preliminary skirmishing of the diplomats was now at an end. The time had come for the common peoples of the world to face this great conflict. Perhaps the dominant note throughout Europe at the time from Carnarvon to Constantinople was the complete bewilderment of the people at the suddenness with which this thing had come upon them.

ON THE HOME FRONT, 1914-1918. Women played a great part in the war. They did men's work, even on the railways and carrying coal, thus releasing thousands for the trenches. Few people realised then that the invasion of industry by women was permanent, and that it would provide post-war Britain with its greatest economic problem.

Women became bus conductors during the war.

Factories were hastily transformed, and existing machinery was adapted for making munitions.
Here girl munition workers can be seen stacking a reserve of shell castings.

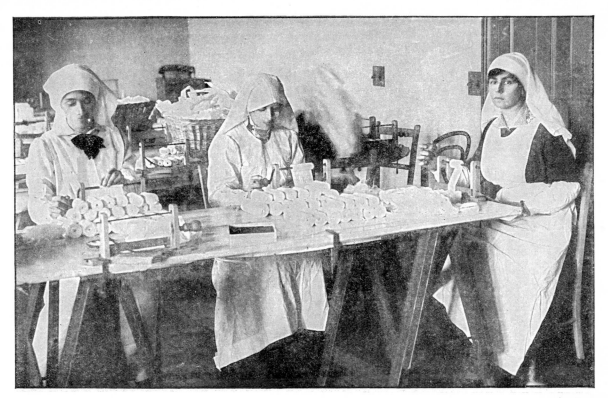

Women making bandages for use in war hospitals.

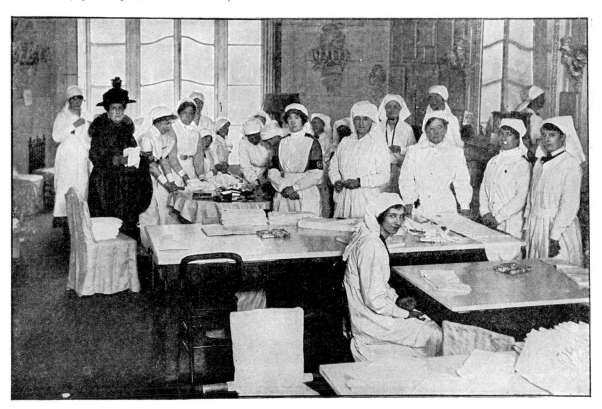

THE FIRST R.F.C. PLANE *to arrive in France for use in the war.*

A R.F.C. SQUADRON COMMANDER *giving orders to his pilots.*

The people of Britain had been enjoying their August Bank Holiday. They were returning from sunshine days at the seaside to find the newspaper headlines screaming alarming reports. Glancing back at those headlines one sees a dramatic kaleidoscope in big type.

"Europe Drifting to Disaster." "Last Efforts for Peace."

"The Archbishops of Canterbury and York appeal for the prayers of the nation."

These were among the first outbursts of headlines in the newspapers. "German yacht withdraws from Cowes" was another headline. This to a sports-loving nation was perhaps the most significant headline of all.

Financiers and traders and commercial men generally were shocked to see the Bank Rate suddenly rise to 8 per cent. and later top 10 per cent. Soldiers and sailors with kit-bags began to be seen at the various London termini.

On Sunday, August 2, the awful catastrophe spread over the front pages of the Sunday newspapers. Extra editions of the Sunday papers brought news that the Germans had crossed the frontiers of France and Luxemburg, and that the rush towards Paris had begun.

Crowds began to gather in the streets of London, drifting about aimlessly, wondering what was going on behind those lighted windows of Whitehall. In the evening a vast mass of people were singing the National Anthem and the Marseillaise outside Buckingham Palace.

Urgent but delayed telegrams began to be received by people who spent their holidays on the Continent. All were rushing at breakneck speed to get across the Channel and within the confines of Britain, their home.

On the actual Bank Holiday, Monday, August 3, the news was being discussed by parties sitting on the beach, watching children paddling and building sand castles, on tennis courts and cricket grounds. Nobody seemed to know whether England was yet definitely engaged in this war. Newspapers were snapped up eagerly as soon as they appeared.

That evening the boat from the Hook of Holland arrived at Harwich, carrying 780 exhausted, excited passengers instead of the usual 100.

Among them were tourists who, only a day previously, had begun their holiday, but had been turned back at the French-German frontiers, and told to get back home as quickly as possible. These people, who had set foot on the Continent only for a few hours, realised too well the huge conflict that was beginning.

Even so, the seaside resorts of Britain remained crowded. The people were on holiday, and in characteristic fashion were determined to enjoy their holiday. Young men in straw hats and white summer suits flirted with jolly girls in hobble skirts. Respectable elderly people sat round bandstands and listened to the Gilbert and Sullivan operas being played.

At Scarborough and Whitby crowds idled beside the sunlit waters of the North Sea, little dreaming that German battle cruisers were already contemplating bombardment of that particular coast-line.

And on the other side of the North Sea the same scenes were to be witnessed. At Ostend, gay Continental crowds lounged along the *plage*. The Casinos were full, dance halls were crowded, orchestral concerts were drawing their huge crowds. Europe, generally, was prosperous and happy. It had been a good year for the crops, and everyone from Calais to Constantinople was looking forward to a bumper harvest.

In the Belgian hopfields and in the wheatlands around Soissons, and along the Marne, the hours were too few in a day for the work there was to do.

They said in the vineyards of Moselle, along the Meuse, and in the Champagne that it would certainly be a year of excellent vintage. There had been little rain on the vine, and in consequence the grapes were small but of a concentrated strength and sweetness, so that 1914 would mean something on a bottle.

Life at that time for the common people of the Continent was simple and pleasant. Never again while they lived would they feel as secure.

Now this terrible thing had broken over these pleasant fields and golden vineyards. Just when the farmers needed their hands there were mobilisation notices.

Under the crossed flags of the Republic, under the heraldic symbols of the monarchies, pasted on public buildings in the villages. Police read out these notices to the simple peasant, while women stood by with their children, whimpering and wondering.

But in the great cities all was excitement. In St. Petersburg the people rushed to the Nevsky Prospekt in such a patriotic demonstration as Holy Russia had never seen. A procession formed with banners made the rounds of the Serbian, French and British Legations cheering. The stout Russian reservists marched singing to their depôts, and the pictures we have to-day show a light on their broad faces as they turned towards the West.

Before them was Tannenberg, and the headlong retreat and the slow agony of disintegration.

In Berlin they crowded the Unter den Linden and filled the great squares round the new Palace. The Kaiser showed himself to his people with his shining sword. They sang the fierce Teutonic warrior hymns and yelled for war—War with England—War with Russia—War with France—War with anybody.

Through the streets marched the fine, tall Germans in their new uniform. To each soldier, his cigar, his grin, and his nosegay stuck in his rifle nozzle. Crowds cheered them as they boarded the troop trains that were taking them towards the Rhine and Paris.

In France it was the same. They tore away the crêpe from the statue of Strasburg, among the great sculptured women that ring the Place de la Concord, and the Mayor of the Arrondissement gave her a symbolic embrace.

He spoke sneeringly to the crowd, of revenge after forty years of humiliation, of the red trousers and of the gay French bugles sounding the charge. He mentioned Altenkirch and Mulhouse.

There were tears of joyous emotion, and the crowd sang the war songs of the warrior race that had burned more powder than anybody in the world. And the soldiers, the little French infantrymen with their long rifles and their too large great-coats buttoned back from absurd red trousers, looked out, while the girls threw them kisses and an occasional bottle of wine.

In Britain the wives of naval men went looking for lodgings in Scotland and on the East Coast, for the Grand Fleet had gone north.

The old men and the boys and the women were to finish off the crops, and presently the stubble fields along the Marne were to be full of dead men, and sleek farm horses from the Île de France and from Hesse were presently to be seen dying of starvation and of overwork and shrapnel fire, whilst they hauled the guns through the sticky Flemish mud.

Yellow men from Asia, black men from Africa, dark, round-headed Mediterranean and tall Nordic blondes were to kill one another earnestly for the next four years. Yet there is abundant evidence that they all went out very gaily twenty years ago.

Throughout the whole of Britain in those early days of August the people watched the machine of war being prepared.

The Government took over the railways, and they were all combined under one general management. Lorries, horse transport, and motor-cars of every kind were suddenly commandeered. The magic letters W.D., meaning War Department, were stencilled on every kind of conveyance.

After the first shock of bewilderment something like panic appeared among some sections of the population. The rumour grew about a possible food shortage. Stories were told of houses packed to the attics with provisions, of grocers' shops cleared out, of motor-cars sent round from shop to shop, even from town to town, to pile up reserves in country houses.

In poorer streets and villages people were doing the same thing on a small scale. Protests against this food hoarding appeared in the newspapers, and the Government were compelled to take action. Hurriedly they set up a Food Prices Committee.

But the real centre of activity had now been transferred from the Foreign Office to the War Office and the Admiralty.

On the outbreak of war the Government had acted quickly. Lord Kitchener, who was then Agent-General in Egypt, happened to be in England on holiday. He was actually at Dover on his way back to Cairo when, on August 3, the Prime Minister sent him an urgent telegram ordering him to come back to London.

On August 5 it was announced that he had been appointed Secretary of State for War. His name still had a great magic with the people of Britain. They looked upon him as the one man who could carry them through this great conflict.

This was the period when there was much talk of the " strong, silent man " type. To the public of England, Kitchener represented that type in its apotheosis.

Very soon Lord Kitchener was installed at the War Office. Generals were in his room studying maps. Plans were being formulated and the famous British Expeditionary Force, the Old Contemptibles, were already being organised to thrust forward into Belgium.

One of the first duties of the War Office, and Lord Kitchener in particular, was to appoint a Censorship. It was considered absolutely necessary that the news from France at this critical period should be censored. Kitchener decided that the one man for this job of Press Censorship was F. E. Smith, later to become Lord Birkenhead.

He mentioned this appointment to Lord Riddell. Later F. E. Smith came over to Lord Riddell and asked what he thought of this particular job.

Lord Riddell replied briefly that there

was only one person who could fill such a job.

"Who is that?" asked F. E. Smith.

Lord Riddell replied, "The Almighty, and even He would be criticised."

In his brilliant War Diary Lord Riddell describes later how he called at the War Office and went into Kitchener's room. He found the War Secretary surrounded by generals and maps—everyone coming and going in a state of great excitement.

"I asked Kitchener what the duties of the Press Censor were to be," writes Lord Riddell.

"His reply was: 'He will see that nothing dangerous goes into the newspapers. Go away with Brade and settle the matter. We must make the English people understand that we are at war, and that war is not pap. At the present moment they do not understand the situation. They ought to act as if we were at war.'"

This was the period, too, when funds were opened for this great conflict and the misery that would inevitably follow in its trail. Again Lord Riddell describes the first appeal meeting in connection with the Prince of Wales's Fund.

It took place at York House. The King and Queen entered the room with Sir Arthur Pearson between them. He being blind, the King held one of his arms and the Queen the other. On the table was a huge pile of cheques—result of the first day's appeal.

Wedgwood Benn, who was present on this occasion, said to the King: "In future there will be no need for a tax-gatherer. Your Majesty will be able to dispense with the Chancellor of the Exchequer. To provide public funds it will only be necessary to make an appeal such as the Prince made yesterday. In two days we have got £400,000, which is more than a good many taxes produce in a year."

Apart from the money that was pouring in for these funds, there was no lack of patriotism among the people. Crowds of men were going round to the recruiting offices, only to find that at that particular moment no recruits were needed. Many barracks were closed. The men did not recognise that the troops had already crossed the Channel and were making their way through France to beat the Germans in their onrush through Belgium.

The whole of Britain waited to hear Lord Kitchener's plans for raising the great army. Lord Riddell describes how he dined with Jack Seeley and his son at the Reform Club, a farewell dinner.

"Seeley said we had a hard job before us and that the mortality would be terrible.

"As we walked back across the park to my house in Queen Anne's Gate we stood on the bridge which crosses the ornamental water. In the distance we could see the Foreign Office, with the anti-aircraft gun on the roof.

"Seeley said, 'I shall often think of this moment as I lie out in the field, looking at the moon and the stars, as one does when one is campaigning.'

"Turning to his son, he said, 'You will have to be a father to the family while I am away. If I don't come back you will have to look after them. I shall rely on you.'

"The boy replied, 'I shall do my best.' Fate decreed that the father should go through the war unscathed, and that the boy, who later on went to France, should be killed. One of the countless tragedies of the war."

Top: *The first R.F.C. aerodrome to be established in France.* Below: *Preparing bombs for use in a raid over German lines. All these bombs were dropped in a single raid.* Inset: *Colonel Bishop, V.C., Britain's most famous war "ace."*

FOR NEARLY TWO YEARS ZEPPELINS INVADED BRITAIN, *and caused considerable damage. Our defences seemed unable to retaliate. But on September 3, 1916, a Zeppelin was brought down at Cuffley, and two more crashed in Essex on September 23. Nine days later another was brought down in flames at Potter's Bar. This one hit an oak tree, and the twelve members of the crew died a terrible death.*

THE KING AND THE PREMIER IN FRANCE.

MR. LLOYD GEORGE *paid several visits to the battlefields to confer with the British and French Generals in command of operations.*

H.M. THE KING *photographed behind the Front Line in France.*

THE KING *paid several visits to the Front, where he decorated soldiers for their bravery.*

THE KING AND THE PRINCE OF WALES *inspecting R.F.C. aeroplanes.*

THE KING AND QUEEN *inspecting the W.A.A.C.'s (Women's Auxiliary Army Corps) at Aldershot. They were recruited to work behind the lines.*

MACHINE GUNNERS *protected with masks from gas attacks.*

A BRITISH BATTERY *shelling the German lines.*

The first news that Britain was at war with Germany nearly caused a panic on the Stock Exchange. The Government declared a moratorium. Several banks also closed. This prevented a run on the banks.

At the same time the Government had time to announce and prepare for a substitution of paper currency for gold. The pound and ten shilling notes, of which the Chancellor of the Exchequer gave notice on August 5, were ready to be handed over the counters of the bank when they reopened on the 7th. Later in the year the pound note numbered A 000001 was sold and resold for the Red Cross, reaching a price of about £250.

In a few days Lord Kitchener revealed his plans. On August 9 came the first appeal for the hundred thousand men.

What seemed to astound everybody was that the enlistment was to be for "four years or the duration of the war." Already many people were quoting Norman Angell's *Great Illusion* and declaring that the war could not possibly last longer than six months. The financial stability of Europe would not stand any lengthier period.

Moreover, they pointed to the fact that the first note of credit was for £100,000,000, and that if this was any indication obviously the war must finish in a few months' time.

Even many members of the Government were inclined to think Lord Kitchener was unduly pessimistic in putting a period of four years as the duration of the war. But, ignoring his critics, Lord Kitchener set to work. The War Office was soon taking huge tracts of land in the country and building those great camps with their hutments which soon became a common feature of the English landscape.

Thousands of men were already en route by train and road to these enlistment camps. The first hundred thousand, who were to set such a splendid example to the many hundreds of thousands who followed them, were already in course of training. In their civilian suits, with sticks for rifles, they were drilling on Salisbury Plain, round Aldershot, and over the whole of the South Downs. At the same time big camps had opened in the North of England.

Behind this first hundred thousand men the new armies were already being organised, a force which with the contingencies from the various Dominions and Colonies was later to amount to more than five million men.

V

What was happening? A nation eager for news of the conflict on the Continent bought every edition of the newspapers that came on the streets. But even these newspapers contained very little information. The Censorship had already got to work, and such facts as could be gleaned were meagre.

Nevertheless, it became known that the British Fleet had received its baptism of blood on August 6 when, in harrying German mine layers away from the French warships, the cruiser *Amphion* struck a mine and went down. On the 9th it was reported that the British cruiser squadron had sunk a German submarine.

Suspense hung like a pall all over Britain. Uncertainty as to whether war would be prevented had given way to an even more terrible doubt as to what this meeting of fully equipped modern armies would mean.

Propaganda was already at work. The Allied and neutral nations were given to understand that the Allies were winning all along the line. Skirmishes between Belgian soldiers and German cavalry patrols were magnified into gigantic victories. Moreover, the French had suddenly gathered six army corps together and invaded Alsace-Lorraine. They had reoccupied Mulhousen, which afforded keen delight to the dramatic French temperament, which was seeking revenge for the lost provinces.

But the whole German Army was coming up like a grey sea over the flats of Belgium. To those who had seen it on the march it did not seem possible that any human force could stop it. Superbly armed, equipped and disciplined, full of fighting spirit aroused by the carefully inculcated belief that Germany's existence as a nation was at stake, it swept forward in sombre magnificence.

To the amazement of all the militarists the super forts of Liège and Namur suddenly fell to the giant howitzers the Germans had brought with them. It was soon realised that this was a war of great mechanism.

But while the German artillery were pounding these super forts to pieces, the rapid onrush of the German forces through Belgium was continued. Very soon Brussels was threatened. The Belgian Government packed up and moved from Brussels to Antwerp. In Brussels itself, meanwhile, life went on as usual, and the cafés and shops were reported to be crowded.

Through the north of Belgium the Uhlans were galloping. Overhead buzzed the first of the military aeroplanes which were soon fairly to darken the skies.

The observers carried pistols or rifles and exchanged shots as they passed. But the days of the air machine-gun were yet to come. Already the French General Staff realised they had made a tactical error in advancing with their main forces into Alsace-Lorraine, instead of trying to stem the German onrush through Belgium.

Those six army corps were made to storm barbed-wire entanglements manned by machine-guns and paid a horrible penalty; 300,000 were swept away in the first three weeks.

In the meantime the first detachment of British troops had been landing in France under the command of Field-Marshal Sir John French. On the 18th their presence was officially admitted, but it was denied that they had been in action or that there had been casualties.

A few days later, on August 24, the Germans occupied Brussels. The news had an ominous sound to the Parisians. They already felt that the Germans were rushing to their very gates.

This was the time when the first mention of atrocities was made. One heard stories of wrecked villages, of ruthless handling of anything that could be called resistance to the advancing troops, of hasty and wholesale executions of peasants and townsfolk, because some individuals had been foolishly violent.

Then came the burning of Louvain. It was reported that this beautiful city, with one of the most famous libraries in the world, had been burned to ashes.

In England for the first time the advancing German hordes were named "The Huns." This phrase, curiously enough, was originated by *The Times* in its leading article on the destruction of Louvain.

The lack of real news was dispiriting

the whole of the British nation. Fleet Street was desperately anxious to secure some news of some kind. Correspondents were hurried across the Channel and told to make their way to the battle-front. But the Censor was already wielding his blue pencil, and nothing really could emerge from that office.

Then on Sunday, August 30, the news was published that British and French forces were in retreat across France and the Germans advancing upon Paris. This was the story of the famous Retreat from Mons.

From the reading of their newspapers the public were inclined to believe that the whole of the British Army had been annihilated. It has since been proved that the message was unduly alarming. And the fact that the French Government had left Paris for Bordeaux rather emphasised the obvious fact that the Germans were winning all along the line.

To some extent this first disastrous shock had its effect upon the British public in the stimulus to recruiting. Crowds of men were now standing in queues outside the recruiting offices anxious to be taken on.

At the same time one saw the beginnings of that mysterious war propaganda. The first of the stories that was circulated at this time was to the effect that thousands of Russian troops had landed in Britain and were being transferred to the Western Front. Russia, in fact, was being proclaimed the salvation of the Allies. For the first time one heard of the famous "Steamroller" which would roll the Germans up and advance steadily on Berlin.

But one story that was not due to the propaganda department of the British Government, or any of the other Govern-ments, but due in fact to the ordinary soldier, arose out of those desperate days when the British Army was retreating from Mons. This was the story, the famous story, of the Angels of Mons. How it arose and how it spread among the troops is well worth recording.

During August, 1914, the British Expeditionary Force was, as we know now, nearly annihilated. It was only by fighting one of the greatest rearguard actions of military history that it managed to escape from Mons and make a stand many miles to the rear.

That the retreat from Mons was not a rout was due to the stubborn fighting qualities of the individual infantryman and his mastery of the rifle. So great a fighter with the rifle is he that the Germans, attacking in mass, held for a time the firm belief that he was armed with a new and secret type of machine-gun.

Whilst the German High Command was discussing this possibility as a way of explaining the dourness of the rear-guard action and their high casualty lists, a very different theory was spreading through Great Britain. We were fighting a Holy War; the German was the Hun, the "blonde beast," the incarnation of evil. All righteousness was on our side. What could be more fitting than that the very powers of Heaven and the angels themselves were our allies?

In all wars each opponent claims that Heaven is on his side. But in this case it was not only on our side but was actually fighting with our men in the line; and thus the strange story spread across from France and percolated into Great Britain that a miracle had happened. To the aid of our hard pressed troops hordes of ghostly bowmen had

II

come into action, the ghosts of the bowmen of Crecy, Poictiers, and Agincourt.

The story was most circumstantial. Our men had seen the bowmen, ranks of ghostly figures facing the foe; they had heard their war cries, "Array! Array!" and had heard the twang of bows and flying arrows. They had seen the German masses melt away before the arrows that hid the face of the sun.

The story had slight variations. In addition to the bowmen, some soldiers had seen the Archangel Michael, some had seen St. George, others had seen hosts of women angels over the trenches whilst the British Army was repulsing the attacks of the German infantry. But all the stories had the same tendency to explain the escape by supernatural means of our force from annihilation and to prove that God was on our side exclusively.

The story was not only believed by masses of people, but it became the subject of scores of sermons in churches, and pamphlets emanating from religious bodies and those interested in psychical research. There is, in fact, a whole library in existence dealing with the mystery of the Angels of Mons. Those writers who are in support of the ghostly aid given to our troops have produced what appears to be documented and irrefutable evidence.

On the other hand, those who were sceptical were able to find many holes in the various stories told. For instance, one soldier claiming to have seen St. George said that he knew it was St. George because he was in shining armour, "just like he is on the golden sovereigns." Unfortunately, the image of this country's patron saint as it used to appear on sovereigns is naked save for the single protection of a flying cloak.

One story told how thousands of dead Germans had been picked up from the battlefield riddled with arrows; another that the Germans were puzzled by the thousands of dead that bore no wounds at all. There was, in fact, great discussion pro and con the appearance of the Bowmen of Mons, even the evidence against it tending to make people believe that "there must be something in it."

This was not the kind of story which could be dealt with by a question in the House of Commons. As far as authorities were concerned, they did not bother to deny it or to carry out any investigation. But, as in the case of the great "Russians in England" rumour, they saw that, far from doing harm, it could do good.

Propaganda is the soul of victory and the more people believed that supernatural powers, even if not Heaven itself, were on our side, the better. Those who have a clear recollection of those days will remember that the story did undoubtedly seize on the imaginations of a vast mass of the population, whilst it even had an encouraging effect on those who did not believe it for a moment.

There are various explanations of the mystery. It is suggested, for instance, that a number of our men, their minds influenced by the terrific experiences through which they were passing, actually "saw visions."

Mass hallucination is a state not unknown to pathologists. The fact that men in a highly emotional and exhausted state saw ghostly bowmen does not necessarily mean that the bowmen existed, and the fact that the bowmen did not exist does not necessarily mean

THE NAVY *made an attempt to block Zeebrugge in order to bottle up German submarines.*
Several ships were sunk in the harbour, their crews being rescued in motor-launches.
The attempt was only partly successful, but was valuable in checking German activities.

MORE PHOTOGRAPHS OF ZEEBRUGGE. *Inset is Admiral Sir Roger Keyes, who was in command of the British Fleet.*

REPEATED ATTACKS *along the Western Front broke the German line, and a retreat began. Soon trench warfare had been abandoned, and the two armies fought in the open for the first time for four years. This photograph shows a British outpost.*

DESERTED *by most of her allies, her own troops in retreat, her navy in mutiny, and with starvation facing its civil population, Germany asked for an Armistice. It was signed in General Foch's railway carriage in the Forest of Compiègne at five a.m. on November* 11. *The memorial below has been erected on the spot where the carriage rested.*

FIRING THE LAST SHOT *of the war, just before eleven o'clock on November* 11, 1918.

TROOPS CHEERING *the announcement that the war has been won.*

THE WAR IS WON. *Huge crowds gathered outside Buckingham Palace on November 11, 1918, when the news of the Armistice was received. The King and Queen can be seen on the balcony acknowledging the cheers of the people. It was a great day for everyone.*

that the men were lying. They related what they thought they saw.

On the other hand, many people believe that there was no foundation whatever for the story as far as the men in France were concerned, and maintain that the rumour arose through a fictional story being mistaken for fact.

Inspired by the doughty fighting of the British soldier on and about August 23, 1914, Mr. Arthur Machen wrote a short fantasy for the London *Evening News*. This fantasy described a British infantryman having a vision of ghostly warriors dispelling with ghostly arrows the grey hordes of Germans that seemed to be about to overwhelm our lines.

Mr. Machen has written a small book in which he lays bare the facts relating to the way in which he conceived the idea of his fantasy and wrote it, and the concrete evidence that it appeared in print cannot be very well denied.

There are, of course, those who maintain that Mr. Machen must have heard something about the occurrences in the fighting line before he conceived the idea. In other words, that the story in the newspapers followed the actual appearance of the bowmen. That, however is a matter for individual choice.

The cynic will take an inevitable view of the whole affair, maintaining that if supernatural powers were on our side and went to the trouble of coming to our aid at Mons, why did they desert us so soon? For in spite of the bowmen and the way the enemy melted before their arrows, we were forced to retreat, and four years of the most strenuous fighting the world has ever known passed before a British soldier entered Mons again.

The question whether angels did or did not actually fight at Mons must

remain a mystery. There are still living men willing to swear that they saw them. And although it is easy to sit back and, by sheer logic, shake their statements, it is doubtful whether it will have the effect of making them alter their evidence.

VI

Kitchener and the War Office were now placarding the streets of Britain with that famous "Your King and Country Need You." The appeal was instantly answered. There was no lack of response from the young men of the country. In fact, hordes of them were eager to enter upon this great adventure, even though the end of it might have meant death.

Something more than posters and rumours was needed to encourage the British public in these dark days. A few of the Fleet Street men, the newspaper special correspondents, had managed to get through to Northern Belgium and brought back some astounding reports of heroism, atrocities, death, and destruction.

Sir Philip Gibbs, later to become the most widely read of all these newspaper correspondents, had reached Northern Belgium, and saw the German armies advancing after they had smashed their way through the forts of Liège.

"It was then that I saw for the first time the agony of war and its terror," he wrote. "The terror leaped upon the civil population. Belgium first, and then Northern France, was like a human antheap overturned by a monstrous boot. The human ants fled. Behind them their villages and homes were in flames.

"The enemy came on with frightful speed. Civilians had hardly time to go piling their babies and household goods on to carts and wheelbarrows and any kind of a truck. The roads were filled with this traffic of refugees—delicate women, old men, invalids, young girls, trudging away from terror until they were fit to drop.

"Those who remained and were caught saw war at its worst. They saw their fathers and brothers shot because they were accused of firing on German troops as *francs-tireurs*. Many atrocity stories were false, but brutal things were done by the German High Command, ruthless and hurried, with no time for mercy and no inclination.

"The French Army was in retreat. The little British Army—the Old Contemptibles — was falling back from Mons, fighting rearguard actions. I met a French sergeant of Sappers who had blown up forty-four bridges to cover the retreat."

The Germans under Von Kluck were driving hard on Paris. They were as close as Meaux, twenty-seven kilometres away. The French Government fled from Paris.

A million people or more fled also from the French capital, and those who remained behind shuttered windows heard the noise of the enemies' guns and waited for the clip-clop of horses' hoofs to tell them that German cavalry had come.

This was the occasion when a new terror of war was first witnessed by the Paris population. On September 1 there was a German air raid over Paris, during which four bombs were dropped. Before the war was over no nation involved was to have clean hands in this respect. But these first attacks upon the civilian population of a great city were everywhere denounced, and everywhere

in neutral countries damaged Germany's position.

These were the dark days in London, too. The rumours of that annihilated British force had had a chastening effect on the crowds who, a month previously, had been shouting and singing in front of Buckingham Palace.

Rudyard Kipling, the poet of the nation at that time, was writing these words:

" Who stands if Freedom fall?
Who dies if England live?"

Those words may have rather an ironic flavour to-day, but there is no doubt that they helped the nation in these days of dark and dreary stress.

Meanwhile the British Army in France was falling steadily back. "You can't mow them down," cried a wounded British sergeant of that moving German Army. "We kill them and kill them, but still they come on."

Yet, during this week, as delayed detailed stories of the great invasion began to flood the newspapers, the myth of German invincibility was to be shaken, and in another week it would be shattered.

The vast sweep of five German armies through Luxemburg, Belgium, and North France had culminated in a southward swing, which had brought Von Kluck's First Army almost to the fortifications of Paris.

Facing Von Kluck were the British under General French, and the rest of the battle line stretched eastward into a great salient at Verdun, then southeastward through Nancy. Two new French armies were coming into the picture, the Ninth, under Foch, which strengthened the French right centre, and the Sixth, to which was assigned the defence of Paris. During their retreat the British had moved south-east past Paris, so that the Sixth Army, whose strength the Germans do not seem to have realised, now held the extreme left of the Allied line.

The original German plan had been to sweep round Paris on the west, invest the city and roll up the Allied line by a final great flanking movement.

It was then occurred the miracle of the Battle of the Marne. But it is possible that it was not that desperate French counter-attack that really defeated the Germans, but the fact that their own success had been so terrific and their advance so rapid that all their time-tables were wrong and, in fact, Von Kluck had lost touch with the rapidly moving detachment.

The Battle of the Marne was a last desperate effort of the Allies, who were almost in danger of being completely encircled by the Germans. That famous French General Gallieni collected an army in Paris and sent them, in thousands of taxi-cabs, round Paris on the road to Meaux, striking Von Kluck's army on its left flank.

At the same time General Foch struck in the centre and sent the Crown Prince's army reeling back. Simultaneously the British Expeditionary Force—the Old Contemptibles that were supposed to have been wiped out—came up with guns and did deadly work against German batteries and transport.

Sir Philip Gibbs has described the drama of those days on the Marne:

"It was in a hot sun that all that happened. The men were parched with thirst. The price of the Marne was frightful for France.

"In Chartres, as I remember, the Medi-cal Officer received a telegram, 'Prepare for forty thousand wounded.' He had already more wounded than it was possible to attend. They were using newspapers to bandage wounds. The wounds were gangrene. The dead lay in heaps beyond Meaux. I saw piles of them being burned. It was only the beginning.

"The Germans fell back and dug themselves in. It was the beginning of trench warfare, which lasted for four years longer, with desperate attempts on both sides to break a way through those earthworks which had made an underground fortress only to be breached at enormous cost of life.

"Millions of men crouched close to each other, divided sometimes by a No Man's Land, a few hundred yards in width, and sometimes, as at Arras and other places, only a few yards away. High explosives replaced shrapnel and smashed through trenches and dug-outs Siege guns were brought up and hurled enormous shells where masses of men were in front-line trenches or in billets behind the line.

"Towns, villages, churches, farmsteads were wiped off the map. All vegetation was blasted off the earth in this battle zone. Every road was under fire, and transport was shelled twenty miles and more away back.

"The daily sum of casualties mounted high, and death reaped its harvest of youth. Their courage, their physical strength, their vitality were at the mercy of this machine-made war."

Such was the desperate position on the Western Front. In the meantime, although the Allied nations were not fully aware of it, the Russian steamroller had crashed. Russia had paid the price of being the most out-of-date of all the fighting powers, and having as its opponent the most modernised army in Europe.

The Russian Generals Rennenkampf and Samsonov were caught with a huge army by Hindenburg, Ludendorff and the Jew military genius, Hoffman, in the Masurian Swamps at Tannenberg.

Hindenburg and Ludendorff had manœuvred among this maze of lakes almost all their military lives. Hoffman had made a plan which was a perfect trap to catch and crush any invader at this spot.

This was the one victory of the war in the grand old smashing style. The Russian army was annihilated at little cost to the Germans. Samsonov committed suicide. It was, perhaps, fortunate that the news of this disaster at Tannenberg was kept from the Allied public, whose nerves were already strained to breaking point.

A victory at sea helped to keep up the courage of the Allies. On August 28 a division of the British Fleet under Rear-Admiral Beatty came in contact with the German Fleet near Heligoland, and in a running fight sank three German cruisers and a destroyer.

It was a period too that saw the first of Mr. Winston Churchill's dramatic war adventures. Two naval brigades, hurriedly constructed by Mr. Churchill out of new recruits, were landed in Antwerp, which was already surrounded by the Germans, but not yet taken.

The presence of these naval recruits undoubtedly helped the spirit of the Belgians, and the arrival of Mr. Churchill himself was also inspiring to them. But from a tactical point of view it had no effect at all. The bombardment of the town began, Antwerp was evacuated, and fell on the 9th to the Germans with the British Naval Brigades having fired hardly a shot.

Numbers of these men could not be re-embarked, with the result that hundreds of them retreated to internment in Holland. The fall of Antwerp was the last phase of this first movement of the war in France and Northern Belgium. Both armies were now digging in, prepared for the winter.

Across the Channel streamed thousands of Belgian refugees to find a home and livelihood of some kind in Britain. These Belgians were soon coming into the country at a rate of six or seven hundred a day.

A War Relief Committee was set up to deal with this enormous influx of people. Empty halls and houses were commandeered to find living accommodation for these people. Food supplies were brought in from all parts of London. Great numbers were dispersed all over the country as guests of individual people, or occupying empty houses under the care of local committees.

Many of these Belgians managed to find work in this country. Hundreds were quartered at the Alexandra Palace in London. Eventually some of them drifted back to the Continent, while others were drafted into the Belgian Army. But the majority of them continued to live and work with the assistance of the local committees throughout Britain. This country showed in many ways its admiration for these refugees.

CHAPTER VI

THE SPY DANGER

Britain's spy service—Karl Lody, first spy to be shot in England—British spies at work—Tricking the Germans.

I

" There are no leaders to lead us to honour, and yet without leaders we sally,

Each man reporting for duty alone, out of sight, out of reach of his fellow,

There are no bugles to call the battalions, and yet without bugles we rally,

From the ends of the earth to the ends of the earth to follow the Standard of Yellow!"

Such is " The Spies' March," by Rudyard Kipling, and more than one hunted man and woman must have been muttering it at this time.

War was but a few hours old when the " spy danger " in Britain was being discussed by everyone. The Germans had hundreds of spies in the country, people said, and behind them were the master spies.

Every foreign waiter, barber, and domestic servant in Britain was a spy, ran the rumours. For years they had been sending to their own country valuable information regarding our most closely guarded secrets. Germany had been preparing for years, and the British intelligence system was but a second-rate imitation of the real thing.

But if German spies were supposedly loose in Britain, it must not be imagined that this country ignored the advantages to be obtained from its own Secret Service.

Actually the British Secret Service is a comparatively new intelligence organisation. It was not formed until sixty years ago. The beginning of our present system was a very tiny section of the Army Office—the " Topographical and Statistical Department." From this developed the present Intelligence Branch.

It is interesting to reflect that at the outbreak of the Great War there were just under twenty men engaged in the work of the Special Intelligence Section at the War Office. Yet by the end of 1918 there were 800 men definitely working in the Special Intelligence group, and something like 1,200 indirectly connected with that work.

This particular department of the War Office, known as " Military Intelligence," or briefly M.I., had its own little group of men working abroad previous to the outbreak of the war.

For instance, in the North Sea, not far from the Kiel Canal, had loafed a little pleasure craft manned by two young Englishmen apparently interested only in deep-sea fishing. In a German garrison town a tailor had specialised in clothes for German officers. In Berlin, in every other important German city, and in many a place which to a civilian's eyes seemed of little importance, men and women were leading obviously respectable lives; but it was a business which the signs on their doors did not reveal.

Two or three years were devoted to building up M.I. with a staff which was sworn never to divulge a single word of what was being done. It became what was to all intents and purposes a detective agency with sources of information in every corner of Britain.

Results began to pour in. Reports were received from all over the country, each one showing how grave was the menace with which the department was dealing. The reports gave full details of those who were anxious to acquire information likely to be of use to Germany in time of war.

Suddenly the German spies found their activities checked. Women agents —and there were many—discovered that information was not so easy to obtain, despite all their fascination. Reports on their way to Germany began to go astray. Headquarters on the other side wanted to know why, but there was no answer known to the spies.

M.I. was at work, but they did not even know of its existence.

War grew nearer. Then it became a question of hours, and M.I. struck. Giant card-indexes which contained details of all the known German agents were consulted. The aid of the naval, military, and civilian police was sought. Messages were sent out, orders were given, and M.I., having thrown out its nets, sat back to await the result.

The catch was heavy. Many agents of all grades of usefulness to their masters at Potsdam were caught and promptly sent to places where they could do no harm. Altogether, in the first few days of the war, twenty-two profes-sional spies and scores of their accomplices were sent off to internment camps.

The British Special Intelligence Service was soon divided into three main sections—one controlled by the War Office, a second by the Admiralty, and the third by Scotland Yard.

Thousands of men and women were set to work in post offices and elsewhere to scrutinise every word that went in and out of England. The whole country was divided into spy districts or "control areas," each under the supervision of a senior intelligence officer.

To each officer was assigned a squad of trained detectives. Each of these in turn employed a varying number of civilian "indicators." It was the task of the latter to report to the divisional chief—discreetly, of course—the arrivals of newcomers in the district and what seemed to be their business there.

In this way the Intelligence Service acquired a working knowledge of the literary style of every German spy in Britain; his or her real name and code number; who their correspondents were; which "canneries" and "cigar factories" in Sweden, Holland, Belgium, or Switzerland were really divisional headquarters of the German Secret Service; which spies used invisible inks and what chemical reagents would bring out the writing; and much other knowledge useful to "Special Intelligence."

When, therefore, the first spies were sent off to internment camps, the British Secret Service was enabled to keep on sending letters and cables abroad as if the German spy-system in England was still functioning with its one-time smoothness and thoroughness. And for some time Berlin did not know what had happened. Then it was shocked to

THE GERMAN SURRENDER. *The British Fleet sailing to receive the submission of Germany's Navy. Below: German sailors leaving their vessels prior to being sent back to Germany.*

THE GERMAN SURRENDER.

On the way out to receive the German Fleet, crews were all at action stations, and arrangements were made for sections to remain on deck to witness the German surrender. The top photograph shows men of a lower deck crew in their flash masks.

MR. LLOYD GEORGE IN 1914.

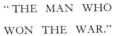

"THE MAN WHO
WON THE WAR."

A grateful nation gave Mr. Lloyd George much of the credit for the Allied victory because of his vigorous work as Munitions Minister, and, later, as War Premier.

Mr. Lloyd George, Signor Orlando, Clemenceau, and President Wilson photographed at the Peace Conference at Versailles.

SIGNING THE PEACE TREATY AT VERSAILLES, June 28, 1919. With this official ending to the Great War, the world settled down to repair the damage that had been done, hoping that nations were weary of strife and would live amicably. But within a few months Europe was again the scene of international squabbles and intrigue.

learn that a whole British Army had been assembled, shipped across the English Channel, and landed on the Continent before the German High Command knew anything about it.

Within three months after the outbreak of the war the Statute Book was packed with emergency legislation, later to be known as "Dora." In secrecy and without any fuss M.I. was given Star-Chamber powers to deal with the national menace. Later, when spy hysteria set in, the department became a military dictatorship acting in secret behind the constitutional mask of the Home Office.

Powers were obtained to enable the Intelligence Service to clear all potentially dangerous people from areas of military or naval importance. Arrests could be made without warrants and the discretion of trial by court-martial was given—with one penalty, death.

Nine thousand Germans and Austrians of military age were handed over by the police and incarcerated as prisoners of war. People who kept homing or carrier pigeons were registered. The houses, clubs, and places of business of all suspect "enemy aliens" were searched for firearms, and in consequence a number of people were imprisoned.

M.I. now had the necessary powers, and, aided by the other members of the Intelligence Service, the department got to work.

II

The first spy who was shot in England in the Great War, and the first man who was executed within the grim, grey battlements of the Tower of London for a hundred and fifty years, was a brave man, but also, alas, something of a blunderer. Karl Hans Lody, the German, blundered from the beginning of his arrival in Britain.

The day before Lody went to face the firing squad on the old miniature rifle range of the Tower of London, he wrote a letter to his relatives in Stuttgart:

"A hero's death on the battlefield is certainly finer, but such is not to be my lot and I die here in the enemy's country, silent and unknown. But the consciousness that I die in the service of the Fatherland makes death easy. . . . I have had just judges and I shall die as an officer, not as a spy. Farewell. God bless you."

He was also gallant to his gaolers. To the officers commanding the battalion in the Tower, he wrote:

"I feel it my duty as a German officer to express my sincere thanks and appreciation towards the staff of officers and men who were in charge of my person during my confinement. Their kind and considerate treatment has called up my highest esteem and admiration regarding good-fellowship even towards an enemy, and if I may be permitted I would thank you to make this known to them."

For his last night on this earth he was invited by Sir Basil Thomson, then head of the Special Branch of Scotland Yard which concerned itself with the detection of spies, to spend it quietly and comfortably in his office.

Lody sat at his ease in a big red morocco chair. The two men smoked and discussed German music and English literature. As cultured men they found much in common.

At dawn they called for Lody. He bade Sir Basil a quiet goodbye, as if they were to continue the night-long chat next time they met. As Lody took his place before the firing squad, he turned to the Assistant Provost-Marshal.

"I suppose you won't shake hands with a spy?" he asked.

"I'll shake hands with a brave man!" said the official, and did.

It appears that Lody was under suspicion from the moment he landed in Britain. For a time, in fact, he was allowed to send his reports to Germany, but those reports were based on wrong information which Scotland Yard had deliberately arranged for him to receive. And yet Karl Lody had been carefully trained for his job. He is said to have been specially selected by the Kaiser.

Before the war he had served in the German Navy as an officer. Because he could not afford the heavy expense of a naval officer he resigned and obtained a job as a guide to tourists with the Hamburg-Amerika line. He lived for a time in the United States and there acquired a complete knowledge of the English language, which he spoke, however, with an American accent. When the war broke out he hurried back to Germany and offered his services for the Navy.

But there was other work, more dangerous work, waiting for Lody. He was told to report to 70, Koenigergratzer Strasse, Berlin, the headquarters of the German Secret Service. Here he was given an intensive training in spy work by Major Steinhauer, Chief of the Service. He was taught how an American tourist would behave and dress in Britain.

An expert taught him the technique of getting people to impart military information. A chemist showed him how to use invisible inks. He was made to memorise ciphers and codes. Veteran spies taught him how to calculate numerical and fighting strength of army and navy detachments. Then, an ordinary bicycle, crated and marked for shipment to England, was prepared for him. Lody was ready to enter upon his great adventure.

But a passport, an unquestionable passport, was needed. In Berlin at that time was an American business man, Mr. Charles A. Inglis, who wanted to leave Germany and get back to the United States. He took his passport to the German Foreign Office for the necessary *visa* to leave the country. He was told to leave it, and come back next day.

When he returned, he was met by a very distressed clerk.

"Herr Inglis," said the clerk, "I am dreadfully sorry, but we seem to have mislaid your passport. In the rush of work it has disappeared.. However, we will do our utmost to rectify the matter and expedite your departure from Germany."

And although the passport of Mr. Inglis could not be found, the German Foreign Office did undoubtedly help him to get back quickly to the United States. Actually, the old passport was being prepared by the German Secret Service. The photograph of the real Mr. Inglis was detached by an expert and replaced by one of Karl Hans Lody. At the same time the written description of the bearer was changed to tally with that of Lody.

A fortnight later he was cycling in Britain. He had successfully entered the country. It was at a time when crowds of Belgian and other foreign refugees were pouring into the country, and proper examination of papers was impossible.

He first committed himself at the North British Hotel, Edinburgh. From thence he sent a telegram to Stockholm, addressed to one Adolf Burchard. This

PEACE PROCLAMATION. *The heralds perform the ancient ceremony of proclaiming that Britain is again at peace, and the terms under which the war has been won.*

SCUTTLING THE GERMAN FLEET IN SCAPA FLOW. *By sinking the German Fleet after it had surrendered to the British Navy, Admiral Scheer thought he had saved his country from disgrace.*

PEACE CELEBRATIONS. *Detachments of troops representing all parts of the British Empire and the Allies took part in the Peace celebrations on July. 19, 1919. It was one of the most remarkable triumphal marches that the world has ever seen.*

THE WHOLE WORLD *began to realise the great future of aviation when Captain John Alcock and Lieutenant Arthur Brown made the first non-stop flight across the Atlantic in 1919. They flew 1,960 miles of ocean between St. John's, Newfoundland, and Clifton, Galway, Ireland, in 15 hours 57 minutes. They were given an enthusiastic reception when they arrived in London.*

telegram caused suspicion, as the address was known to the authorities. From that moment all his letters were opened and read by the postal censors.

He blundered, inasmuch as he used no cipher or shorthand. His letters to Sweden were in plain English or German. They described coast defences, ships' armaments, and other confidential matters, and these communications alone were sufficient to justify his immediate arrest. But Scotland Yard decided to wait.

A young Canadian journalist, who seemed to be well informed about the movements of troops, struck up a chance acquaintance with Lody in a Scottish hotel. Actually, the young Canadian was a British Intelligence officer. The Canadian moved about with Lody, engaged, so he said, in pursuit of "copy" for his newspaper.

He also provided Lody with exciting bits of information about military matters, which the German spy faithfully forwarded to Sweden. All the information was false. The Canadian even took Lody to a Scottish railway station and let him see a succession of trains racing southwards. All these trains had the blinds of the compartments closely drawn.

"Russian troops being rushed to the Western Front," whispered the Canadian. "Over two hundred thousand men landed this morning."

Lody was impressed. He sent an urgent telegram to Sweden. The telegraph officials tapped it over the wires with a smile on their faces.

He arrived in London on a bright moonlight night. An air raid was in progress. Through the streets sounded the siren wail of alarm. In the distance was the heavy crash of bombs dropped from the sky and also the barking of the anti-aircraft guns.

Lody seized the opportunity. He calmly went about studying the means taken to protect various public buildings from air raids, the location of anti-aircraft guns, and the places devastated by the bombs dropped. Then he returned to the little hotel in Bloomsbury where he was staying, and prepared another report.

But his end was near. He went to Liverpool to discover how the Atlantic liners were being armed. Then came his first suspicion that he was being watched. He decided to escape the friendly Canadian journalist and get over to Ireland. He managed to reach Dublin, but no sooner had he settled in a hotel than he glimpsed from the window a burly man quietly pacing up and down the street. He was being shadowed.

Hurriedly he stole away from the hotel and reached the railway station. He was still ostensibly an American tourist, and so he booked a ticket for a spot that all tourists visit—Killarney. Once the train steamed out of the station he leaned back in the seat with a sigh of relief. He was certain that he had escaped his shadowers.

But they had merely played with him. As the train steamed into Killarney three men of the Royal Irish Constabulary entered his compartment.

"Very sorry, sir, but we've instructions from Scotland Yard to arrest you," said one of them.

Lody had made a vain effort to reach his automatic pistol and shoot himself. But the men had given him no chance.

"Very well," he replied quietly.

He was taken to London. There had been no subtlety in his methods and no concealment of evidence. His bag contained nearly £180 in English money, besides Norwegian notes and German gold coin, also a notebook containing information about the latest naval action in the North Sea and copies of his communications to Burchard.

The evidence was complete. But he died a brave and gallant man. In his native village in Germany there thrives an oak tree, planted in his memory and called by his name, so that the tale of Lody will be told to future generations.

III

But the real desperate business of Military Intelligence was conducted on the actual battlefield, as well as in the big cities behind the lines.

British Headquarters on the Western Front was situated during most of the war at Montreuil, a tiny walled town on a hill with a landscape that was as peaceful and pastoral as the Wye Valley in England.

"Walking among its walled gardens," wrote C. E. Montague, "where roses hung over the walls, or sitting upon the edge of the rampart, your feet dangling over among the top boughs of embosoming trees, you were not merely out of the war; you entered into that beatitude of super-peace which fills your mind as you look at a Roman camp on a sunned Sussex down, where the gentle convexities of the turf seem to turn war into an old tale for children. . . ."

Nevertheless, in this peaceful pleasant atmosphere Military Intelligence was busy concocting maps and pictures of the whole area that lay immediately behind the German front-line trenches. Its first and easier task was to mark out correctly the place where every enemy unit was, each division, each battery, each railhead, aerodrome, field hospital, and dump. Next it had to mark each movement of these, the shiftings of the various centres of gravity, the changes in the relative density and relative quality of troops and guns at various sectors, the increase at any sector of field hospitals, the surest harbingers of heavy attacks. The trains on all lines had to be counted, their loads calculated.

It was necessary to know the spirit of the enemy. Did the men believe in their officers? What sort of letters were the enemy troops receiving from their civilian relatives in the background? Were the enemy soldiers themselves cheerful? Were any deserting? Did the German Army shoot its deserters?

To obtain this sort of valuable information, raiding parties crawled at night through the barbed wire across that welter of mud known as "No Man's Land," and seized some isolated member of the enemy's forces and dragged him back to their own trenches to be searched and questioned.

But all information about either side was of value to the other. News of the outbreak or settlement of a strike in a Welsh coalfield was of military value to Ludendorff. News of the day's weather in Central Europe was of military value to Sir Douglas Haig. News of anything that expressed in any degree the temper of London or Berlin, of Munich or Manchester, helped to eke out that accurate vision of our enemy's body and mind which was the basis of success in combat.

In that brilliantly written book _Disenchantment_, Mr. C. E. Montague has told the story of one clever exploit that Military Intelligence in France had to

When the Flanders battle of July 31, 1917, was about to be fought, we employed the old ruse of the Chinese attack. We modernised the trick of medieval garrisons, which would make a show of getting ready to break out at one gate when a real sally was to be made from another. The enemy was invited to think that a big attack was at hand. But against Lens and not east of Ypres.

Due circumstantial evidence was provided. There were audible signs that a great concentration of British guns was cautiously registering west of Lens. A little scuffle on that part of the front elicited from our side an amazing bombardment—apparently loosed in a moment of panic.

"I fancy a British Staff Officer's body —to judge by his brassard and tabs— may have floated down the Scarpe into the German lines. Interpreted with German thoroughness, the maps and papers upon it might easily betray the fact that Lens was the objective. And then a really inexcusable indiscretion appeared—just for a moment and then was hushed up—in the London Press.

"To an acute German eye it must have been obvious that this composition was just the inconsequent gassing of some stupid English general at home on leave; he was clearly throwing his weight about, as they say, without any real understanding of anything. The stuff was of no serious value, except for one parenthetic accidental allusion to Lens as the mark. As far as I know this ebullition of babble was printed in only one small edition of one London paper.

"Authority was then seen to be nervously trying, as Uncle Toby advised, 'to wipe it up and say no more about it.' Lest it should not be observed to have taken this wise precaution, some fussy Member of Parliament may have asked in the House of Commons how so outrageous a breach of soldierly reticence had occurred. And was there no control over the Press? It all answered. The Germans kept their guns in force at Lens, and their counter-barrage east of Ypres was so much lighter and our losses so much the less."

But the stories of Military Intelligence would in themselves provide a fascinating history, and, for the time being, one must leave them.

CHAPTER VII

ON THE HOME FRONT

Recruiting—The Dominions send troops—"Business as usual"—Britain's war songs—The Germans bombard Scarborough—First Zeppelin air raids—Bombs fall in the Strand—Shell scandal—Northcliffe's attack on Lord Kitchener.

I

RECRUITING in Britain was now in full blast. The first hundred thousand had already been trained and many of them were on their way to the battlefield. The Government was now talking in millions. Ships were bringing men from all over the Dominions and the Colonies. Canadian units were in training camps and many more being recruited.

Australians and New Zealanders were on their way. South Africa, too, was sending large contingents. The need for more and yet more men was seen when the first casualty lists were published. The total loss in killed and wounded was given in mid-November as fifty-seven thousand, and the worst of the Flanders fighting had yet to show its results.

This was the time when the name of Ypres first came into the news. "Wipers," of course, was what the British Tommy called it. But not only were men being trained all over Britain, in the many camps that had sprung up, with the intention of taションng their place on the Western Front. Men were also being trained for the defence of Britain itself. Thousands enlisted in the Special Constabulary. There were also Volunteer Training Corps, which were recog-

nised by the Government and War Office.

A great Red Cross service had also been formed. Women as well as men were offering themselves for every form of service. The Y.M.C.A. was appealing for funds for huts to make training camp life more comfortable. In every village women were forming parties for making socks and mufflers for the troops.

The Suffragettes had formed their own very useful working corps, and day after day troop trains were thundering along the road to Southampton, where the men boarded ships and were taken across the Channel to add to the great War of Attrition, as it was now known, that was taking place in Flanders and France.

"Business as usual" was the plea of the business men in Britain. They took the first war Budget calmly, with the doubling of the income-tax and the heavy stiffening of the duties on intoxicants. At the same time they handsomely over-subscribed the first War Loan of £350,000,000.

The shop windows of the London streets were full of the things which could be sent to troops in France. Occasionally mud-stained figures wearing those extraordinary fur coats of the soldiers in the early days were to be

188

seen in the streets of London, taking a few hours' leave from the Western Front.

II

The war suddenly came to Britain in a devastating fashion. On December 16, 1914, German warships shelled Scarborough, Hartlepool and Whitby for some hours, killing over a hundred people. It was the first loss of civilian life in England, and it added violent fuel to the outcry about German atrocities. The people of Britain were now beginning to suffer what the Belgians had been describing to them.

The newspapers, which until then had been full of the photographs of the war at the front, were now filled with "Scenes of the English Bombardment." It seemed incredible that an English girl at Scarborough should be killed by Germans whilst cleaning the doorstep; that a British family of eight at Hartlepool should every one of them be slaughtered by Germans.

When the wreckage was removed from the homes of these unfortunates, the dog and the canary were found crushed, but the cat, the only living thing to escape, was sleeping unharmed beneath the washing copper.

The Queen's Hotel at Scarborough was very badly damaged. Ten thousand sightseers visited Scarborough to see with their own eyes the almost unbelievable wreckage of an English town by the guns of German ships.

Beside the 127 civilians killed there were 567 injured, in addition to 35 soldiers and sailors.

Lord Riddell in his War Diary describes a talk with Lloyd George on Walton Heath regarding this bombardment.

"Do you remember that I prophesied this weeks ago?" said Lloyd George. "At the Committee of Defence I said, 'Why should they raid Lincolnshire? What objects have they got in bombarding haystacks? If I were a German I should bombard Middlesbrough, Hartlepool and Sunderland, the great industrial centres where we were making steel, etc.' At first Balfour was inclined to agree with me, but ultimately he thought that the danger from long-distance firing was comparatively small.

"Kitchener thought that there was something in my theory. He wanted the Admiralty to mind the coast. He said, 'I have nothing but six-inch gun at Hartlepool and that is little use.' I don't believe the Admiralty did mind the coast.

"When the last meeting of the Committee opened Captain Hankey, the secretary, commenced proceedings by saying 'Lloyd George's raid has taken place.'"

The result of this raid by the Germans on the English coast led to them being stigmatised by the newspapers as "Baby-killers." But this was only the beginning. The Germans were preparing a series of Zeppelin raids on this country which, later to be followed by aeroplane raids, were to bring terror and destruction in many of the big cities.

It was the early months of 1915 that brought the first Zeppelin raid—at Yarmouth, Cromer and King's Lynn on January 20, on Tyneside and at Lowestoft in April, and at Southend in May.

III

Although it cannot be said that the Zeppelins that bombed England achieved anything of any great military value, they did undoubtedly have a great moral effect upon the people of this country.

When their visits became a regular feature many householders abandoned their homes on the East Coast and came inland. For the most part, however, the people of this country took the bombing by Zeppelins with the phlegm of true Englishmen and were apt to stand out of doors on roofs or other vantage points and regard the whole affair as a spectacular show well worth watching.

It is little known that the German Fleet had only a single airship at the beginning of the war, the L 3.

But from 1914 until 1918 the Friedrichshafen works built sixty Zeppelins for the Navy, besides nine Schutte-Lanz ships.

Fourteen of these were shot down in land attacks, and four over the sea were so hit by shrapnel that they could not return. Two were destroyed in their sheds by English flyers, thirty were wrecked because of unfavourable circumstances or burnt in their sheds. Some were discarded as being out of date, and so only a few airships existed towards the end of the war.

A dramatic description of the bombing of England from a Zeppelin was broadcast some time ago by a German, Kapitänlieutenant D. Joachim Breithaupt. He was in the great engagement near Terschelling and in the bombing attacks on London in 1915, on Sheffield and Liverpool in 1916, and on London March 31, 1916.

On the last occasion he was shot down over Rainham and forced to descend at the mouth of the Thames. He was made a prisoner until the end of the war. It was as Captain of the Zeppelin L 15 that he made his attack on London in October, 1915.

A graphic description of this same raid, in which thirty-eight people were killed and eighty-seven injured, has been given by James Wickham, call-boy at the Gaiety Theatre, in the Strand, on the night of the raid.

"London did not know," wrote James Wickham, "that three hours ago on this fatal evening an urgent message had been flashed from France to the War Office that five Zeppelins had been noticed making for the East Coast.

"I heard it from Jupp, the stage doorkeeper. We often heard things of that kind at the Gaiety. Marconi House is next door.

"A clock struck nine.

"Twenty minutes to go to the first interval.

"A few minutes later I heard my name being called. It was the stage-manager, who wanted me.

"'Just run across to the post with these letters, Jimmy,' he said. 'We've a special rehearsal call for the morning and they must go off to-night.'

"As I went out of the stage-door I met Billy, the page.

"'Come over to the post with me, Billy,' I said. He was a bright little lad of fifteen; I was three years older.

"Only too glad of a little relaxation, he readily agreed.

"The nearest pillar-box was at the top of Catherine Street, which lies immediately opposite the stage-door of the Gaiety, and together we crossed Aldwych and made our way alongside the Strand Theatre.

"I stopped a moment to light a cigarette, carefully screening the match. Billy waited.

"'They say the Zepps are on their way; the swine!' I remarked.

"As though my words had released

BRITAIN WAS SURPRISED *to learn in August, 1919, that its police force, upon which it had learned to rely in emergencies, had gone on strike. Members of London tubes stopped work in sympathy with police strikers, but the dispute was soon settled.*

RAILWAY
STRIKE, 1919.

Railway transport was paralysed for nine days in September and October by a strike. Eventually the Government intervened, and secured a settlement.

Above: *A non-striking porter has a few moments' rest.*

Below: *The public volunteered for work during the strike. Even women helped to unload trucks.*

Fully equipped troops guarded parts of the line where trouble was feared. This sentry was posted on the G.W.R. main line at Slough.

DURING THE RAILWAY STRIKE *the clerical staff at Euston Station became porters and unloaded trains carrying food.*

A FOOD CONVOY *in Hyde Park during the railway strike.*

There were several big boxing matches in London just after the war. Joe Beckett fought Carpentier upon two occasions, but was knocked out by the young Frenchman in the first round in 1919, and in 1923 he retired from the ring.

ten thousand furies, there was the sudden crackle of anti-aircraft gunfire; simultaneously a dreadful sound that London knew only too well—a sound like no other on earth.

"It was the mournful wail created by the velocity of a descending bomb.

"In the one brief terrible moment before the impact I instinctively knew it was coming directly where we stood.

"I was not wrong.

"It exploded three yards from where we were standing. It flung me against the wall next the pit entrance to the Strand Theatre. It sucked me back again. It dashed me to the ground. Masonry fell. Glass rained. I felt unhurt. Only dazed. Yet I had twenty-two lumps of shrapnel embedded in me. They carried me downstairs into the bar of the Strand Theatre. The streets were pandemonium. I asked for Billy. But he had been blown to pieces. I could hear screams in the street outside. The dull vibrant thud of more bombs. Others were brought in and laid beside me. Some were moaning, some calling for missing friends and relatives. Someone rushed in and said a London General omnibus had been blown to bits in Aldwych opposite the Waldorf.

"It was true.

"More injured were brought in. They were carried on theatre boards.

"There was the ring of ambulance bells, the imperious clang of fire alarms. And above it all a terrible, insistent thudding.

"The Zeppelin—it was the L 15 on her maiden voyage to England—had manœuvred herself into line with the Strand and travelled directly eastward, dropping bombs at short intervals.

"Two fell barely a second before the one that hit me, in a narrow street running parallel to the Strand between the Lyceum and Covent Garden.

"The little street was crowded. As the first bomb exploded people were flung in all directions. One woman was blown to pieces. Another was cut in two by a sheet of glass blown from a shop front.

"When those in the vicinity who were unhurt recovered sufficiently to lend help they found thirty-eight people prone on the pavement, in the roadway or the gutters.

"All around was the glitter of glass. It lay everywhere in millions of pieces.

"There was an old orange seller who had been standing at the gallery entrance to the Lyceum. She lay huddled against the wall still clutching her wares. She was dead.

"A man from the audience had hurried down the staircase into the street when the firing began, leaving his wife in her seat. He never returned. He was instantly killed by a flying fragment of shell from our own anti-aircraft guns.

"One man, terribly mutilated, yet still clutching a glass and sandwich, was discovered half inside and half outside a public house whose walls had been shattered by the explosion.

"Nine other people in the saloon had been wiped out. A barmaid was killed.

"When official help arrived it was found that seventeen had been killed and twenty-one injured by that one missile.

"No single bomb dropped from a Zeppelin during the war claimed a greater death-roll."

IV

At the end of some eighteen months effective means were invented for the destruction of Zeppelins in the air, and several raiders were brought down in flames. But the Germans had developed a new weapon in the aeroplane. Early in 1917 London began to experience daylight raids.

The most impressive air raid of all occurred on the morning of June 13, 1917. A squadron of thirty or more German bombers crossed London from end to end while the citizens were going about their business. The spectacle of this massed formation of planes was so surprising that the raided forgot the oft-repeated warnings to "take cover," and, instead of cowering in cellars and tube railways, they stood in the streets watching the raiders. Yet this raid, borne so carelessly, produced more casualties than any other; about 580, including more than 150 deaths.

On September 29, 1917, a bomb struck the pavement outside the Eaglet public house in Holloway, blowing up the building and killing and wounding a number of people who were sheltering in the cellars. At the same time a nurse and baby on the top floor escaped uninjured.

On January 28, 1918, a still more terrible tragedy occurred when a bomb, falling through a pavement light in front of Odhams Printing Works in Long Acre, exploded in the basement, which was being used as a public shelter.

The lower part of the main walls was undercut, with the result that the floors collapsed, and heavy printing machinery and the immense rolls of newsprint stored on the upper stories fell through into the basement, where some scores of women and children from the surrounding tenements were crowded together. Nineteen women and ten children

were killed, some of them being drowned, and thirty-eight women and fourteen children were injured.

V

The German air-raiders did not have it all their own way. There was in Britain, as well as on the Western Front, a group of brave young flyers who, if their machines were technically less advanced than those of the Germans, were soon to give a good account of themselves. Furthermore, towards the end of the Great War the Royal Air Force was to be the greatest and most powerful in the world.

In the beginning it was known as the Royal Flying Corps, wearing khaki flap jackets and soft caps, which only some years later were to be changed to the sky-blue uniform of to-day.

As an indication of how this force grew, it has been pointed out that at the outbreak of war the R.F.C. consisted approximately of 150 officers and 550 other ranks. At the cessation of hostilities the R.A.F. had a strength of 28,000 officers and 264,000 airmen.

By the end of 1919, 26,000 officers, 21,000 cadets and 227,000 airmen had received their discharge papers. Moreover, in the war the British flying services destroyed 8,000 enemy aeroplanes and 300 balloons; dropped 8,000 tons of bombs on hostile objectives; fired 12,000,000 rounds of ammunition at targets on the ground.

The first four squadrons flew to France in August, 1914. The first British aeroplane to land on the Western Front was flown by Lieutenant H. D. Harvey-Kelly, an officer destined to survive three years of war in the air before he fell, commanding No. 19 Squadron, in 1917. He was probably the first British officer to exchange shots with the enemy in the air, when on August 25, 1914, he helped to drive down a German aeroplane.

The first squadrons to land in France were numbered 2 to 5 and were led by Majors Burke, J. Salmond, G. H. Raleigh, and J. F. A. Higgins.

An administrative wing was left in England, under Major H. Trenchard, who had trained a good proportion of the R.F.C. personnel at the Central Flying School.

This nucleus, destined to amazing development, then consisted, as its Commanding Officer said later, of: "One clerk and one typewriter, a confidential box with a pair of boots in it, and a lot of unpaid bills incurred by various officers in the Flying Corps during the rush to the front."

Major Brancker was at the War Office and Lord Kitchener was suggesting—what seemed almost incredible then—the raising of a hundred squadrons.

In 1915 General Trenchard assumed the command of the Flying Corps in the field. He was one of the successes of the Great War. Of him an officer in a great fighter squadron wrote:

"The pilots trusted him implicitly, and with reason, for he never asked of them impossibilities and he never let them down.

"Tall and commanding in appearance, with black hair and a complexion inclined to be pallid, he looked less than his age, but one had only to glance at the strong face, with power and determination so clearly shown in every line, to realise the strain to which he was subjected. In times of severe stress he looked, indeed, drawn and haggard.

"But the encouraging word or message was always given, the unfailing sympathy, alas, so frequently called for, and the spontaneous appreciation of work well done or a fight well fought, never faltered or flagged.

"He could fling a squadron into action determined to achieve or not return. The wildest of pilots recognised in him the Master Spirit. It was not that he inspired fear—it was that he inspired the desire to merit his approbation."

Very soon the Germans began to hear of our flying aces. There was Albert Ball, who had a startling series of successes in aerial combats.

Despite the supremacy of the enemy's Fokkers, this youngster, who had joined at the age of 17, brought down machine after machine belonging to the Germans.

One of the leading fighter pilots of 1918 admired Ball's dashing methods so intensely that to sustain his courage in times of strain he pinned on his instrument board a card bearing the words:

He must fall.
Remember
BALL.

There is also the epic story of the first air V.C., Lieutenant R. A. J. Warneford.

Warneford, flying a tiny Morane aeroplane, fell in with a German Zeppelin that was returning from a scouting trip along the Belgian coast. The scene of the combat was in the neighbourhood of Ghent and Brussels at three o'clock one morning in June, 1915.

Warneford accepted combat. He flew alongside the Zeppelin, firing at it with a rifle from his baby machine. The rifle fire made no impression upon the airship, and the crew of the Zeppelin were using machine-guns in reply.

Warneford zoomed up in his machine

and when above the airship dropped his six bombs in rapid succession. There was an explosion in the Zeppelin and Warneford found his baby machine flung skyward, and out of control until it fell in a nose-dive. The Zeppelin also crashed in flames.

Warneford was lucky enough to get back with his machine to the British lines and report. Alas, ten days later he was killed at Buc Aerodrome while flying a machine destined for Dunkirk. He was 23.

From the spring and early summer of 1916 Britain's air defences steadily developed. London's aeroplane defence was then centred mainly on Sutton's Farm and Hainault Farm. The value of these defences against the raiding Zeppelins was proved in the autumn of 1916, when one of the German airships fell in flames over Cuffley, its fiery descent seen by millions in London. The hero of this exploit was Lieutenant Leefe Robinson.

Flying a B.E. 2C at an altitude of 11,500 feet, Robinson manœuvred his 'plane so that he was about 800 feet below the gas bag. He fired one drum after another from his machine-gun without any apparent effect. Then he dropped behind the Zeppelin and fired another drum into the underside of the stern. Exultantly he saw a red glow creeping stealthily along the belly of the ship.

In a few moments the whole of the rear of the airship was a blazing furnace. It began to break and fall. Robinson in his 'plane dodged the mass as it roared earthwards. The young Englishman, overwhelmed with excitement and victory, fired off a few red Very lights and dropped a parachute flare to add more colour to the event. Then he glided back to his base at Sutton's Farm.

For his great performance the King awarded Robinson the V.C. But he was not long to survive. On April 5 the following year he made a forced landing behind the German lines and was taken prisoner. His health was undermined by his imprisonment, and when repatriated in 1918 he was a victim to the influenza plague and died.

It was about this time that the famous Scandal of the Shells burst upon England.

The deadly battle of Neuve Chapelle had been fought, and the terrible casualties suffered by the British, as was revealed in the dispatches which subsequently appeared, showed that something was definitely wrong.

Colonel Repington, the military correspondent of *The Times*, had already sent several messages, supposedly inspired by General French, to the effect that the British troops lacked a number of high-explosive shells, which the Germans were using in big quantities.

Even a month after the battle of Neuve Chapelle, Mr. Asquith, the Prime Minister, was denying that the British attacks had been crippled by lack of munitions and that the casualty list had been swelled by that lack.

At the same time Mr. Lloyd George was giving figures of a remarkable development of the munition output. Yet the British public was not entirely satisfied by these speeches. It was a period when the strong, silent man, Lord Kitchener, at the head of the War Office, was being very much criticised. This criticism reached its peak with an article in the *Daily Mail* which was a definite attack on Lord Kitchener's position at the War Office.

This article in the *Daily Mail* alleged that Kitchener had neglected the manufacture of high-explosive shells and had

AN EARLY BROADCAST. *It shows Miss Olive Sturgess broadcasting from the seventh-floor studio at Marconi House.*

THE FIRST BROADCAST TRANSMITTER *operated in Great Britain, installed at the Marconi Works, Chelmsford, in 1919 and 1920.*

THE GROWTH OF WIRELESS.

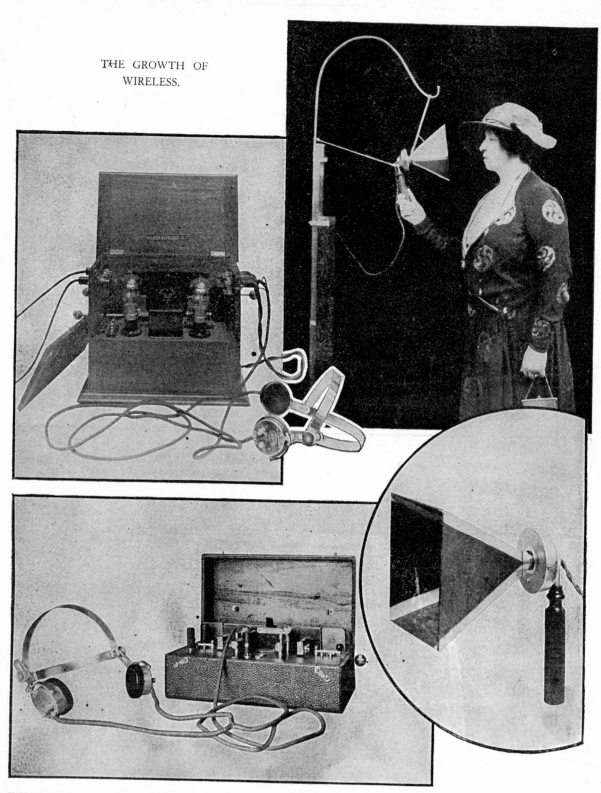

WIRELESS *began to interest the public after the war. Dame Nellie Melba broadcast from the Marconi Works in 1920, and autographed the microphone* (bottom right photograph). *Other photographs show the early Marconiphone wireless sets.*

THE CENOTAPH, erected in Whitehall to the memory of the Glorious Dead, was unveiled by H.M. the King on Armistice Day, 1920. It was designed by Sir Edwin Lutyens.

THE UNKNOWN WARRIOR. *The body of a British soldier who died in France—a nameless hero of the battlefields—was brought to London and buried in Westminster Abbey on Armistice Day, 1920. The King and Prince of Wales, field-marshals and generals followed the coffin, and soldiers, with arms reversed, paraded the route.*

THE NATION'S PILGRIMAGE. *Four sentinels guarded the Tomb of the Unknown Warrior whilst the nation paid homage. Over a million people filed past in the few days following his burial.*

THE PRINCE OF WALES *visited Samoa in 1920, where he received native chieftains and their families and was presented with small gifts.*

IN AUSTRALIA, 1920, *where the Prince of Wales was given a great welcome.*

supplied the Army with too much shrapnel. Needless to say, this attack on the leading figure in the war conducted by Britain shocked a good many people. A few days later the *Daily Mail* was burnt publicly on the Stock Exchange.

Lord Northcliffe, however, persisted in his attacks. He began by saying: "Kitchener must go." Later he was to change this attitude and bring forth a new slogan: "Asquith must go."

Nevertheless, the Government, and also the people, were perturbed over this disclosure of a munition scandal. The Government were of the opinion that General French should have made his request for shells to the Prime Minister and not to the Press, as he had apparently done, through the military correspondent of *The Times*.

Criticisms also began to appear in the Press and elsewhere that Lord Kitchener was much too autocratic and was holding information from the Government. *The Times* itself, controlled at this period by Lord Northcliffe, was frank enough. In a leader it wrote: "The War Office has sought to do too much. It cannot hope to organise a nation which its own chief has in many ways curiously failed to understand."

Mr. Bonar Law asked why use was not made of the business man. Newspapers at the same time urged the organising of the employers instead of concentrating on the habits of the wage earners.

It was realised that something had to be done. In the beginning, a business man, Mr. Booth, was appointed to a new War Office committee on munitions. But it was seen that even this would not solve the great problem of providing the British Army in France with sufficient munitions.

On April 16 an outside committee on munitions, mainly composed of the heads of great engineering firms, was appointed. Mr. Lloyd George was made the Chairman. This was the beginning of his successful career as Minister of Munitions.

Lord Riddell describes an interview he had with Kitchener at the War Office.

"This has been a sad and worrying time," said Kitchener. "It is terrible to think that such a breach of discipline should have taken place in the Army and that such lies, such damned lies, should have been circulated. Under ordinary circumstances I should have taken measures, but in the face of the Germans what can I do? French has plenty of ammunition at Havre. Why does he leave it there? Here are the figures."

Kitchener then read the details from a paper on his table, from which it appeared that General French had 689 rounds of high-explosive shells per gun, in addition to shrapnel and so forth.

Kitchener added: "I am sending him 23,000 rounds to-night, and the consignment is forwarded every night. I would rather have been kicked from one end of the country to the other than have the Army dragged through the mire in this way."

But while this conflict was going on regarding the production of high-explosive shells for the British Army, a new phase of the war had opened.

Mr. Winston Churchill had begun a dramatic adventure in the attempt to force the Dardanelles and capture Constantinople.

CHAPTER VIII

THE DARDANELLES DISASTER

Winston Churchill's great idea—Bombardment of the Turks begins—Several ships sunk by mines—The Gallipoli landing disaster—The massacre—The greatest evacuation in history.

I

ONCE again Mr. Winston Churchill was in the limelight. This time with the Dardanelles campaign.

Strategically the idea of attacking Constantinople and capturing the Straits of the Dardanelles was sound. Mr. Winston Churchill had always been an admirer of Napoleon. It was said that he kept a bust of him in his rooms at the Admiralty. It was Napoleon, however, who said of Constantinople: " Priceless key! In herself she is worth an Empire. Whoever possesses her will govern the world."

The need for a blow at Turkey at this particular moment was obvious. Apart from the fact that the Turkish Army was menacing our occupation of Egypt, by troops on the other side of the Suez Canal in the Sinai Desert, it was also essential that the Allies should link up with Russia, and the barrier between Russia and the Mediterranean was, of course, the Dardanelles.

As First Lord of the Admiralty, Mr. Winston Churchill was confident that the scheme could be carried through successfully. It was he who discovered and appointed Beatty, recalled Fisher to the Admiralty, and entrusted the Grand Fleet to Jellicoe.

But when the War Council met on January 28 to discuss the proposed expedition to the Dardanelles, it was soon obvious that Fisher and Churchill were at odds.

As Churchill was speaking, becoming more and more eloquent and insistent, and winning the adherence of the Council, Lord Fisher rose abruptly and threatened to hand in his resignation.

Kitchener hurried after him, reasoned with him in a corner by the window, and led him back almost by force to the table. Fisher bowed, and promised to do " his best." At bottom he remained fundamentally, irreconcilably hostile to the adventure.

However, Churchill's views won. Orders were given to Admiral Carden to prepare for a big scale naval attack on the Dardanelles. The naval forces under the command of Admiral Carden were indeed powerful. Besides several dreadnoughts, he possessed that latest ship of which the British were so proud, the *Queen Elizabeth*. There were also eleven torpedo boats and three submarines.

The British Admiralty asked the French Ministry of Marine to supply a reinforcement consisting of two fairly modern battleships, and these were promptly despatched under the command of Rear-Admiral Gue Pratte.

The story of that naval attack, as revealed by the Commission which eventually investigated the whole of the operation, is by no means pleasant reading. It revealed not only bad mismanagement of the operation, but also bad shooting on the part of the British ships.

But the thing which really brought this naval operation to a disastrous end was the employment by the Turks of mines. The Straits of the Dardanelles, which are thirty-three miles long by two miles broad, contracting to about 1,300 yards at their narrowest point, are very well adapted to the employment of mines.

They are traversed by two currents flowing in contrary directions. Not only were the waters extensively anchored with mines, but the Turks also used floating mines, sending them down by the current. Just at the moment when the attack was almost ready to be launched, Admiral Carden was taken suddenly ill, returned to Malta and resigned the command to De Robeck.

De Robeck telegraphed to London on March 17: "Weather permitting I will proceed with operations to-morrow."

The Admiralty replied with explicit instructions for the demolishing of the forts and the procedure of the fleet, which was to advance into the Narrows and batter the further forts.

"To cut the Turkish Empire in two," was Mr. Churchill's declaration to the War Council, who were hesitating now that the moment for attack had come.

On the morning of March 18 the *Queen Elizabeth*, the *Agamemnon*, the *Lord Nelson*, and the *Inflexible* opened fire at a distance of some nine miles. The attack waged fast and furious. Several of the Turkish forts were demolished, blown sky-high by the huge shells shot out by *Queen Elizabeth* and the other battleships. But the floating mines were the real victors of the day.

When evening came it was seen that the losses of the Allies had been severe. Three battleships were sunk — the *Bouvet*, the *Irresistible*, and the *Ocean* —and four disabled, including the *Inflexible* and the *Agamemnon*.

The day had ended badly for the Allies. They had lost seven big ships out of eighteen. Eight enemy guns had been destroyed out of 176, and forty soldiers had been killed. It was a sorry balance sheet. Yet the Turks were in despair, for they were almost devoid of ammunition.

II

But it had been realised from the outset that even should the warships succeed in attaining their object, land forces would sooner or later be required to aid in the campaign, if only to secure the communication with the Fleet after it had passed into the Sea of Marmora.

Before the failure of the naval attack of March 18, Allied troops had been set in motion for the Ægean. Some were already in Lemnos, and Sir Ian Hamilton, chosen as Commander-in-Chief of the military contingent, had arrived in time to witness the fight of the 18th. In view of its result, the Allied Governments decided that from this time onward the gathering army must assume the principal rôle in the efforts to secure possession of the Straits.

Hamilton was unable to initiate land operations at once. The Turks were making preparation to repel landings on both sides of the Straits, while the troops at his disposal were partly in Egypt, partly at Lemnos, and partly on the high seas en route from the respective bases in England and France.

Sir Ian Hamilton decided, therefore, that his army must, in the first place, be concentrated in Egypt, to be organised for the hazardous undertaking to which it was about to be committed, and that it must then be disposed in transports in accordance with tactical requirements in anticipation of a landing in face of the enemy.

A month was lost in consequence. During that month the Turkish Army was formed to guard the Straits. Marshal Liman von Sanders, head of the German Military Mission in Turkey, was appointed Commander-in-Chief. Under his instructions the defence system organised in consequence of the warning offered by the naval operation was overhauled and developed.

The Allied force was composed of five divisions—two furnished by the United Kingdom, two formed of Australian and New Zealand troops, and one composed of French Colonial troops. Against this force Liman von Sanders could pit six divisions, but these were dispersed all over the Gallipoli Peninsula.

The Expeditionary Force concentrated in Mudros Bay, Lemnos, in the third week of April. After a short delay enforced by bad weather, the Armada put to sea during the nights of April 23-24 and 24-25, so that the transport of the covering warships should arrive at their various rendezvous at or before dawn on the 25th.

The landing at Cape Helles on the night of April 24 may be said to be one of the greatest tragedies in the whole history of the British Army.

On the beach marked "V" on the Staff maps, one of the largest convoys of the Allied Armada was steered. On board the convoy were crowded several battalions, among them some of the pick of the British Army; the Dublin Fusi-liers, the Munster Fusiliers; and some veterans of the Naval Division.

To the right a stout collier, the *River Clyde,* landed full on the beach. Its commander, Edward Unwin, had been ordered to run it aground. It was to provide a landing platform for hundreds of infantry enclosed within it.

In the deep silence of the night the men began to come forth from the ship. They did not realise that the slopes above them were slit with trenches, fortified with barbed wire, behind which were machine-guns, pom-pom guns, and crowds of Turks—five hundred of them.

The Turks waited like hunters until the British advance. Once they were within rifle fire the massacre began. Rifles, machine-guns, and pom-poms opened. The Fusiliers were mowed down in bunches, so thick that several men were suffocated beneath the dead. Other lighters carrying numbers of troops were riddled with shot. Sailors manœuvred desperately and tried to land their lighters. The waves broke red on the sand.

The Irish troops managed to reach one vantage point and were then mowed down by machine-guns. Only twenty-five returned.

Commander Unwin himself, of the *River Clyde,* plunged into the sea and worked desperately with his officers to restore the gangways so that the troops could reach the beach. By eight o'clock in the morning they had succeeded in this.

But with the dawn a dreadful sight was revealed. The boats were scattered and destroyed, manned by corpses. In spite of the machine-guns concealed by sandbags in the bows of the *River Clyde,* the Turkish fire had never

THE PRINCE OF WALES IN THE UNITED STATES. *The Prince of Wales paid two visits to the United States. The first was in 1919, and the second was five years later. Upon each occasion he was given a warm reception by the Americans.*

THE PRINCE OF WALES *became known after the war as " the Travelling Prince." He paid visits to Canada, Australia, New Zealand, India, South Africa, the United States, Japan, and South America. Wherever he went he was received with the same enthusiasm, and he made many friends.*

THE IRISH RISING. *The rising in Ireland was the main event of 1920. Regiments of soldiers, artillery, and tanks were rushed to Dublin to maintain order.*

BRITISH TROOPS ON GUARD. *Ironically, the wall they guard is plastered with a Sinn Fein advertisement.*

THE IRISH RISING.

Suspects being searched in Dublin.

THE IRISH RISING.

A sentry on guard in Dublin Castle.

THE IRISH RISING. *Many of Dublin's chief buildings were partly destroyed by shell fire.*

Dublin ablaze during the riots.

THE IRISH RISING.

SENTENCING A MURDERER TO DEATH. *This photograph is unique, for it is the only photograph ever taken in a British Court of Justice showing a judge wearing the dreaded Black Cap. It shows Mr. Justice Avory giving sentence of death upon Thomas Allaway, 1922.*

ceased. Landing had to be interrupted. All the day groups which had managed to reach the shore lay hidden behind a fold in the ground over which poured a rain of bullets. Not until the fall of night did the few parties of men creep up to the outer walls of the old fort. The remainder of the troops landed under cover of darkness.

In the meantime messages were received from the other landings. They all told the same story of the desperate massacre.

The Australians had managed to effect some sort of a landing at a point on Cape Helles, known as Anzac Cove. At the end of several days' operations, Hamilton could look round and realise that he had gained a somewhat precarious footing on two points of the Peninsula. The two forces were some fifteen miles apart, and what amounted to little more than a patch of ground had been won in either case.

His intentions were now completely exposed to the enemy, and the great advantage of surprise had passed away without his force having established itself in a dominating position, capable of being turned to satisfactory account in subsequent operations.

In both areas the Turks enjoyed the tactical command. They were at least equal in force to the Allies. Their guns were able to bear with effect upon the beaches used as landing places and advance bases, and, although at this time of the year the weather was generally calm, these beaches provided but inadequate facilities for the landing of ammunition, armament, or stores.

It was not possible to disguise the tragedy of these operations to the people in Britain. True, they had only had the news that the landing had been "strongly opposed," but the people by this time began to realise that these official phrases meant disaster.

Mr. Winston Churchill was strongly criticised. He had unfortunately to stand most of the blame for this particular operation. Actually the practical idea was sound. Where it had gone wrong was in the fact that the enemy had been given plenty of notice of this particular landing. They had had months, in fact, to prepare for it.

In May, 1915, Mr. Winston Churchill resigned. Lord Riddell in his War Diary reports a conversation he had with Winston Churchill as they left the Admiralty together to walk to the Bath Club.

As he stepped outside the doors of the Admiralty Winston Churchill said:

"I leave the nation and Navy in a state of perfect efficiency. I cannot say more."

He then talked of the political situation, concerning which he made a few bitter remarks. Finally, he said:

"I shall give the Government my support. I shall make a few speeches and then I shall go to the front. I could not continue to hold a sinecure office at such a time."

III

On the desperate campaign that followed one need not dwell. There was the tragic landing at Suvla Bay, where the military operations were in some confusion. This failed materially to alter the situation.

In the middle of September of the same year the Paris Government had come to the conclusion that there was now no hope of victory in the Dardanelles theatre. But the British Cabinet, influenced by anxiety as regards the prestige in the East and by disinclination to abandon an enterprise in which great sacrifices had been incurred, and from which much had at one time been expected, could not make up its mind to cut losses and withdraw.

On General Sir Ian Hamilton being advised to give his views concerning the question of evacuation, he pronounced himself as emphatically opposed to such a step. So Sir Charles Munro was sent out from England to take his place.

The new Commander-in-Chief, impressed by the very unsatisfactory positions occupied by the Allied troops, by the impossibility of their making any progress at their existing strength, and by the risk the army ran by clinging to such a shore without any safe harbour to depend on for a base in stormy weather, declared unhesitatingly in the closing days of October for a complete withdrawal, after examining the situation on the spot and consulting with Birdwood, Byng and Davis.

The British Cabinet would not accept the recommendation, and sent Lord Kitchener to investigate and report. He had viewed proposals to abandon the campaign with alarm; but after visiting the peninsula he realised that evacuation was the only justifiable course, and reported to that effect.

All this time winter was drawing nearer and the need for a prompt decision was becoming more and more urgent. But the authorities in London lost another fortnight before, on December 8, they at last sent instructions to Munro to withdraw from Suvla and Anzac while retaining Helles.

On December 19, at sunset, the last guns at Suvla fired their last salvos. Two large detachments of five thousand men left the front line. A certain number were left to hold the second and third lines. Small picket attachments remained at their posts. Rifles discharged automatically by means of candles which set light to strings, kept up a spasmodic fusillade in the deserted trenches. The sappers were the last to leave. They closed the barbed wire gates behind the infantry, cut the telegraph wires, and set contact mines.

At another point 250 men with six machine-guns had received orders to sacrifice themselves to the last man to keep off the Turks from the beaches.

But the Turks had not the slightest inkling of the departure. They went on exploding mines. An aeroplane hovered in the night sky and dropped a few green stars. Aviators saw the usual glimpse of light from the British hospital tent, though not a soul was inside. At the landing stage the feverish activities continued to the subdued rattle of chains, winches, and machinery.

The last 200 defenders made their way down the path to the beach, leaving behind them vast piles of biscuits, canned food, and condensed milk.

The last man to leave Suvla was General Byng.

The withdrawal from Anzac was carried out with equal skill. 20,000 men were safe in Mudros by December 18. During the latter night 10,000 more were evacuated. The last 6,000 men had been distributed among three positions. Australians and New Zealanders stole silently over sacking spread on planks from every corner of the fan-shaped expanse.

On the 20th, at three o'clock in the morning, only 800 diehards were left quite close to the Turkish line. The Australians invented all sorts of cunning devices. Rifles discharged by sand running out of buckets continued to fire to the very end. The Turks, completely gulled, turned their new guns upon the enemy trenches, which they bombarded furiously. The naval guns retorted and pounded the hills.

It was then decided at long last to evacuate Helles. Troops were embarked with even greater speed than at Anzac —7,000 men on the last night but one, and 15,000 on the last night.

Between December 31 and January 8, 16,000 men, eighty-five guns, 2,667 horses and mules, and enormous quantities of material, munitions, and provisions were taken off.

On January 8 the weather broke. There were still over 16,000 men to be embarked. At seven o'clock in the evening troops were massed on the beaches. Meanwhile the mines prepared in the trenches were already exploding and the rifles continued firing mechanically.

General Maude arrived last of all, having failed to discover the openings in the lines of barbed wire. The men leaped on the barges, which were already swept by the waves. Luckily the sea did not become seriously rough until much later, but if it had the troops would have been left on the shore.

The British were obliged to leave immense quantities of material on the beaches; a dozen old and useless guns, 500 animals, which were slaughtered by a special staff detailed to destroy all that had to be left behind.

Up to the last moment they were cutting cables, telephone wires, killing mules, throwing petrol on heaps of clothing, setting time fuses to bombs. At length the Turks understood.

British organisation and discipline, and the wind, which continued favourable almost to the last moment, had made possible the success of a gigantic operation, unparalleled in military history—the evacuation of a whole army under the very eyes, and actually within a stone's throw, of the enemy.

Thus ended the tragic chapter of the Gallipoli campaign.

CHAPTER IX

THREE WAR TRAGEDIES

Nurse Cavell's arrest—Her execution—Sir Roger Casement arrested in Ireland—His trial for treason—His execution—Lord Kitchener leaves for Russia—H.M.S. Hampshire strikes a mine—Sailor's last glimpse of Lord Kitchener.

I

IT was on October 16, 1915, that there appeared in the newspapers a paragraph to the effect that an Englishwoman, Miss Edith Cavell, a nurse who had for some years been living and working in Brussels, had been shot on a charge of assisting war prisoners to escape.

This was the first time many people in this country had heard of Edith Cavell. The story of her trial and execution, which was subsequently told, aroused a new revulsion of feeling against Germany.

It was shortly after her arrest on August 5, 1915, that the matter first came to the attention of Brand Whitlock, the United States Minister to Belgium.

It was reported that she had been taken into custody on the charge of aiding stragglers from the Allied armies to cross the Belgian frontier into Holland. It was alleged that she gave them money, clothing, and information concerning the route to be followed.

One of her fellow prisoners was Dr. Hostelet, of Brussels. He escaped with a five years' sentence, and when the Armistice was signed was released.

Like all who came in contact with the heroic Englishwoman, he was filled with admiration for her calm courage. He had known her before her arrest, and was familiar with the whole circumstances surrounding the case. Writing of those earlier days in Brussels, he says:

"In my frequent visits to Miss Cavell, I was able to see the risks she was running. The presence of a lot of men was obvious as soon as one entered the house—voices, songs, cries. I often pointed this out to her, and she replied calmly and resignedly: 'What would you? I cannot impose silence on them.' She even consented to let them go into town to amuse themselves. I remember her fright when one night some of them came back singing and disorderly, scandalizing the neighbourhood.

"It was then that I and some other friends determined to put these dangerous guests in private houses or with reliable innkeepers. But the more we housed the more came . . .

"In her trial she was accused of recruiting, but she only spoke the truth when she replied: 'My object was to get the men sent to me across the frontier; once there, they were free.'

"She was also accused of espionage. Denial here was absolutely justified. That espionage was facilitated through her is certain, but she never took an active part in it. Absorbed in her work as head of a nurses' school, she never dreamt of running a recruiting office or a spy service. She wished to save men; Englishmen first, then Allies, and she gave herself up entirely to this humanitarian and patriotic work."

We have no account of the execution beyond the fact that the heroic nurse was shot early the next morning.

The officer in charge of the firing squad noticed the pale, drawn face of some of the men. He said: "It is very sad to have to shoot a woman, but she is not a mother; and, therefore, you will do your duty as soldiers."

The rifles spoke. A brave, gentle woman died; and the manner of her dying sent a shudder of horror round the world. Her execution and the sinking of the *Lusitania* were the two greatest crimes committed during the war.

II

But the British themselves were to execute a traitor shortly afterwards, one of their own countrymen. This was Sir Roger Casement, an Irishman, who had served in the Consular service and had been knighted by King Edward.

On April 25, 1916, the newspapers published details of what was called "an armed raid" on Ireland. A German ship carrying munitions had been captured, a convoying submarine had got away, but two men landed from her in a boat had been traced to hiding and arrested.

The next day Dublin was in revolt. It was the famous Easter Rising. The streets of the Irish capital echoed to the thudding of field guns, the rattle of machine-guns, and the crackle of rifle shots. The rebels seized the Post Office and the Four Courts. There were also signs and rumours of risings elsewhere.

Then, on May 1, came the official report that "the back of the rebellion was broken," and the rebels surrendering.

In the meantime, the British had Sir Roger Casement under arrest in the Tower of London. The story of his discovery after that adventurous landing on the wild Irish coast is worthy of being told again.

At four o'clock on the morning of Good Friday, John McCarthy, a farmer living at Curraghane, found an apparently abandoned boat on the shore. Filled with curiosity, he made an examination and discovered a dagger, a tin box full of pistol ammunition, and other articles. Nearby, buried in the sand, were three Mauser pistols, two handbags filled with ammunition, six maps of Ireland, a flash-lamp, and three coats.

In the pocket of one of the coats was a railroad ticket from Berlin to Wilhelmshaven, dated April 12, 1916. The authorities afterwards made a great deal of this bit of pasteboard. It was photographed and shown to the jury as part of the proof that Sir Roger Casement had been in Germany at the time indicated.

The story is next taken up by Mary Gorman, a farm servant, who saw three men passing along the road in the direction of Ardfert. The police were notified at this stage of the proceedings, and Sergeant Hearne searched the neighbourhood in the quest for three suspicious-looking characters.

They were located finally in what was called McKenna's Fort. McKenna's Fort was in reality a cave where the three men had sought refuge. The leader of the trio, when asked to give his name, said:

"I am Richard Morton, of Denham."

"What is your business?" inquired the officer.

"I am a writer—an author."

The sergeant was plainly sceptical. He wanted more detailed information.

"What have you written?"

"Well, among other things, the *Life of St. Brendon*."

"Where do you come from?"

"I came to Kerry from Dublin, and arrived at Mount Brandon on the nineteenth. I left there on the twentieth, slept at a farmhouse, and intended to go to Tralee."

The man was not Richard Morton, but Sir Roger Casement, and most of his statements were the products of his imagination.

He was taken to Ardfert Barracks, where he was charged with landing arms and ammunition in county Kerry.

On the way to the barracks he was seen to drop a piece of paper. When this was recovered it proved to be a code.

On April 27 Casement was conveyed to England and handed over to Inspector Sandercock of the Metropolitan Police. He was tried for treason in the High Court of Justice, London, beginning June 16, 1916.

The Lord Chief Justice of England (Viscount Reading, who for a time during the war acted as Ambassador from Great Britain to the United States) presided, and associated with him were Mr. Justice Avory and Mr. Justice Horridge.

The counsel for the Crown was the Attorney-General, Sir Frederick Smith, assisted by the Solicitor-General and a competent staff.

Mr. A. M. Sullivan, an eminent member of the Irish bar, was counsel for the prisoner, and he was assisted, among others, by Michael Francis Doyle, of the American bar.

The first move of the Attorney-General was to prove by documents and oral testimony that Sir Roger Casement had been in Germany in 1914. In December of that year prisoners of war belonging to various Irish regiments were removed from the different camps in which they were then imprisoned, and were collected into a large camp at Limburg, Lahn. It was claimed that this was being done for a purpose.

And so it seemed, for when the stage had been fully set Sir Roger Casement suddenly appeared on the scene.

Why was he there? What did he do? Let the answer to these questions be given in the words of the Attorney-General in his opening speech for the prosecution. Says Sir Frederick Smith:

"He introduced himself to them—such was the tenor of his address on more than one occasion—as Sir Roger Casement, the organiser of the 'Irish Volunteers.' He stated that he was forming an Irish Brigade, and he invited all the Irish prisoners of war to join it. He pointed out repeatedly, and with emphasis, that in his opinion everything was to be gained for Ireland by Germany winning the war; and that the Irish soldiers who were listening to his address had the best opportunity they had ever had of striking a blow for Ireland by entering the service of the enemies of this country.

"He said that those who joined the Irish Brigade would be sent to Berlin. They would become the guests of the German Government. And in the event of Germany winning a sea battle he (the speaker) would land a brigade in Ireland to defend the country against the enemy England. And that in the event of Germany losing the war either he or the Imperial German Government would give each man in the brigade a bonus of

THE ROYAL BRIDE *is pelted with confetti by her three brothers in the Buckingham Palace courtyard. A scene at the wedding of Princess Mary to Viscount Lascelles, now Earl of Harewood.*

PRINCESS MARY'S MARRIAGE. The bride and bridegroom photographed with the best man and the eight bridesmaids. It will be noticed that the bridesmaid standing on the Earl of Harewood's right is Lady Elizabeth Bowes-Lyon, now Duchess of York.

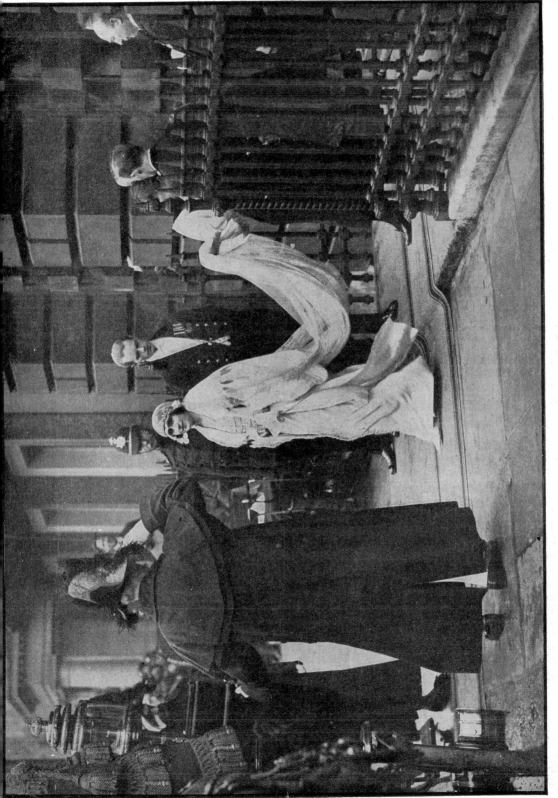

THE MARRIAGE OF H.R.H. THE DUKE OF YORK, *the King's second son, to Lady Elizabeth Bowes-Lyon, daughter of the Earl of Strathmore, on April 26, 1923, delighted the whole nation. His bride was nicknamed " the Smiling Duchess."*

A FAMILY GROUP, *taken after the wedding of the Duke and Duchess of York.*

THE PRINCE OF WALES *became very fond of hunting after the war. Most of his holidays from public duties were spent at Melton Mowbray. He had one or two minor accidents, but on one occasion broke his collar-bone in the hunting field. In 1929 he decided to give up hunting, and sold his stable of hunters.*

WHEN THE NEW STADIUM *at Wembley was first used for the Cup Final in the match between Bolton Wanderers and West Ham in 1923, the ground was packed. Barriers were broken down and turnstiles were put out of action. The match started late because the crowds overflowed on to the field, and the pitch had to be cleared by police. For subsequent Cup Finals a system was instituted by which only ticket-holders were admitted to the ground.*

from £10 to £20, with a free passage to America. . . .

"Gentlemen, to the honour of Ireland, let it be recorded that the vast majority of the Irish prisoners treated the rhetoric and the persuasions, and the corruptions of the prisoner with contempt. He was received with hisses, and was on at least one occasion driven from the camp.

"The Munster Fusiliers were particularly prominent in their loyal resentment of the treacherous proposals made to them. One private in that regiment actually struck, so it is recorded, the prisoner, who was saved from further violence by the intervention of an escort of Prussian Guards, who had been assigned to him for his protection by a nation which thinks of everything."

The prosecution had six or seven soldiers as witnesses, men who had been prisoners at the Limburg Lahn camp. They testified to the facts recited in the indictment and in the speech of the Attorney-General; also they identified a copy of a leaflet which had been widely distributed in the camp.

There is no need to go into all of the details of the trial. There was an agreement upon the main facts of the case. At one point Sir Roger Casement arose to contradict the statement of certain witnesses who claimed that he was responsible for reducing the rations of those soldiers who had refused to join the Irish Brigade.

He declared the assertion to be an abominable falsehood. He also emphatically denied that he had ever asked any Irishman to fight for Germany.

"Finally," he concluded, "I resent the imputation of German gold. From the first moment I landed on the Continent until I came home again to Ireland I never asked for nor accepted a single penny of foreign money, neither for myself nor for any Irish cause."

The Attorney-General in the closing speech for the Crown, and the Lord Chief Justice in his summing-up, both declined to accept the justification pleaded by the counsel for the prisoner.

The case went to the jury on June 29, 1916. It was 2.53 in the afternoon when they retired for deliberation. Twice they sent for documents in the case, and at 3.48 they returned with the announcement that they had agreed upon a verdict.

"What is your decision?" asked the King's Coroner.

All eyes were on the foreman of the jury. He cleared his throat and replied:

"We find Sir Roger Casement guilty of high treason, and that is the verdict of all of us."

An appeal was made, together with a petition for mercy, by many leading intellectuals, writers, and other celebrities in this country. But the Prime Minister declined to interfere with the action of the Court, and the date of the execution was formally fixed.

After his trial Sir Roger Casement was "deknighted" by the Government, and he went to his death without the title which, under the circumstances, was probably not a matter of great importance to him.

He was executed in the Pentonville gaol on August 3, 1916, and one who was present on that occasion testified that he ascended the scaffold "with the calm courage and inflexible bearing of a martyr."

III

Used as they were to a succession of shocks and horrors, few events in the war staggered the nation as did the death of Lord Kitchener, at the time Secretary of State for War.

On June 5, 1916, while on his way to Russia, in H.M.S. *Hampshire,* an armoured cruiser, the ship struck a mine off the Orkney Islands, between the Brough of Birsay and Marwich Head.

She sank in a few minutes. Nearly 800 officers and men and Lord Kitchener and his staff were drowned. There were only twelve survivors.

The fact that disaster was looming over Russia was the real reason for Lord Kitchener's visit. The Czar himself had invited Lord Kitchener to visit the Russian Front and obtain a first-hand knowledge of the situation.

The importance of the projected visit was recognised in London by the War Cabinet. Lord Kitchener, too, was anxious to go. The arrangements for departure were pushed through at top speed. The party accompanying Lord Kitchener was to consist of Sir Frederick Donaldson, General Ellershaw, Colonel Fitzgerald and Mr. O'Beirne of the Foreign Office, Mr. Robertson, Second-Lieutenant McPherson, one clerk, one detective, and three servants.

After a meal at Thurso with Admiral Sir John Jellicoe, the party was taken to H.M.S. *Hampshire,* the cruiser which had been detailed for the voyage to Archangel; and which, as soon as the passengers were aboard, weighed anchor and steamed off.

Meanwhile, the weather had become more stormy, and tremendous seas were running. In accordance with Admiral Jellicoe's personal instructions, the *Hampshire* shaped her course west of the Pentland Firth, hugging the west coast of the Orkneys, so as to enjoy for a space such shelter as the islands could afford from the north-easterly gale which was blowing.

She was travelling at full speed, and after a while the escorting destroyers found that they could neither keep up with her nor, indeed, make any sort of headway in such wild weather. In the end they gave up the attempt and returned to Scapa Flow, leaving the *Hampshire* to continue her voyage alone.

Shortly after eight o'clock that evening, the commander of the Western Patrol at Stromness reported by telephone that a cruiser was in difficulties. It was the *Hampshire.* Between 7.30 and 7.45 she had struck a mine. Fifteen minutes later she sank; and although she was only a mile and a half from the shore between the Brough of Birsay and Marwick Head, only twelve men escaped with their lives. Lord Kitchener, his staff, and all the ship's officers perished.

When the explosion occurred Lord Kitchener was resting and reading in his cabin. Four boats were at once lowered, but these were swamped or smashed to pieces almost immediately.

Three rafts were then got away, with rather better results. But the evening was bitterly cold and many of the men, who were half clad, died of exposure. On one of the rafts alone forty-three dead bodies were found; another raft was dashed against the rocks close to the shore, and a number of men were killed or drowned.

It seems, however, that Lord Kitchener made no attempt to enter either boat or raft. He came up on deck and there he stayed until the end, when he went down with the ship.

His body was never recovered.

CHAPTER X

THE WAR IS WON

*First gas attack—Allied commands were warned—German soldier tried in
1932 for revealing details to the French—Sinking the* Lusitania*—Riots in
London—War in the Middle East—Battle of Jutland—Food shortage in
Britain—Rationing for everyone—The Russian Revolution—No change on
the Western Front—Capture of Jerusalem—The German line on the Western
Front breaks—The war is won.*

I

TOWARDS the summer of 1915 the stalemate which had existed on the Western Front was suddenly broken. There was heavy fighting by the British forces against Germans in the neighbourhood of Ypres. The whole of this sector leading up through Flanders to the coast became a series of heavy bombardments. It seemed obvious that the Germans were trying to break through to the Channel port of Calais, turn the British line, outflank it, and drive again to Paris.

It was in this series of battles that the first gas attack was launched by the Germans. On April 22, 1915, one sector of the battle front at Ypres seemed uncannily peaceful just before sunset. Suddenly an inexplicable mist appeared in front of the German trenches, and crept towards the Allied lines.

Clouds of gas travelled over the trenches of two French divisions just on the left of the Canadians. One division was composed of elderly French territorials, the other of African native soldiers, Senegalese and the like.

When that cloud of gas had passed, both these divisions had virtually disappeared, leaving a yawning four-mile hole in the Allied front. But the Ger-

man General Staff gazed blankly at this opening. They had neglected to provide reserves to drive through in this break on the Western Front.

In the meantime British reserves were rushed up and barred the opening. The Canadian troops in particular had stood firm, yet they did it under terrible torture. They had no respirators, no gas masks. Nothing, except handkerchiefs and towels which were suddenly wetted as a makeshift protection and held over their mouths.

Just as the line was cracking, the situation was saved by the appearance of two battalions of Yorkshire Territorials, whose counter-attack was supported by Canadian batteries firing over open sights.

Other British reserves were rushed up, and by the time the Germans had entrenched themselves, further progress was impossible.

Only recently, a few months ago, in fact, was it known that the plans for this gas attack were in the hands of the French General Staff and nothing was done to prepare for what was undoubtedly coming.

This is the story. Private Jaeger was captured on the night of April 14 by a patrol of French Chasseurs near Langemarck. But on March 30—15 days previously—a bulletin of the French Tenth Army recorded the following facts which are quoted in the Official British History of the War:

"According to prisoners of the 15th Corps there is a long supply along the whole front in the neighbourhood of Zillebeke (this was where the enemy first intended to use gas) of iron cylinders which were stored a little in rear of the trenches in bombproof shelters. They contain a gas which is intended to render the enemy unconscious or to asphyxiate him.

"It has not yet been made use of, but the pioneers have received instruction regarding its employment. The cylinder is laid on the ground, pointing towards the enemy, and is opened by withdrawing the cap. The gas is forced out by its own pressure and remains near the surface of the ground. In order that the operations should be without danger to the operator, a favourable wind is necessary.

"The pioneer detailed to open the cylinder has a special apparatus attached to his head. All the men are supplied with a cloth pad to be placed over the nostrils to prevent the gas being breathed in. The inventor has been promoted Lieutenant."

The Official History adds the following note: "No action seems to have been taken with regard to this warning."

And there would seem to have been little action taken when, sixteen days later, a report was handed into Second Army Headquarters from a British Liaison Officer attached to the staff of the two French divisions under the command of General Putz, who died in 1925, which were on the left of the British line, next the First Canadian Division.

This report stated that a prisoner of the 234th Regiment, 26th Corps, taken on April 14 near Langemarck, declared that an attack had been prepared for noon, April 13. "The Germans," it was said, "intend making use of tubes of asphyxiating gas, placed in batteries of twenty tubes for every forty metres along the front of the 26th Corps."

This prisoner was apparently Private Jaeger. He was found to have in his possession "a small sack filled with a kind of gauze which would be dipped in some solution to counteract the effect of this gas."

The report continued: "It is possible that the attack may be postponed if the wind is not favourable."

The British Command seemed to have been sufficiently impressed to send a squadron of the Royal Flying Corps to "observe the German lines for the express purpose of verifying the presence of any special apparatus."

Reconnaissances carried out over a number of days failed to find any trace of this apparatus, but General Plumer, as he was then, felt impelled to pass on this information "for such as it was worth" to the various commands in the 5th Corps, which was next to the French, on which the first gas attack, delivered on April 22, partially fell.

The Official History includes in an appendix the paragraph: "Whether the warnings were sent to London remains in doubt; letters and telegrams to the War Office seem to have been drafted, but there is no record of their despatch or receipt."

The German private, Auguste Jaeger, was recently tried for the crime of having given away the plans of the gas attack in Germany. Jaeger's story ran that he was captured by a patrol of

THE BRITISH EMPIRE EXHIBITION *at Wembley was the great event of 1924 and 1925. It was opened in State by the King on April 23, 1924, and was attended by almost the entire Royal family and members of the Cabinet.*

THE KING AND QUEEN *paid several visits to the Exhibition at Wembley, and were photographed whilst travelling on the miniature train on " Treasure Island."*

LORD DERBY'S DERBY. *When in* 1924 *the Earl of Derby's horse Sansovino won the Derby, it was the first time that a holder of the title had won the race which his family founded. It was naturally a popular victory. In* 1933 *Lord Derby won again, with Hyperion.*

FIRST LABOUR GOVERNMENT. *History was created in 1924, when Britain's first Labour Government came into power. It had a short life, however. On October 8 it was defeated in the House of Commons on the question of its Russian policy, and at the General Election on October 29 Labour was hopelessly defeated.*

THE HIT OF THE CENTURY. *Playing against Somerset at Taunton in 1925, Jack Hobbs, Surrey's famous batsman, equalled W. G. Grace's great record of scoring 126 centuries in first-class cricket. Hobbs has since increased his record to nearly 200 centuries. This photograph shows him scoring the run he needed to equal " W. G.'s " achievement.*

Chasseurs, who saw his queer unheard-of gas mask and asked questions.

Jaeger was actually tried and acquitted by the Leipzig Supreme Court twelve years ago, and all would have been serene had not the French general, Ferry, who had commanded in the sector involved, relet the cat out of the bag in a recent magazine article in which he said Jaeger had come over and told everything.

The general did this not to get at Jaeger, but at the French Staff, which had ignored the most vital of all advance warnings; and making due allowance for early days of constant learning, it does seem that this Staff was grievously to blame.

At the last moment a hitch did occur on the German side, and they had to postpone their secret frightfulness from the 15th, the day of Jaeger's revelation, to the 22nd. In other words, the French —and ourselves and the Belgians— would have had one whole week in which to devise some form of crude preparation instead of the ultimate moistened handkerchiefs and pieces of wet cloth pressed to the mouth to ward off hideous suffocation in agony.

The French Colonial troops, 10,000 of them, ran back in rout through Elverdinghe to Poperinghe, and one can hardly blame their African terror. The Canadians in a neighbouring trench stood firm with their moistened rag.

It was in December, 1932, that the trial of Auguste Jaeger was opened in Leipzig. Jaeger was only 25 when, as a lorry driver in the German Army, he was accused of having deserted to the enemy and then told them all the details of the proposed attack.

After hearing all the evidence, the German Court sentenced Jaeger to ten years' penal servitude.

Although this new form of frightfulness had a distinct moral effect on the civilised world, it was necessary for the various war departments to counteract it in some form or other.

From the War Office in London Dr. J. S. Haldane was sent over instantly to diagnose the nature of the gas and reported it as some form of chlorine or bromine.

The German troops coming behind the gas wave had been observed to be wearing respirator pads over the mouth, and an appeal was issued for the provision of similar pads for our men.

These were easily made, and within two or three days an ample supply had been received. But they were only primitive precautions, and a week later it was announced that the War Office was considering forms of defensive equipment, which took shape as the once familiar " Ph " helmet of greyish flannel, impregnated with protective solution and provided with talc eyepieces.

It was an awkward safeguard, for a long neckpiece had to be very carefully tucked into the collar all round, and this was a slow, cumbrous job for a man loaded with his equipment. But it served its purpose while the use of gas was still occasional and experimental.

Later and more and more potent forms of poison gas were to be used and invented, and equally effective or non-effective gas masks were also to be produced. Gas warfare, in fact, became one of the tactical uses on the Western Front.

Medical men, scientists and chemists generally are apt to argue that gas in warfare is less brutal than explosives. Dr. Herbert Levinstein, for example,

President of the Society of Chemical Industry, has given an entirely new outlook on gas warfare.

The casualties of this great war, according to Dr. Levinstein, showed that the military results desired could be obtained more easily and with less human suffering from gas than from high explosives. Gas maimed or killed a much smaller proportion of those it put out of action than any other weapon used in the war. In proportion to the military results it caused far less human suffering, temporary or permanent.

From January 1 to September 30, 1918, the number of German gas casualties was in round figures 58,000; of those only 3 per cent. died. From August 1 to 10, 1918, the French had 14,578 gas casualties; of these 2·9 per cent. died. The total British casualties from gas from September 15, 1918, to the end of the war was 24,363, with 540 deaths. The percentage of deaths was 2·2.

Of the American gas casualties, less than 2 per cent. died, and very few were permanently injured. Out of every hundred casualties from all forms of warfare other than gas, more than twenty-five died, and of those which survived, two to five were maimed, blinded or disfigured for life. It was estimated that mustard gas killed one man for every forty put out of action, while shells killed one for every three.

While not suggesting that gas warfare was anything but dreadful, Dr. Levinstein argued that it was less wasteful of human life and property than older forms of warfare.

It only remains to add that the experience of troops on the Western Front during gas attacks, the agonies they suffered, and the resulting disabilities in civil life, have caused this form of warfare still to be regarded as a form of frightfulness, and one which is still condemned by the civilised world.

II

While the Allies were facing this form of frightfulness the Germans loosed another shock. This was the sinking of the *Lusitania* on May 7 with the loss of over 1,000 lives.

This torpedoing of the great liner as she was returning from America was one of the worst tactical errors the Germans ever made. It did, ultimately, bring the United States of America into the war on the side of the Allies, and hastened the inevitable German defeat.

It was a few minutes after two o'clock of a glorious spring afternoon that the Cunard liner *Lusitania* sank, with a gaping hole in her side, off the South Coast of Ireland. Only eighteen minutes passed from the time she was struck by a torpedo from a German submarine, until her mast disappeared. 1,195 of her passengers and crew lost their lives.

The story has been recorded of a certain German spy who was responsible for this sinking of the *Lusitania*.

This is the German's story. "In April, 1915, I received orders in Vienna to report in Berlin. I went to the Admiralty, where I was given a large sum of money and instructed to go to England and see one of our agents there. A few hours later I was walking down Shaftesbury Avenue. Next day I telephoned my colleague and fixed an appointment in Hyde Park.

"Our meeting lasted exactly three minutes. He was a clever man who had wormed his way into English society. The money I gave him went to ferment trouble in Ireland, and to pay for the coastal service of the German U-boats' equipment, fuel, trawler-guides.

"On May 3, the necessary information having arrived from England, ten U-boats left harbour under sealed orders. I saw the report of the captain of the victorious U-boat to Admiral von Tirpitz.

"Here it is. 'Information reliable reached me. *Lusitania* due 11 a.m. Weather hazy. Visibility bad. Irish trawlers could give no precise information. On communicating U 16 and U 11 I decided to submerge and wait.

"'Three hours passed. I was about to give up hope when I saw her heave in sight, zig-zagging. I fired. The torpedo struck her amidship. The explosion was so violent that it seemed as if her cargo of munitions had been hit. A second shot struck her bows. She sank at 2.12 p.m. I stood by for two hours.'

"I read this despatch at the dinner given in honour of the captains and crew of the two U-boats who claimed the victory. To avoid ill-feeling both the crews were feted and decorated. All received substantial financial reward."

Yet to-day there is one man who knows the real truth about that terrible sea tragedy. He is Captain W. T. Turner, who was in command of the doomed liner. For some years he has been an invalid. From his bed he recently told the vivid story of the *Lusitania's* end.

"First," he said, "read this. I wrote it years ago." It was an old ship's log that he handed over. In bald sentences it gave the simple history of the facts: "Arrived in New York April 23, 1915. During the time in New York the Germans put in the papers a warning to passengers not to go in the ship as she would be torpedoed. Arriving in the Irish Sea off Kinsale at 2.10 p.m., May 7, 1915, the ship was torpedoed and sank."

"Yes," Captain Turner went on. "All the time we were in New York warnings kept coming to me that my ship would be caught by submarines. Even the Admiralty sent word that we should have to take the greatest care because of the threats.

"Most of the passengers were still in the dining-room at 2.10 p.m. on May 7. I was on the bridge looking forward to getting a decent sleep when I reached Liverpool.

"When, from out of the empty sea, came that one messenger of death, there was no warning. I did not see anything, although some passengers said later that they saw a submarine's periscope just before we were hit.

"The torpedo caught us amidship. The 32,000-ton ship quivered and slowly heeled to starboard. Officers on the bridge turned to me. No one spoke. A hole had been torn in our side large enough for a tramway car to pass through, and the water just rolled in.

"I turned to the telegraph and my officers went away to their jobs. The watertight doors were closed, and messengers sped to calm the passengers. Like lightning the lifeboats on the starboard side were manned. In the steerage there was a panic. Officers had to rush and fight to keep the ways clear.

"Then from every companion-way there burst an endless stream of passengers. The boat deck was crammed with a silent crowd—mothers and fathers clasping their little ones, some searching for their parents, sweethearts clinging to each other, all wide-eyed with terror.

"The ship sank lower and lower. More boats got away. But still the deck was black with people. By this time frayed nerves were giving way, and terrible hopeless confusion reigned.

"Helplessly I turned away. The waves seemed to jump on our decks. Soon it was all over. The whole ship seemed to be cut from my feet by a giant hand, and I found myself being dragged down into the depths.

"It seemed an age before I broke the surface again. And what a ghastly sight met my eyes! Hundreds of bodies were being whirled about among the wreckage. Men, women, and children were drifting between planks, lifeboats, and an indescribable litter. The instinct to live kept me swimming until I was picked up by a lifeboat. Then I lay exhausted until destroyers came and rescued us."

The tragedy of the *Lusitania* was used all over the world for propaganda purposes. A powerful cartoon appeared in the *New York World* depicting the piteous forms of little children rising from the sea, holding up their hands and asking of the Kaiser, "But why did you kill us?"

This had a great effect upon American opinion. The Germans pointed out that on April 30 this warning was published in New York newspapers:

"Vessels flying flags of Great Britain and her Allies are liable to destruction. Signed, Imperial German Embassy, Washington."

Whether or no the *Lusitania* was a defenceless passenger ship flying the American flag and bearing only civilian passengers and an ordinary cargo possibly now will never be known.

Mr. Winston Churchill in his book, *The World Crisis*, admits that included in her cargo was a small consignment of rifle ammunition and shrapnel shells weighing about 173 tons. The Germans declared that she was carrying concealed guns and Canadian troops. Captain Turner, in the course of the enquiry which was held, denied this.

The result in Britain of the sinking of the *Lusitania* was to inflame public opinion bitterly against Germany and those Germans who, until this time, had remained unmolested and in possession of businesses.

Mobs in London and other towns attacked hundreds of shops and restaurants which bore German or Austrian names so thoroughly that for a day or two there was something like a bread famine in East and South London, where very many of the bakers were of those nationalities.

In Liverpool it became necessary to intern all Germans and Austrians for their own protection. Shops were wrecked, and the police had to be called out to protect their owners.

The need for keeping order in the streets of the great cities at this time was left almost entirely to the special constables. These specials created a fine corps of their own, with an equally fine sense of duty.

They were nearly all over military age —many, indeed, were over sixty—or rejected by the Army doctors for physical reasons. They had long night hours of duty in addition to their daily occupation. No small strain in these times of great strain. There was, however, never any difficulty in securing volunteers for additional duties at times of emergency.

In London alone the special constables freed 4,350 men for the Colours —that is, the regular constables—and

LOCARNO TREATY. *When Dr. Stresemann signed the Locarno Treaty on Germany's behalf in London, December 1, 1925, Europe heaved a sigh of relief. It was hoped that peace might be assured, but quarrels soon broke out again between Continental Powers.*

THE ENTIRE COUNTRY *mourned the death of Queen Alexandra, widow of Edward VII., in November, 1925; and, despite a snowstorm, huge crowds gathered at her funeral to pay a last tribute. She was buried at Sandringham, which had been her home for so many years.*

Troops were on guard at omnibus garages, and each bus had a police escort

THE GENERAL STRIKE. *Troops paraded in Hyde Park in service kit, and armoured cars patrolled the London streets, ready to quell any riots. The strikers, however, caused little trouble.*

THE GENERAL STRIKE. *An auxiliary police force called the Civil Constabulary Reserve was formed to help the Metropolitan Police. Many of their members were recruited from army regiments, and they performed valuable duties during the crisis.*

"helped to preserve the King's peace and therefore to ensure the continuity of the City's activities."

By their unpaid services they saved the ratepayers a very large sum of money, and were thanked by the King on June 14, 1919. "You have to your credit a clean record of work well done," he assured them, and in that sentence voiced the opinion of the nation.

Towards the end of this first half of the war years came the political crisis, which swept the Liberal Government from power and brought in what was known as a Coalition Government.

When the new Government was formed it was found to include Mr. Bonar Law at the Colonial Office, Mr. Balfour at the Admiralty, Mr. Austen Chamberlain at the India Office, Mr. Walter Long at the Local Government Board, Lord Curzon as Lord Privy Seal, and Lord Lansdowne as Minister without portfolio.

Mr. Arthur Henderson, chosen for the Board of Education, brought Labour into the Coalition. Sir Edward Carson became Attorney-General. Mr. Asquith was still Prime Minister, but Mr. Lloyd George began to concentrate his immense energies on a Ministry of Munitions that was formed, with himself as First Minister.

In February and March, 1916, the Western Front blazed up again, and the Germans made an attack upon Verdun, which was held by the French.

The German High Command allowed the Crown Prince to try his luck at this ring of forts. Attack after attack of the Germans collapsed in a squalor of destruction, beyond anything humanity had so far achieved in the whole of its history of violence.

The French lost 350,000 men, the Germans 500,000. At the end of it all both armies fell back.

III

Failure of the British at Gallipoli turned the eyes of the world towards the Middle East generally. In fact the campaign seemed to be waxing more furiously in these parts than on the Western Front, where a state of stagnation existed.

An Allied force, for example, had landed at Salonika in Greece and had pushed inland towards Monastir, but it was unable to render any effectual assistance to the Serbians, who had come into the war on the Allied side, and were now overwhelmed by Austro-German attacks.

It was this Salonika plan which really sealed the fate of the Gallipoli expedition. At the same time, further east, in Mesopotamia, the British, using Indian troops chiefly, made a still further flank attack upon the Central Powers.

An army, very ill-provided for the campaign, was landed at Basra in November, 1914, and pushed up towards Bagdad in the following year. It gained a victory at Ctesiphon and managed to travel within twenty-five miles of Bagdad.

But the Turks were heavily reinforced. There was a retreat to Kut, and there the British army, under General Townshend, was surrounded and starved into surrender on April 29, 1916.

It was this same year that saw the biggest naval engagement that has been witnessed in modern times—the Battle of Jutland.

The sinking of the *Lusitania* had caused President Wilson to begin his series of famous notes to various Governments. The threat of an ultimatum from President Wilson had decided Germany to abandon her unrestricted campaign by submarines against the shipping of the world.

The release of these submarines decided Germany to attempt her big naval engagement.

On May 30, 1916, the British Grand Fleet left its bases on one of its periodical sweeps through the North Sea, but with reason to expect hostile encounter.

On May 31, early in the morning, the German High Sea Fleet also put to sea, in the hope of destroying some isolated portion of the British Fleet.

For such an encounter the British Admiral Jellicoe had formulated an outline plan in the early months of the war. Its basis was the cardinal necessity of maintaining the unimpaired supremacy of the Grand Fleet, which he viewed as an instrument, not merely of battle, but of grand strategy, the pivot of the Allied action in all spheres, economic, moral and military.

Hence, while desirous of bringing the German Fleet to battle under his own conditions, he was determined not to be lured into mine and submarine invested waters.

Early in the afternoon of May 31, Beatty with his battle cruisers and a squadron of battleships, after a sweep to the south, was turning north to rejoin Jellicoe, when he sighted the German battle cruisers, five in number.

In the initial engagement two of Beatty's six battle cruisers were hit in vital parts and sunk. When thus weakened he came upon the main German Fleet under Admiral Scheer. He turned north to lure them in reach of Jellicoe, fifty miles distant, who raced to support him.

It is not possible to describe the intricate evolutions and the naval manœuvres which followed the meeting of the two battle fleets. Mist and failing light put an end to an indecisive action, which, however, left the British Fleet between the German and its bases.

During the night Scheer broke through the destroyer guard and, although sighted, was not reported. Then he slipped safely through a net which Jellicoe dared not draw too close, in view of his guiding principle and the danger of torpedo attack.

Flaming headlines in the newspapers on June 3 startled the country. The first impression was that the British Fleet had suffered a severe disaster. The Admiralty announced that we had lost six cruisers and eight destroyers, and knew of the sinking of only one German battle cruiser, one light cruiser and an unspecified number of destroyers.

Next day certainly brought better news—two German battleships as well as two battle cruisers had been sunk, and we had lost no ship of those classes; the respective losses were now put—ours at fourteen vessels, the Germans at eighteen.

But, on the other hand, the Germans were claiming a great victory, and it was difficult to discover which particular country could claim the real victory of Jutland. It could certainly be counted a tactical advantage to the Germans, but it had no effect on their strategic position.

Britain's command of the sea was intact, the grip on the blockade of Germany unrelaxed.

From the German standpoint the Battle of Jutland caused that country to fall back on submarine warfare, and the first development was an extension of range.

In July one of their large new submarine cruisers appeared off the American coast and sank several neutral ships. In British and Mediterranean waters the pressure began seriously to affect the seaborne trade and food supplies of the Entente. Various remedies were tried—the most effective being a system of sailing in convoys—but the only truly adequate measure, that of penning the Germans in their bases, by closing minefields, was debarred by Britain's failure to obtain a decisive battle success.

But if Britain was feeling the strain of economic pressure, so also was Germany, and her leaders feared that the race between decisive success on land and economic collapse would end against her.

The naval authorities of Germany, therefore, declared for a renewal of the "unlimited" submarine campaign. It is now possible to say that they fully realised that this would bring America into the war against her.

This is the time when the food shortage in Britain became really acute. A Food Controller was appointed, and all kinds of restrictions were forced upon the public.

Undoubtedly many of the poorer people were in absolute want, and a series of National Kitchens were opened by the Ministry of Food.

The Queen opened the first National Kitchen and, helped by Princess Mary, served a number of customers.

In those days people had not learned the art of buying their dinners at public kitchens and many of them omitted to bring any kind of receptacle, and in order that they should not be too late to be served by the Queen, rushed madly home again to fetch a jug or basin.

While the Queen was ladling out food a very old man shambled up and bought meat, vegetables, and pudding, which he proceeded to place all together on a very dirty plate and cover them with a still dirtier piece of newspaper.

He then shambled out, never having realised who it was who had served him. The fact that it was the Queen must have been pointed out to him by the crowd outside, for shortly afterwards he returned, edged his way back to the service counter, and solemnly waved his hat three times at her.

Very soon rationing was in full force. All kinds of rules and regulations were instituted to stop the wastage of food. To throw rice at a wedding became a summary offence, and the sale of luxury chocolates was stopped.

No sweetmeats over 2d. per ounce or chocolates over 3d. per ounce were permitted. The use of starch in laundry work was restricted. Horses and cows, and even the London pigeons, were rationed. No corn was allowed for cobs, hunters, carriage horses, hacks, most of which had by then been commandeered for Army use.

A man was fined £50 for collecting bread crusts for pig food, and in defence said that otherwise they would have been wasted, as navvies would not eat crusts.

The amount of bread or cake which might be sold at tea shops for afternoon teas was reduced to two ounces. It became an offence to adopt and feed stray dogs.

Local Food Controllers were appointed. Butchers were ordered to display price lists, and bakers were forbidden to bake any but Government regulation bread. Grocers would not sell to people who were not registered with them for sugar, and, it was said, insisted upon other purchases being made in addition to sugar. Milk was also controlled.

The time came when so great were the discomfort and ill-feeling caused by the food queue and the suspicion that the rich were obtaining more than their fair share of eatables that the demand for compulsory rations became more and more insistent.

In the bitter cold and rain of these depressing winters of the Great War, women and children waited outside the shabby shops common to the poor districts of all towns.

They carried baskets, string bags, bags made of American cloth, and babies, and stood shifting their burdens from one arm to another to ease their aching. Women used to go from shop to shop trying to find one at which they could buy meat or margarine, tea, and possibly a little extra sugar.

The time came when meat cards and ration cards of all kinds were in force. The public were also required to register for bacon. The rations served to the troops to Britain were reduced and it became legal to inflict a fine up to £400 for hoarding food.

The price of fish in those days was a nightmare to housewives. Sole was up to 4s. per pound, and turbot 3s. An old account book of these days shows that in the autumn of 1917 milk cost 9d. per quart, butter 2s. 6d. per pound, tea 2s. 6d. per pound, a cauliflower 1s., a fowl 12s. 6d., bananas 5d. each, a tin of peaches 4s. 6d., and a flat sponge sandwich cake the size of a teaplate 2s. 3d.

IV

In the beginning of 1917 the World War began to break up into a real international chaos. Russia was the first to go smash. The many bloody defeats which the Russian Army had suffered under the German advances had had their effect. The troops were disgusted with Czardom and their leaders.

It was said at the time that the Czar, like several of his ancestors, had now given way to a crazy pietism. The Court was dominated by a religious impostor, Rasputin, whose cult was one of unspeakable foulness, a reeking scandal in the face of the world.

It is said that many of the leaders were in league with the Germans, and that Rasputin was working on behalf of the German Government.

The Russian common soldiers had been sent into battle without guns to support them, without even rifle ammunition; they were wasted by their officers and generals in the delirium of military enthusiasm.

On December 29, 1916, the monk Rasputin was murdered at a dinner party at Petrograd. It was a desperate attempt by some of the higher but patriotic classes to put the country in order. It did not seem to have much effect. By March things were moving rapidly; food riots in Petrograd developed into a revolutionary insurrection; there was an attempted suppression of the Duma, the representative body, attempted arrests of Liberal leaders, and the formation of a provisional Government under Prince Lvoff.

This led inevitably to the abdication of the Czar himself on March 15. A new figure was flung into the limelight by the revolution, the picturesque leader

THE GENERAL STRIKE, 1926. *Buses and trams were run with volunteer drivers and conductors. Many young undergraduates enjoyed themselves at this work. The strikers showed admirable self-control at these efforts to defeat them, and there were only a few ugly incidents.*

PLEASE PASS ON THIS COPY OR DISPLAY IT

The British Gazette

Published by His Majesty's Stationery Office.

LONDON, SATURDAY, MAY 8, 1926.

ONE PENNY.

ORGANISED ATTEMPT TO STARVE THE NATION

Orders By Leaders Of The Railway And Transport Trade Unions.

SUBSTANTIAL IMPROVEMENT IN THE TRAIN SERVICES.

Government's New Steps To Protect The People.

SITUATION BECOMING MORE INTENSE.

OFFICIAL COMMUNIQUE.

May 7.

No serious disorder has occurred in any part of the country. The work of feeding the people and of maintaining light and power and essential communications is being successfully accomplished. Over 2,000 trains were run on May 6, or nearly double the day before.

A further substantial improvement both on the main lines and in the metropolitan and suburban services is arranged for to-day.

The protection of 'buses in London proved yesterday most satisfactory and they are constantly increasing in numbers.

As was to be expected, the situation is becoming

FALSE NEWS.

Printer And Street Sellers in Court.

The following announcement is made by his Majesty's Government:

A WARNING.

Prompt Action By The Police.

The public are advised to pay no attention to alarmist rumours which may be spread by disaffected persons. Typical cases are the circulation of such reports as that the Post Office Savings Bank has suspended payment, and that mutinies have occurred among his Majesty's Forces. Such reports are wholly untrue. Their circulation is a criminal offence.

This notification, which appeared in the official communiqués in Thursday's *British Gazette*, had a sequel when the printer and sellers of a leaflet containing false news of the Liverpool police leaving control on strike appeared at the Marylebone Police Court.

Henry William Atkins, of 3, Sele Street, Paddington, was charged with committing an act likely to cause disaffection among the civil population of Great Britain.

Detective-inspector Jessett, of the Special Branch of Scotland Yard, described his arrest at his home on Friday morning for printing the leaflets and

---

You are on strike.

Have you been consulted by your Union?

FOURTH DAY IN THE PROVINCES.

Tendency to Return In Some Industries.

All ranks of the Armed Forces of the Crown are hereby notified that any action which they may find it necessary to take in an honest endeavour to aid the Civil Power will receive, both now and afterwards, the full support of his Majesty's Government.

CREWS FOR LINERS.

Volunteer Dockers Busy At Liverpool.

Southampton Sailings.

A return to normal shipping conditions is gradually being made both at Liverpool and Southampton.

The position at Liverpool has improved beyond all that was indicated on Thursday. Volunteer labour is being employed in unloading and loading the great liners.

870 Engineers Back at Leeds.

Exciting Level-Crossing Scene.

The outstanding feature of the latest reports from the provinces is the indication of a desire to return to work, in many industries. For instance, 870 engineers have already gone back in Leeds.

NORTH-EASTERN DIVISION

The West Riding is reported quiet. Essential services are maintained, and railways and road transport are improving. Fifty transport workers returned to work in Halifax and 270 engineers at Armley and 170 at Pudsey went back to work. Large supplies of food went to Pontefract to-day.

Independent 'buses have restarted at Halifax and 57 trains and 'buses were running in Leeds on Thursday. Forty trams ran through Doncaster on Thursday. A large number of men in the building trade have ceased work at Sheffield, but there has been dissension at their meetings, and there is some talk of a return to work.

Many are seemingly obliged to die rather than face a level crossing. The gates were stormed and a cordon thrown in front of a train, but rescued. Order has been restored by the police. Three thousand men tried to hold up trains in Leeds and were supported by the police.

Over 2,000 volunteers have been enrolled at Sheffield, a further 300 men

---

GENERAL STRIKE. *Newspapers ceased publication owing to the printers' strike, and the public had to rely upon the wireless and publication of the Government "British Gazette" for its news.*

LORD OXFORD AND ASQUITH'S MESSAGE.

British People On The Rack.

STRIKE WEAPON AIMED AT DAILY LIFE OF THE COMMUNITY.

Must Be Sheathed Before Negotiations.

There could be no greater misunderstanding of the attitude of our people at this moment than to suppose that it implies any hostility to the right of combination in industry. Strikes and lock-outs, though they always inflict a certain amount of inconvenience on the public, may be, and often are, in the last resort justifiable and even necessary. But the challenge which has now been thrown down and taken up is of a totally different kind.

A General Strike, such as that which it is being sought to enforce, is directly aimed at the daily life of the whole community. The people who suffer the least from it are the capitalists and the plutocrats. They have at their command the whole apparatus of opulence, and the petty discomforts to which they are exposed are not more than pin-pricks, easily endured, rapidly forgotten.

The real victims of a General Strike are what is called the common People—the men and women who have to labour hard day by day for their own livelihood and that of their families, for whom steady, regular transport between their homes and their work is a prime necessity, and to whom any contraction in the supply, or rise in the

T. W. BURGESS *swam the Channel on September 5, 1911. It was his sixteenth attempt, and he was in the water for 22 hours 35 minutes.*

THE CHANNEL *was not swum again until* 1926, **when Gertrude Ederle, an American girl,** *crossed in* 14 *hours* 39 *minutes.*

RUDOLPH VALENTINO *was the film idol of the period. His sudden death in August, 1926,*
was followed by hysterical scenes of hero-worship by film fans. Meanwhile GRETA
GARBO, *who was to be the world's next idol, was on the threshold of her great career.*
Her first Hollywood film, " The Torrent," was made in 1926.

FUNERAL OF EARL HAIG, 1928. *For nearly three years of the war he was Commander-in-Chief of the British Armies. After the war he was given a grant of £100,000 for his services, but he refused to accept it until better provision had been made for disabled and discharged soldiers. He was founder and President of the British Legion.*

ANOTHER BIG EVENT *of 1928 was the visit to England of King Amanullah of Afghanistan. He was impressed by all he saw, and upon his return tried to Westernise his own country. This led to civil war, and Amanullah was forced to leave the country.*

THE MEDICI COLLAR *was much favoured in 1930, with a slight indication of a train to the rather full skirt.*

THE BARE-BACKED EVENING GOWN *was one of the most discussed fashions of the day. This is a 1927 beaded model.*

Kerensky. But it was soon revealed that Kerensky, although a powerful speaker, and with many of the arts of the demagogue, was unable to control the mass of disillusioned, dissatisfied, and even desperate Russian soldiery.

Germany, in the meantime, had sent, in a closed compartment right through Germany from Switzerland to the Russian frontier, two obscure agitators, Lenin and Trotsky. They were deposited on the Russian frontier and left to fend for themselves.

They did so with remarkable success. In a few months Lenin and Trotsky were in full command of the Bolshevik revolution. The Russian Army turned their backs upon the German forces and marched towards Moscow and Petrograd.

The Germans took full advantage of the situation. They imposed a peace, the Peace of Brest-Litovsk, which, despite Trotsky's protest, was rigorously enforced. Russia had lost a huge slice of territory, the whole of Poland, and her army was mutinous and crippled.

It seemed that the Central Powers were winning all along the line. The British Forces were still licking their wounds after the huge offensive that a year previously they had conducted on the Somme. This huge offensive had been begun in order to relieve the German attack against Verdun, which the French were only just managing to withstand.

The battles of the Somme had been conducted on very orthodox military lines. A huge preliminary bombardment of several days gave full indication to the Germans as to where the attack was coming from. They had ample time to prepare. It was thought that the Germans could be shelled out of their position. Only after these battles did military commanders realise that men could endure days of bombardment and survive providing their dug-outs were adequately protected.

When the British forces advanced against the barbed wire and machine-guns that had been well prepared by the German forces, they paid heavily. Altogether 475,000 men were victims of these great battles of the Somme.

At the end of 1916 General Joffre had been superseded by General Nivelle, who speedily framed a grandiose plan to break the deadlock in the West, and rashly persisted in it when its foundations had been upset by the Germans' cleverly staged withdrawal to a massive and shorter line of defence in the rear—the famous Hindenburg Line.

The only thing about Nivelle's new system was that it lost men even faster than any of the older systems—200,000 in a few days. This disastrous repulse had as its sequel a widespread series of mutinies among the French troops, sick of being thrown against unsubdued machine-guns.

The full story of this French mutiny has never been told. It is still shrouded in mystery, and not even the leaders of France have been able to give details of it.

Regarding the mutiny, we do know that 115 units in the French Army were affected, and that all that stopped it were the wholesale executions which followed the raising of the red flag by a regiment at the Cœuvres depôt.

For that one day's mutiny, one mutineer out of every five was chosen by lot for execution.

With this great mutiny occupying their attention, the French appealed to the British to make an attack to draw off

German attention. The British obeyed. The slaughter round Passchendaele was the price. The Germans killed two Englishmen to every man they lost, but it is also said that Earl Haig had the conviction that the British could defeat the German Army single-handed in Flanders.

Tanks were used in these attacks, but they stuck in the waterlogged ground and mud. Rain made matters worse.

Yet for more than three months Haig continued to pour the strength of Britain into the mud of Passchendaele. Not only did he fail in his own bigger aims, but he did not prevent the Germans from sending reserves to force peace on Russia, and also to reinforce the Austrians in striking a deadly blow at Italy.

Italy's front collapsed, and, although her defeated forces managed to hold fast on the Piave, covering Venice, she was crippled for a year to come.

The only offset to these multiple disasters was the capture of Jerusalem by the British, and their surprise stroke at Cambrai in November—with a swarm of tanks in place of a warning bombardment.

And in that capture of Jerusalem by General Allenby and his forces there emerges that strange, mysterious, and adventurous figure of Colonel Lawrence, often termed the Uncrowned King of Arabia.

V

The exploits of Lawrence of Arabia have made him a legendary character. He certainly achieved a remarkable success, which considerably helped Allenby in his drive towards Jerusalem.

On the outbreak of the World War Lawrence, being below standard height, obtained at first no more active service than a post in the Geographical Section of the War Office, in London. But soon after Turkey had joined the Central Powers, he was sent by Lord Kitchener to Egypt and attached to a rudimentary Intelligence Section.

It was at that time when an Arab revolt broke out. The Sheriff Hussan of Mecca, a guardian of the Holy Places, decided to overthrow the yoke of the Turks. Incidentally, he was promised support by the British, with their headquarters in Cairo.

Lawrence at this time was working in what was known as the Arab Bureau in Cairo, an organisation which produced daily an Arab newspaper, and saw that the nations of Arabia, from the Red Sea across to the Persian Gulf, were well prompted with Allied propaganda.

Lawrence applied for permission to go to Jidda on the Arabian coast. There he heard of the Emir Feisal, one of the sons of the Sheriff Hussan, who was endeavouring to lead a real military revolt against the Turks.

Lawrence went on a special camel journey and met Feisal. He was singularly impressed by this Arab, and induced him to reorganise his army and move north, so as to threaten the communications of Medina, by attacking the Hejaz Railway.

Lawrence then began his association with the Arab forces. He rode off into the interior to raise the northern tribes, and so extend the area to be held and defended against the Turks. He even went behind the enemy lines in Syria, and on his return picked up another tribe under the famous raider, Auda Abu Tayyi. He fought his first battle at a place called Maan, and forced a passage to the coast, at the Gulf of Aqaba, which was occupied by Feisal in August, 1917.

For this exploit Lawrence was promoted to Field Rank and given decorations, British and French, which, however, he would not accept.

Lawrence went back to Cairo for a meeting with General Allenby, and obtained consent for his real assistance with munitions and men.

Lawrence began to build up a considerable army. In the meantime he turned his attention in particular to train wrecking. He had such success that Medina became virtually isolated, and a large reward was advertised by the Turks for his capture.

Early in 1918 he made a desperate attempt to cut the Turkish Palestine Army's railway communications with Damascus, and failed only by a hair's breadth. In that summer, in concert with Allenby, he induced Feisal to move up north and organise a new force to advance on Damascus.

This duly moved up in the autumn, side by side with Allenby, and after breaking up the enemy's Transjordan Army, entered Damascus several hours ahead of the British.

Lawrence took charge of the city until Allenby could reach it, and suppressed attempts at reaction.

Allenby, in fact, was the first British general to whom big successes came. He had taken over in July, 1917, on the Palestine Front, and devoted the first three months to intensive preparations for an autumn offensive.

By complete secrecy and ruses he deceived the Turks as to the main point of attack. While he bombarded Gaza, his real blow was towards Beersheba, which was seized by a manœuvre which

broke through the enemy's weakened centre.

The German general, Falkenhayn, now in command at Aleppo, had also been planning an offensive, but the better communications of the British had decided the race, and although Falkenhayn tried to stem the tide by a counter-stroke against Beersheba, the breaking of his centre compelled a general retreat.

The pursuit was hampered owing to lack of water, but even so by November 14 the Turkish forces were driven apart in two divergent groups.

The Port of Jaffa was taken, and Allenby wheeled his main force to the right for an advance inland on Jerusalem. He gained the narrow hill passes before the Turks could block them, and after a necessary pause to improve his communication, brought up reserves for a fresh advance, which secured Jerusalem on December 9.

By the time the winter rain set in, the British had expanded and consolidated their hold on the region. As a moral success the feat was valuable. Yet viewed strategically it seemed a long way round to the goal.

At the same time events were undoubtedly moving in the Middle East. The British had also entered Bagdad, which gave them enormous prestige throughout India and the Far East, and particularly impressed all the Mohammedan population through whose countries they were moving.

The campaign in the Middle East had, in fact, started a series of successes for the Allies. Even so, on the Western Front the Allies were still reeling under fresh German attacks. Desperately the Germans realised that they must take the offensive now or be smashed in a welter of defeat. There was every indication that America was coming into the war.

Actually the United States declared war on Germany on April 6, 1917. The German military leaders made a desperate effort. The first attack was upon the British in the Somme region. On March 21 came "Gough's Disaster." A British army was driven back in such disorder as no British army had ever known before.

Thousands of guns were lost and scores of thousands of prisoners taken. The British were driven back almost to Amiens. General Gough was severely criticised for this retreat.

Throughout April and May the Germans continued to rain offensives on the Allied Front. They came near to a break through in the north, and they made a great drive back to the Marne, which they reached again on May 30, 1918.

The citizens of Paris could hear the guns coming nearer and nearer. But this was a climax of the German effort. Foch unleashed his counter-stroke on Ludendorff, in which the sudden advance of a mass of tanks on the Cambrai method paved the way for the attacking troops.

Then came the second Battle of the Marne, in which seven strong American divisions took a leading part. The initiative had definitely passed to the Allies.

On August 8 Haig struck at the Somme salient with the use again of a great mass of tanks. This attack came as a nerve-shattering surprise to Ludendorff, so much so that he confessed: "August 8 was the black day of the German Army in the history of the war."

It led him to abandon hope of victory. Foch again struck further south, and under this pressure from British and French the Germans were forced back to the Hindenburg Line.

The Battle of Château Thierry, July 18, proved the quality of the new American Armies. In August the British opened the great and successful thrust into Belgium, and the bulge of the German lines toward Amiens wilted and collapsed.

Germany was finished. The fighting spirit passed out of her Army, and October was a story of defeat and retreat along the entire Western Front.

Early in November British troops were in Valenciennes and Americans in Sedan. In Italy also the Austrian Army was in a state of disorderly retreat. Everywhere the Central Empire forces were collapsing. It seemed that the newspapers in Britain could not keep pace with the succession of victories which were being reported from all the various fronts. In September the great Allied offensive against Bulgaria had produced a revolution in that country, and peace proposals.

Turkey followed with a capitulation at the end of October and Austro-Hungary on November 4. An attempt was made to send out the German Fleet for a last fight, but the sailors mutinied.

At this time German towns were being heavily bombed. The people were desperately short of food, bankrupt of hope and forsaken of their Allies. At this moment Ludendorff, the super-chief, broke. He sent for the Reichstag and told its representatives to make what terms it could, locked himself in, and would see no one.

Prince Max of Baden went to see the

GREYHOUND RACING *suddenly became a national sport. This photograph shows the first meeting at White City in* 1927, *but it was not until some months later that it attained its amazing popularity.*

SPEEDWAY RACING *followed as another national sport. Introduced into the country in* 1929, *soon it had millions of supporters. This shows riders practising for the first meeting.*

A TRAGEDY *of* 1928 *was the overflowing of the Thames. Fourteen people living near the Embankment were drowned, and thousands of pounds worth of damage was done. Many valuable paintings in the Tate Gallery were spoiled.*

WOMEN'S SKIRTS *got shorter and shorter after the war until in 1927 and 1928 they had reached the knee. Then they began to get longer again, and for evening wear the skirt reaching to the ankle became the vogue once more.*

ARCOS RAID. *Police raided the London offices of the Soviet Trading Corporation (Arcos) in 1927. Safes were forced open, and many documents were confiscated. The Government never published these papers, but a few days after the raid diplomatic relations with the Soviet were broken.*

Kaiser. He advised Wilhelm to abdicate. Always a nervous and vain man, the Kaiser hesitated. Prince Max announced the abdication, and when it was obviously accepted with relief the Kaiser signed and fled into Holland.

It was a sorry departure of the Captains and Kings of Germany. Ludendorff fled with a forged passport and green spectacles into Sweden. Von Tirpitz shaved his hawk beard and also ran. Ballin, the shipping king, the Kaiser's friend, went into his office and shot himself. Only Hindenburg, with massive calmness, went to his small house in Hanover. Germany, even when Republican, remembered that.

On November 11 an Armistice was signed. The war was at an end.

Upwards of ten millions of people had been actually killed through the fighting, another twenty or twenty-five million had died through the hardships and disorders entailed. Scores of millions were suffering and enfeebled by under nourishment and misery, and now, as maroons were fired at 11 o'clock on November 11, 1918, it had all ended.

Extraordinary scenes were witnessed in London on that day. Into the streets crowded masses of people who had left every office empty, every house deserted. They packed motor buses, taxis, private cars, anything that was moving. Military lorries set out upon journeys of their own devising, with picked up loads of astounded and cheering passengers, going nowhere in particular and careless whither they went.

Crowds of people surrounded Buckingham Palace, and had the King and Queen out on the balcony in the middle of the morning, and fairly mobbed the Royal carriage driving along The Mall in the afternoon. They drifted to and fro hour after hour, increasing as the evening came.

But, despite this spontaneous gaiety, there was more a sense of intense relief than anything else.

There was indeed a hope that the days of ordeal, terror and endurance were at an end. But those jubilant crowds of November 11 did not realise that years were coming that would tempt their endurance still further, that the country would be wracked again, if not by war, at least by civil strife, economic disasters and even more tragedies to face.

The military battle was over. The economic battle had only just begun.

CHAPTER XI

EVENTFUL YEARS FOR THE ROYAL FAMILY

The King's work in the war—The Prince of Wales at the Front—His tours abroad—" The Ambassador of Commerce "—Marriages in the Royal family —The King's illness.

"AT least the King is doing without his beer," was the remark many a soldier blurted out during the war when groups of men were apt to discuss the shortcomings of those people safely entrenched in high circles in London.

That spontaneous gesture of King George during the war was one that appealed to the individual soldier. It gave him to understand that Royalty was prepared to set an example to others. But King George, as also the Prince of Wales, did much more during those years than forgo little luxuries. They placed themselves with the Army, in France and Flanders.

Not only that, but the King visited the Grand Fleet at frequent intervals, and we are told that on many naval matters his advice was eagerly sought. From the beginning to the end of hostilities no naval manœuvre or move was outside his knowledge, and few took place without their being the subject of his well-judged comments.

And so it was with the Army. Every new invention and new suggestion for the equipment or comfort of the men in the line or the precise field strength in each theatre of war were subjects on which he demanded close and constant information.

On frequent occasions during the war Royal visits were paid to important factories and workshops at the munitions centres throughout Britain, as well as to shipbuilding yards, hospitals and other institutions engaged in war work of one kind or another.

Early in the war the Prince of Wales was eager to take his place on the Western Front. He wanted no easy and safe job at the base, but because he was heir to the Throne it was insisted that he be attached to General Headquarters.

Even so, constant watchfulness by those responsible for the safety of the Prince did not prevent him from escaping into the battle zones again and again. On many occasions he was under fire, and was able to prove himself. He early displayed an unusual and able interest in military tactics, and was able to study the military operations from the beginning to the end.

After a period of apprenticeship at G.H.Q., the Prince succeeded in getting posted to the Staff of the Guards Division.

This was not quite what he wanted. He would have liked to have commanded a platoon and gone over the top at the head of his men, but as he could not attain his heart's desire he settled down to really hard work on the " Q " side— that is, in the branch of Divisional Headquarters controlled by the Assistant Quarter-Master General, who is responsible for the quarters and general comfort of the troops.

THE FIRST R.A.F. PAGEANT, HENDON, 1927.

GREETING
THE VICTOR
OF THE
ATLANTIC.

CHARLES LINDBERGH *flew solo from New York to Paris in 1927. This achievement
made him the idol of America, and to-day his position there is the equivalent to the
popularity of the Prince of Wales in Britain.*

FIRST TALKIES. *It was only in 1928 that the first talking film, "The Jazz Singer," was shown in London. Al Jolson appeared in it, and followed shortly afterwards with "The Singing Fool." This film, notable for the "Sonny Boy" theme song, has been one of the greatest box-office successes in cinema history.*

NOVEMBER, 1928, *was an anxious month for the nation. The King caught a chill at Sandringham, and his illness became serious. Crowds waited anxiously for the latest bulletins, which were posted up outside the Palace gates. A Council of Regency was appointed, consisting of the Queen, the Prince of Wales, the Primate, and the Prime Minister.*

WHEN THE KING *had partly recovered from his illness, he was taken to Craigwell House, Bognor, to recuperate. Eventually he made a complete recovery. The seaside town became Bognor Regis as a mark of the King's appreciation.*

SUZANNE LENGLEN, *photographed before the war. She was ladies' champion at Wimbledon from 1919 to 1923. She also won in 1925.*

From 1927 until she retired from tennis in 1933 owing to injury, MRS. WILLS MOODY *only lost one match. She was never beaten at Wimbledon.*

In 1931 Britain won the Schneider Trophy outright. We had already won at Venice in 1927, and at Calshot in 1929. Shortly afterwards, on September 29, 1931, Flight-Lieut. Stainforth created a world record of 408 m.p.h. in a Schneider Trophy aeroplane.

The Prince was appointed Staff Captain of the Mediterranean Expeditionary Force in 1916 and promoted D.A.Q.M.G. in the same year. He attained his twenty-first birthday in 1915, whilst serving in the field, but naturally that year was not a time for any sort of public rejoicing, and the event passed almost unnoticed.

The Prince came in for a useful sphere of activity during the winter of 1915-1916 when the British Government appointed a National Committee to make permanent provision for the care of British graves in France and Belgium. The Prince was appointed President of this new body and took an active interest in its important duties.

There was no lack of work for the Prince, but it must be admitted that during the whole of his service on the French Front his complete disregard of personal danger continued to be a constant source of anxiety, and, popular as he was with all ranks, it was with a sigh of something like relief that the High Command witnessed his departure from France.

Subsequently the Prince visited the Italian Front, and took with him that same keenness and interest in military operations. Thus, by the time the Armistice came, the Prince of Wales had a wider experience of war than any man of his generation.

Even so, he decided his work had only just begun. He was tremendously interested in the growth of the war comrade movement. He had experienced that camaraderie of men under fire, and he believed in it, profoundly. He determined to tour the Empire, to visit the outposts, to meet again those men with whom he had rubbed shoulders in the war zone. And in the years that followed the Prince obtained a greater knowledge of the British Empire, its men and women and its problems, than had ever been vouchsafed to any other member of the Royal Family.

It is worth while setting out just what countries the Prince has visited within the period following the war. Here they are:

Canada	Brazil
Australia	Panama
India	Gambia
South Africa	St. Helena
New Zealand	Trinidad
Malta	Grenada
Gold Coast	St. Lucia
British East Africa	Barbados
Kenya	Montserrat
Tanganyika	British Guiana
Rhodesia	Bermudas
Nigeria	Fiji
Sierra Leone	Samoa
Malaya	The Philippines
United States	Borneo
Chili	Straits Settlements
Uruguay	Aden
Peru	Hong Kong
Bolivia	

Some of these countries the Prince has visited more than once. He has reconnoitred at every point of the compass.

But the Prince has treated the world less as a playground than as a mighty harvest ground of experience. His is the type of intelligence that gains richly and quickly from observation and talk; he understands, say, the native question in Kenya more truly than any student of Blue Books. Mechanical things he grasps readily also.

No effusion of "sights" bewilders the Prince. They are all sealed in separate compartments of his memory so that he can recall readily when he saw a thing and where. His memory for faces and names is even better, and it holds him in good stead when he sees again people he has met on his travels.

This happens often. People come to sign the visitors' book at St. James's Palace and the Prince seldom fails to remember them at once. He has a succession of visitors whom he has met abroad. Sometimes he sees from the newspapers that they are in London, sometimes the Colonial Office let him know, and an invitation to call at the Palace is the result.

On his trip to South America the Prince appeared more conspicuously than before in the rôle of unofficial trade ambassador, and though he would deprecate any attempt to measure the value of his work there in terms of money, there is no doubt that his personal éclat has done British trade in South America an immense amount of good.

He is renewing the tradition of the Prince Consort on a grand scale. Who can gainsay that the two pieces of counsel he is constantly giving as the result of his travels, " Adopt, adapt and improve," and "Let the heads of businesses themselves go and see," are eminently sound?

It should be added that the State does not pay for all these tours, but only for those which the Government itself suggests. The trip to South America, for instance, though entirely a business one, was paid for by the Prince.

Many events have occurred within the circle of the Royal Family since those war days. On February 28, 1922, the King's only daughter, Princess Mary, was married in Westminster Abbey to Viscount Lascelles, eldest son of the Earl of Harewood. Two sons resulted from this marriage.

Then, on April 26, 1923, the Duke of York was married to Lady Elizabeth Bowes-Lyon, fourth daughter of the Earl of Strathmore and Kinghorne. A first daughter, Princess Elizabeth, was the result of this marriage, to be followed some years later by another, Princess Margaret Rose.

At both these marriages great celebrations revealed the popularity and respect with which the Royal Family was held in the hearts of the people. This patriotism reached its peak when on April 23, 1924, the British Empire Exhibition at Wembley was opened by the King.

The close of 1928 was darkened by the serious illness of the King, creating the gravest anxiety for more than two months. The King had neglected a chill caught at Sandringham, and continued for many days to work painfully when all work should have been denied him.

By the beginning of 1929 it was possible for the King, accompanied by Queen Mary, to journey to Bognor and begin his convalescence. Throughout that period of anxiety Queen Mary had devoted herself day and night to looking after the King.

To-day this small, bearded man with the deep-set tired eyes, who rules over fourteen million square miles of the earth's surface, is the living symbol of the British Commonwealth of Nations, the greatest force for peace that has ever existed.

CHAPTER XII

THE ECONOMIC WAR BEGINS

Problems of demobilisation—Riots in camps—Red tape—Cost of living too high—Housing Shortage—Jazz era—Scuttling of German fleet at Scapa Flow—First Atlantic flight—First woman M.P.—Women's fashions change—Mystery of the Unknown Warrior.

I

AT the signing of the Armistice about three million Britishers were still under arms. Three-quarters of a million of young Britons had died of wounds or disease, and something like a million had been incapacitated.

By the end of January, 1919, one million of these three million men had been demobilised. But there was still a considerable British Army in occupation on the Rhine. But those troops who marched across the Rhine and entered the old German city of Cologne were a tired and dispirited army. They had fought through the long years, many illusions had gone, and now that victory had come to them they found it bitter fruit.

Nevertheless, throughout the long years of that occupation of the British Army in Cologne, the record of our troops was very high. The Germans themselves have been the first to admit that the British Army behaved as one could only say, "like English gentlemen."

Demobilisation was a tremendous problem which faced the country. Hundreds of thousands of men were anxious to return home, and millions of people were anxious to welcome them back as quickly as possible.

In fact, the whole country had but one desire, to get back to the normality of pre-war times. Actually they were never to see those pre-war times and the normality again.

The War Office realised the serious economic difficulties of flinging thousands of men suddenly upon the labour market. They therefore worked out a scheme which could only work slowly, and allow for the gradual absorption of men into industry.

Under this slow system the men became restive. Demobilisation bases in France grew more and more difficult to handle, even when they did not break out in actual disorder.

In England the early days of January, 1919, brought riots in camps at Dover, Folkestone, and Osterley, and angry demonstration of troops outside the War Office.

Tremendous difficulties were experienced with the Colonial troops, as transport had to be provided to take them to their countries beyond the seas. These were delayed for too long, and in March Canadian troops at Kimmel Park mutinied. Five were killed and over twenty injured before order was restored.

A few days later there was a riot near an American Y.M.C.A. hut in London. In the meantime Mr. Lloyd George as Premier, in consultation with Mr. Bonar Law, leader in the House of Commons

18

had decided upon an immediate khaki election.

Mr. Lloyd George wanted a national mandate before going to Versailles to discuss the terms of the Peace Treaty. Thus, only 11 days after the Armistice, on November 22, 1918, a manifesto was issued jointly by the Prime Minister and Mr. Bonar Law appealing for the votes of the country.

"A land fit for heroes to live in" was the great slogan of that day. In addition the hoardings carried posters demanding "Trial of the Kaiser; Punishment of those responsible for Atrocities; The fullest Indemnities from Germany; Britain for the British Socially and Industrially; Rehabilitation for those broken in the war, and a Happier Country for All."

These were the things promised by the new Coalition Government. Needless to say they were voted into power with enormous majorities.

The Coalition numbered 478 members, and there were fifty-nine Labour members and a mere scrap of Liberalism.

Thus, while the great politicians and statesmen, the generals and advisers and the diplomatic giants of Europe were preparing for the long-drawn-out drama of Versailles, the people of this country were rapidly trying to adjust themselves to the peacetime problems.

There was an immediate desire to shake off the many restrictions that wartime had imposed. People began to complain of the officiousness of officials, from the policeman down to the ordinary underground tube conductor.

There was also a desperate demand for a lessening in the cost of living, which was still exceedingly high. But the fact that money was still plentiful,

that officers were leaving the Army with large gratuities, and men were coming home with arrears of pay, sent the cost of living up still further.

Rationing and control of prices was still in force. As soon as the restrictions on the sale of bread were abolished, the price rose from 9d. to 9½d. the quartern loaf. In October, 1920, it had reached 1s. 4d. In September, 1921, it was 1s.; February, 1922, 10d.; and thereafter it fluctuated between 8d. and 10d.

Granulated sugar cost 1s. per lb. in May, 1920, but with increasing supplies sugar rationing was abolished in November that year, and the price was reduced 2d. per lb. In October, 1920, butter which in June cost 2s. 8d. per lb., went up to 3s. 4d. In the winter of 1920 to 1921 milk cost 11d. per quart.

The newspapers at this time were full of complaints at the still rising prices. Eggs, for example, were still costing 9d. each. Buyers also complained of the bullying attitude of shopkeepers. Altogether a new phase in class warfare had been developing in the circles of democracy itself.

There came also at the same time the terrific problem of housing. The thousands of men returning, many of whom had married, wanted to set up homes for themselves right away. There were no houses to be had. Building had been practically at a standstill during the war, and even repairs to the old houses had been neglected.

At the census of 1921 there were more than 750,000 families in England and Wales in excess of the number of structurally separate dwellings. The rise in prices, and also the cost of labour, sent up the price of houses to an exorbitant figure.

An ordinary working-class house with-

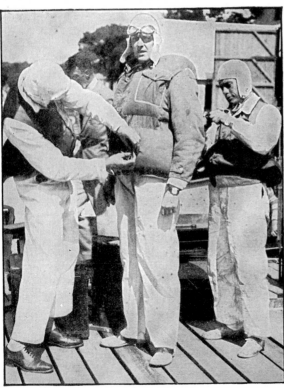

ANOTHER GREAT DISASTER of 1930 *was the death of Sir Henry Segrave, speed king.*
He lived for thrills. In the war he was an R.A.F. pilot, and was shot down. After the
war he won the world's land speed record for Britain, putting the pace up to 231 m.p.h.
In Miss England II. he unofficially broke the speed-boat record on Lake Windermere,
but his boat was wrecked when it struck a log. Sir Henry died from his injuries a few
hours later. His last words were, "Have I broken the record?"

THE PRINCE OF WALES *is called* "The Flying Prince" *because of his practical interest in aviation. He has his own aeroplanes, and frequently uses them when travelling about the country.*

JIM MOLLISON *flew from Australia to London in 8 days, 22 hrs. 25 mins. in 1931.*

Without any publicity, Amy Johnson started off on a record flight to Australia on May 5, 1930. When she reached India ahead of Bert Hinkler's time, every detail of her flight was followed eagerly. But she failed to beat the record, and reached Australia in nine days.

These two famous aviators were married in July, 1932. Later, Mrs. Mollison made a record solo flight to the Cape, and her husband flew the Atlantic. In 1933 they made a joint flight across the Atlantic, but crashed on landing. Both were injured.

ON OCTOBER 5, 1930, the R 101 set out from Cardington on a flight to India. Lord Thomson, Minister of Air; Sir Sefton Brancker, Director of Civil Aviation; and Britain's greatest airship experts were aboard. A few hours later the ship was a mass of broken metal just outside Beauvais, France. This composite picture shows clearly the contrast between the airship in flight and its wrecked shell. Only six survived out of a personnel of fifty-four. The bodies of the dead men were laid in Westminster Hall, where the public were allowed to file past, and after they had been borne in procession through London, they were buried in a common grave in Cardington

MIDGET GOLF
was one of the crazes of 1930. Introduced from America, it did not survive long in this country. But several fortunes were made by promoters whilst it lasted.

BEACH PYJAMAS—*a fashion from the Continent—were seen at English seaside resorts for the first time in 1930.*

BLACK AUGUST *saw the fall of the Labour Government. Britain's increasing financial difficulties made rigid economy necessary, but at the Cabinet meetings of August 20 and 21 there were differences of opinion over cuts in unemployment pay. Top picture shows Mr. Clynes, Home Secretary, discussing the situation in Downing Street. Below, Mr. Montagu Norman, Governor of the Bank of England, drives to Downing Street for a conference with the Prime Minister.*

out a parlour cost £860 to build, exclusive of the purchase of the land on which it stood and the roadmaking charges. The Government had to face this big problem.

In 1919, therefore, the Director General of Housing was appointed, and the Government came to the assistance first of local authorities, and afterwards of the private builder, granting subsidies and long term loans to facilitate the building of houses which could be let at a rent within the means of the people most needing them.

175,000 houses were built at a cost to the Treasury of £175,000,000. Many of the demobilised soldiers and sailors began building their own houses. One saw the rise of hutments and bungalows of extraordinary structure in the waste parts of England. Biscuit tins, petrol tins, and soap boxes were used by many.

The new Government that had come into power was rather like the old one, with just a few changes. Sir Eric Geddes became one of the Ministers without Portfolio. Mr. Churchill went to the War Office. Sir F. E. Smith became Lord Chancellor as Lord Birkenhead.

The prospect of a new policy for India was seen in the appointment of Sir S. P. Sinha as Under Secretary of State for India. He was the first native of India to become a member of the British Government, and was very soon the first native of India to take his seat in the House of Lords.

Perhaps it is safe to say that at this time, when the various Ministers and statesmen were getting themselves ready for Versailles, and preparing for the problems they would have to face there, they were oblivious to the plain fact that the real problems were to be in this country.

The miners were the first to bring their grievances to a head, to make the country realise the squalor and danger in which they lived and worked. They demanded a 30 per cent. advance in wages, a six-hour instead of an eight-hour day, and nationalisation of the mines.

The miners also added to their demands the payment from State funds of full wages to all demobilised miners until they were re-absorbed. The Government had to face this spreading discontent among the miners. They endeavoured to come to terms. They offered an immediate advance of a shilling a day on wages, and proposed a Royal Commission to consider the more general demands.

There was also a Land Settlement Bill going through the House, which was an attempt to do something for the returning men and settle them agriculturally on plots. Many of these men who had left office stools, clerks and the like, had no particular desire to go back to office life. The war had taught them the value of an open-air existence. They had roughed it. They returned with a contempt for what they called the softness of civilian life.

To help them in this new outlook the Government bought large tracts of agricultural land where training centres were established and small holding colonies developed. Thousands of men were learning to farm for the first time in their lives, and seemed to be enjoying it.

All these reconstruction programmes were being carried on at tremendous expense. Money was still being spent like water, and the growth of the Civil Service, the hordes of secretaries, typists, and clerks, was a subject of constant criticism. Nevertheless, money still seemed plentiful, and generally speaking labour was being well paid for its work.

The post-war craze for amusement had also come into being. Night clubs, dance-halls, and theatres and restaurants were opening everywhere, and being crowded. All the pent-up emotion of the war years seemed to be let loose in this new freedom, particularly among the young.

Dancing became nothing more nor less than a national craze. It was the era of jazz. Morals, too, seemed to have taken on a new freedom after the war, and cigarette smoking women were now to be seen everywhere.

But in June, 1919, a dramatic incident in the north of Britain brought the minds of the public back to the war again.

On June 23 the Germans scuttled their surrendered ships lying in Scapa Flow. Within practically a few minutes all went to the bottom, except one of the battleships and five of the light cruisers.

It had been a clever and concerted plan of the sailors left in charge of the ships at Scapa Flow. The German Admiral, Von Reuter, took full responsibility.

He explained that the surrender of the fleet had been part of the terms of the Armistice, and the Armistice terms being superseded by the acceptance of the Peace Terms, he regarded himself as free to carry out the orders given at the beginning of the war, that no German ship was ever to be surrendered.

Perhaps this action brought some satisfaction to the interned German sailors. The British public merely regarded it as a crazy action altogether. *Punch* at this time had a cartoon depict-

ing the top of a mast sticking out solitarily from the waves, flying the signal: "Germany expects every man this day to do the dirty."

Politics and peace terms were suddenly forgotten by the opening of the great drama of the Atlantic flight. Lord Northcliffe, through the *Daily Mail,* had offered £10,000 for the first successful Atlantic flight.

The first adventurers on this most adventurous of all flights were Harry Hawker and Lieutenant-Commander Grieve. Their attempt was a failure, a very gallant and dramatic failure. They were picked up by the *Mary,* a Danish steamer.

The two gallant fliers were transferred to H.M.S. *Revenge* and were landed at Thurso. They travelled up to a tremendous reception in London, to be decorated by the King and publicly lunched in London.

The excitement of this gallant effort had no sooner been known than the prize of £10,000 was won by the first two Britishers to cross the North Atlantic.

It was accomplished on June 14, 1919, by Captain Alcock and Lieutenant Brown. Both afterwards were knighted.

They left St. John's, Newfoundland, in a Vickers-Vimy Rolls biplane and landed at Clifden, Galway, Ireland, the next morning after a flight of sixteen hours.

In spite of bad weather during the flight, an average speed of 120 miles an hour was maintained. It must be remembered that in 1919 aeroplane engines were nothing like so reliable as they are in present days, a fact which adds greatly to the credit of Alcock and Brown's achievement.

About this time, too, there was a

triumphal peace procession through London.

A great march of troops headed by General Pershing and the Americans, followed by Lord Beatty leading Navy detachments and Lord Haig leading the Army, with Marshal Foch riding beside him, were meant to impress the crowd with the reality of the great victory which had been won over the Central Powers.

But Labour troubles were looming large on the horizon. In March, 1919, unemployment had topped a million.

Even the police forces decided to strike. This led to trouble in Manchester and rioting in Liverpool. At the same time the Sankey Commission issued their report on the mines, and Mr. Lloyd George informed the House of Commons that the Government had definitely rejected the policy of nationalisation.

Despite these desperate labour troubles, there seemed to be no difficulty about raising money. A victory loan, which was opened in June, raised £250,000,000. Budget figures, like prices, were still rising, instead of falling; the estimated revenue at that time was £1,160,000,000.

II

On September 1, 1919, the House of Commons itself saw a revolution happen in its midst. This was the introduction of the first woman member.

One of the last acts of the War Parliament had been to pass a Bill known as The Representation of the People Act, giving women over thirty the vote. And a further Government Bill which became law just before the general election made women over twenty-one eligible for return as Members of Parliament.

Sixteen women were nominated for this particular election. Only one of them, the former Suffragist leader, Christabel Pankhurst, stood as a Coalition candidate.

Of the many who put up for election, only one of them, the Countess Markievicz, was returned.

But as she was an Irish Republican she was not able to take her seat at Westminster. She had been one of the leaders of the Easter rising of 1916, commanding the volunteers who occupied the College of Surgeons at Dublin.

But that first woman member who entered the House of Commons on December 1 was not the result of any great feminist movement. It was accounted for by a Mr. Astor being elevated to the peerage, and his wife therefore stood for the vacated seat.

Lady Astor was successful at the poll, and a good deal of interest was aroused as to how she would actually appear in the House: whether she would retain her hat, if she would dress in a deliberately masculine or feminine fashion, and so forth.

Lady Astor, wearing her hat, was introduced to the House by Mr. Balfour and Mr. Lloyd George. A painting was made of this auspicious occasion and subsequently hung in the Hall of Bedford College for Women.

To go back to the definite advance of the Women Movement in 1919, this was the year also that the Sex Disqualification (Removal) Acts of 1919 gave women admission to the legal profession.

Miss Olive Clapham, the first woman barrister, passed the final bar examination on May 25, 1921. During 1922 over thirty women were called to the Bar.

Not all the women who passed the examination, however, went into practice, and it was not until December, 1924, that a woman appeared for the first time as an advocate in the Court of Criminal Appeal.

Another great gain for women was the passing of the Matrimonial Causes Act of 1923, which made adultery of either party a sufficient cause for divorce. Previously the wife petitioner had had to prove some other misdemeanour (*e.g.*, cruelty or desertion) in addition to adultery.

Other acts relative to property owned by women also came into force about this time.

It was obvious that woman was achieving an independence for herself and was boldly making a bid for positions in the various professions.

Further down in the social scale there was a struggle going on between the returned soldiers and the women who were still holding the jobs which they had taken up during the war. Many of these women were very loath to leave their work. At the same time many employers were equally loath to part with them. They had proved their usefulness and efficiency.

Returning men who found their jobs held by women were particularly bitter about this.

The war too had increased in remarkable fashion the number of surplus women. Casualties provided the country with many young widows.

It had also increased the proportion of women to men, and at this particular time the struggle for existence was such that many of the men hesitated before taking on the economic disadvantages of marriage.

These surplus women insisted on continuing their industrial life. They had to, or starve. They had nothing to look forward to but a lonely middle age, and, as they had sacrificed husbands or intended husbands, they demanded the right to live.

In years to come these surplus women were to influence entertainments, fashions, modes of transport, and even the reading of periodicals. As they were in the majority, so the plays, magazines, books, films, and other entertainments of the period had to provide for them.

But perhaps most startling of all was the change in fashions in dress at this period. The hobble skirts and enormous hats of 1914 had given way to the utilitarian short skirt and the type of slouch hat that seemed to be worn by everyone from women of fashion down to the ordinary working girl.

Most of these fashions had one definite aim—to preserve the illusion of youth. Perhaps the large majority of surplus women, many of them approaching dangerous middle age, were responsible for this. They had to preserve their youth, appear alert and efficient.

Beauty preparations, make-up, lipstick, rouge, and all the cosmetics of the toilet table began to boom. It was soon discovered that the women of Britain would spend a fortune on their toilet tables, and manufacturers were not loath to take advantage of this desire.

The boyish appearance of women went so far as to introduce the bobbed hair fashion, and also the Eton crop. The older generation gazed askance at this transformation of the modern young women. Articles and denunciations appeared everywhere on the immodesty of it all.

The revolution in women's fashions proceeded apace.

AFTER THE CRITICAL CABINET MEETINGS of the Labour Government, the King hurriedly returned to London from Scotland. Next day the Government resigned, and Mr. Ramsay MacDonald formed a National Government. Mr. Philip Snowden (left), Chancellor of the Exchequer, was one of the few Cabinet Ministers to support him. Mr. Stanley Baldwin (right) pledged the support of the Conservative Party.

THE NEW CABINET. *A provisional Government was formed on August 24 to introduce a supplementary Budget and carry on until a General Election could be held. Reading from left to right: Mr. (now Lord) Snowden, Chancellor of the Exchequer; Mr. Stanley Baldwin, Lord President of the Council; Mr. Ramsay MacDonald, Prime Minister; Sir Herbert Samuel, Home Secretary; Lord Sankey, Lord Chancellor. Standing: Sir Philip Cunliffe Lister, President of the Board of Trade; Mr. J. H. Thomas, Dominions Secretary; Lord Reading, Foreign Secretary; Mr. Neville Chamberlain, Minister of Health; Sir Samuel Hoare, Secretary for India.*

A GRIM FIGHT *between the National Government and the Labour Opposition took place at the General Election in October. Mr. J. H. Thomas, former trade union leader, fought for his old seat at Derby as National candidate, and was elected.*

VIGOROUS PROPAGANDA *was conducted on behalf of Mr. Ramsay MacDonald, who was bitterly attacked by Labour for having left the party. His supporters retaliated by calling him " The Captain who stuck to his ship." Even aeroplanes were plastered with bills.*

TWENTY-FIVE YEARS OF NEWSPAPER DEVELOP-MENT. *The old offices of the "Daily Chronicle" as they were at the beginning of King George's reign.*

TWENTY-FIVE YEARS OF NEWSPAPER DEVELOPMENT. *The greatly extended offices
of the "News-Chronicle" in Bouverie Street as they are to-day.*

LONDON HAS CHANGED RAPIDLY. *Here are the new buildings which have sprung up along the Embankment. On top is the new Thames House and the building which houses Imperial Chemical Industries. Below, the new Lambeth Bridge, opened by the King in 1932. In the background is Lambeth Place, home of the Archbishop of Canterbury.*

With short skirts to their knees they sat in smart little sports motor-cars and drove at breakneck speed along the new arterial roads which were being built in Britain.

Even the evening dresses were short. The silk stockinged legs inspired the dance teachers to introduce such complicated dances as the Charleston. Jazz musicians composed these hectic dances. Josephine Baker, Creole artist of Paris, had introduced the Black Bottom to Europe. Gaby Deslys, decorated with ostrich feathers, paradise plumes and diamonds, danced with her partner, Harry Pilcer, in a frenzy of modern jazz. The boyish girls of Britain took to this new hectic existence with avidity.

III

The Unknown Soldier is still the greatest mystery of the Great War. Who is he? Where actually was he found? Who was responsible for the idea of the exhumation and the solemn procession through the London streets together with the impressive burial in Westminster Abbey?

Few people to-day realise that there were actually six bodies of soldiers dug up from nameless graves in order that the Unknown Warrior might be selected.

The Rev. G. Kendall, who in the year 1920 was Senior Chaplain to the 63rd Naval Division, was placed in charge of these exhumations. He has since related the measures taken by the authorities to ensure that no one should even guess the identity of the body which rests to-day in the Abbey.

Bodies, he says, were taken from unknown graves on six different sectors of the fighting area—Ypres salient, the Marne, Arras, Cambrai, and two points further south. No one knew whose bodies they were; neither whether they were those of humble soldiers or men of higher rank, nor whether they were soldiers, sailors, or airmen.

Each of the six bodies was placed in a coffin, each coffin being of identical size and pattern. The coffins were then placed in a row in a hut, each being covered with a Union Jack. The hut door was then locked, and on the following morning a general officer, who had not seen the arrival of the cortège or any of the coffins before, was asked to unlock the hut, enter and place his hand on one coffin. This he did, and the coffin he touched contained the body of the Unknown Warrior. The other five bodies were reburied.

Of the procession of the Unknown Warrior back to England, the newspapers of November, 1920, give us details of the solemnity and impressiveness of the occasion.

Draped with the Union Jack, the coffin was placed on the deck of a British destroyer at Boulogne, carried across the Channel, and, with guns thundering a salute, entered the harbour at Dover. The number of guns fired equalled the salute due to a field-marshal.

Soldiers and sailors carried the coffin reverently to the train, which then steamed towards London. It remained with a guard of honour throughout the night, and the next morning, placed on a gun-carriage, was slowly trundled through the streets towards Whitehall. Huge crowds lined the pavements. Ranks of soldiers, bowed over reversed arms, guarded its progress.

The gun-carriage, drawn by six black horses, came to a halt in Whitehall, where the King, attended by his sons and Cabinet Ministers, statesmen, generals, admirals, and all the panoply of troops standing stiffly to attention, solemnly unveiled the Cenotaph, which was to be the centre of all Armistice Day celebrations in the future.

Then the King led the procession towards Westminster Abbey, where an impressive religious service saw the Unknown Warrior lowered into the tomb. Finally, a black marble engraved stone sealed the tomb.

The inscription reads:

Beneath this Stone Rests the Body of a
British Warrior
Unknown by Name or Rank
Brought from France to Lie Among
The Most Illustrious of the Land
And Buried Here on Armistice Day
11 Nov. 1920. In the Presence of
His Majesty King George V
His Ministers of State
The Chiefs of His Forces
And a Vast Concourse of the Nation
Thus are Commemorated the Many
Multitudes Who During the Great War
of 1914-1918 Gave The Most That
Man Can Give Life Itself
For God
For King and Country
For Loved Ones Home and Empire
For the Sacred Cause of Justice and
The Freedom of the World
They Buried Him Among the Kings Because He
Had Done Good Towards God and Toward
His House.

The impressive idea of a shrine to an Unknown Warrior appealed to other nations. France, Italy, and the United States followed the example of Britain. Subsequently the Unknown Soldier was to inspire writers in various countries, and one French dramatist at least wrote a great play about the Unknown Warrior of France. This was quickly followed by novels and plays in English on the same theme.

Some time ago an American newspaper published a report that Mr. George Bernard Shaw contemplated writing a play suggesting that the Unknown Soldier buried in Westminster Abbey was a German.

The idea in Mr. Shaw's mind, according to the American newspaper, was that Christ comes back to the earth in the distant future and is asked by a British Cabinet to raise the Unknown Soldier from the dead in the hope that here they may find the one last symbol that England may adopt, follow, and worship.

Christ consents, descends into the tomb, and, in a brief and touching scene, the Unknown Soldier arises from the dead. When he appears, he makes a speech, not one word of which can be understood by the populace. Then an erudite scholar of this future period is able to solve the puzzle. The Unknown Soldier was a German.

A daring suggestion. Anxious to get at the truth of the matter, the Editor of *Pearson's Weekly* wrote to Mr. Shaw and received the following reply:

" *This is a very stale piece of inaccurate news.*

" *When the Unknown Warrior ceremony was new I suggested in the course of conversation, as a plot for a play on the subject, a political comedy centred on the resurrection of the Unknown Soldier and the discovery that he was a German.*

" *There was no question of writing such a play: I have often thrown out such suggestions for fun . . .*"

But even more difficult is it to discover the person who first conceived the idea that England should have an Unknown Warrior. There seems to be more than one claim in this direction.

The question was first raised in the

House of Commons by Sir Harry Brittain. He asked the Prime Minister, then Mr. Lloyd George:

" Whether, in view of the fact that no commemoration had ever been held in this country which so touched the hearts of the people as had the burial of the Unknown Warrior, it was possible to record for future history the name of the individual who first made this very beautiful and appropriate suggestion."

The Prime Minister replied:

" I am sure the individual, whoever he may be, will be quite satisfied with the *result* of his suggestion."

Sir Harry Brittain then further asked:

" Might I ask whether this suggestion was not first publicly made by Mr. J. B. Wilson, the news-editor of one of the great metropolitan dailies?"

No answer was given to this suggestion.

Interviewed recently, Sir Harry Brittain recalled the circumstances of his questions in the House of Commons.

" I am almost certain," he said, " that this very fine suggestion was made in the course of a discussion in the editorial offices of the *Daily Express* when I was present. A group of us were discussing the war and the war graves in France. Then Mr. J. B. Wilson, one of the men in that group, suggested it would be a splendid symbol of our dead warriors to bring a body of an unknown soldier back to England. That was the first occasion I heard the suggestion mooted."

Richard Haestier, in his book, *Dead Men Tell Tales*, points out that several reports gave the credit for the suggestion to the Rev. David Railton, who was at one time senior curate at Folkestone Parish Church.

Mr. Railton is reported to have said that he first conceived the idea while serving in France. He went into the garden of a partly demolished house behind the lines and there saw a tiny wooden cross marking the grave of an unidentified soldier.

Some time later he talked it over with a Folkestone friend, and as the result of that chat wrote to the Dean of Westminster suggesting a national memorial in the form of an Unknown Warrior buried in the Abbey. The Dean was sympathetic, and took steps to place the suggestion before the proper authorities, with the results we know.

One of the newspaper reports says that it was Mr. Railton who anonymously presented the Union Jack which covered the Unknown Warrior's coffin on its journey from France to Westminster.

The Unknown Warrior of Britain was awarded the Victoria Cross, the Congressional Medal of America, and the medals from the other Allies, all symbolic of the bravery of the men who died in the colossal slaughter.

CHAPTER XIII

THE GENERAL STRIKE

I

IN the meantime, Ireland inevitably was giving more trouble to the British Government. Absorbed in their own affairs, English people had thought little of what was happening on the other side of the Irish Sea.

There had been some amusement and excitement when it was learned in March, 1919, that Mr. de Valera, who had been one of the Sinn Feiners arrested in 1918, had escaped from Lincoln gaol. The amusing part of it was in the stories of two beguiling girls who had used their good looks to help his escape.

Since then there had been constantly recurring accounts of attacks upon police barracks, and upon post offices, and the ambushing and killing of constables.

By December the seriousness of what was going on became apparent. The sporadic attacks were growing more frequent, more determined; and then came a murderous attack on General French, the Viceroy; his car was ambushed on a road, and his escape was extraordinary.

Assassinations of the Irish Constabulary began to be horribly frequent. In a desperate attempt to save the situation, the Government organised an auxiliary police known as the "Black and Tan."

Terrorism began to stalk throughout the Irish countryside. Mr. Lloyd George, ingenious as usual, tried to stem the tide of terrorism by producing an entirely new scheme of Home Rule for Ireland, one which would also placate Ulster.

His idea was two separate Parliaments with a single Federal Council of forty for the whole of Ireland, elected with equal proportions by the two legislatures.

But the proposal was not received favourably in Ireland itself. The Sinn Feiners refused to take their seats in Parliament and entered upon the new feud and civil war with a desperation that suggested that they intended at all costs to create a Republic.

But England was facing her own desperate problems, economic ones. Although money was flowing freely and everybody seemed to have plenty to spend, there were indications which economists might have realised were going to lead to the greatest slump in history.

In 1920 the effect of the war on prices was at its worst. The Budget for this year was as depressing as that of the year before; the revenue to be raised was over £1,340,000,000; letter postage went up to 2d., telegrams to one shilling, and spirits and beer were more heavily burdened than ever.

Moreover the railways added a further 25 per cent. to the 50 per cent. increase on fares. Nevertheless, the temper of the people was still frivolous. Restaurants and theatres were crowded. The great hit of 1920 was *The Beggar's Opera*, which ran night after night to packed houses.

Also the cinema had come into its own. Every cinema in these days was crowded with people who were discovering Charlie Chaplin, Douglas Fairbanks and Mary Pickford, the first great film idols of the British public.

In October, 1922, Mr. Lloyd George resigned. It brought to an end that Coalition Government which had tried, unsuccessfully, to grapple with the enormous problems of post-war existence.

The instinct of the people was that the great economic war had now begun, Although the Conservatives held office for a few months, soon the Labour Party was given control of the Government for the first time.

The Labour Party could only govern with the help of the Liberal Party in order that they should have a clear majority over the Conservative Party.

Mr. Ramsay MacDonald was appointed Prime Minister, and they entered upon a short, but stormy, period of office. Actually this Labour Government lasted for less than a year.

Appealing to the country the Labour Party found the electorate suddenly and unexpectedly biased against it by a letter purported to have come from Zinoviev, then an important Moscow commissar, telling the English Communists how to act.

Naturally England as a whole did not pay much attention, but many who voted against Labour did so because they believed foreigners were interfering with the national concerns.

In consequence, Mr. Baldwin, who now reigned since Mr. Bonar Law's death, ruled with his Conservatives.

Early in its period of office the Baldwin Government was called upon to deal with a very grave industrial crisis, which arose from the situation in the coal industry. It had long been obvious that the settlement reached in 1921 was no solution of the problems of the industry. The competition of oil and electricity had hit the coal industry hard. The miners had suffered. Many were out of employment. Others were working on rates of pay which compared badly with previous years.

The Trade Union Congress supported the miners in demanding redress and threatened a General Strike unless their demands were met.

In the summer of 1925 that crisis was reached.

Playing for time, Mr. Baldwin promised a subsidy to the mining industry, until an enquiry could be carried out which might possibly have been undertaken beforehand. The subsidy lasted eight months and cost the taxpayers £23,000,000.

While it was going on a Royal Commission, under Sir Herbert Samuel, investigated the problems of the industry, and made a series of proposals, some of which involved legislation, while others depended upon agreement between miners and mine-owners.

But the miners and the mine-owners both rejected the scheme, and in the absence of agreement the Government refused to legislate, except that it restored the eight-hours day. Thereupon the Trade Union Congress again intervened, with a definite threat of a general strike unless a satisfactory solution was reached before May 2; but they had no clear idea as to what the solution was to be.

There were two days of fevered negotiations; and at midnight of May 2 the long dreaded General Strike began.

May Day fell on a Saturday that year, and a crowd of 25,000 took part in demonstrations in Hyde Park. Two days later the *Daily Mail* failed to appear. The printers, members of the National Society of Operative Printers and Assistants, had anticipated the start of the General Strike by twenty-four hours by refusing to set up the leading article dealing with it.

At the same time the Government announced that Hyde Park was closed to the public. It appeared that it was to be used as a centre for London's milk supplies. Some of the evening papers failed to appear. Special constables materialised in the streets. Troops were seen marching up and down Whitehall. The War Office was again a blaze of light. Men in Fascist uniform also appeared at certain centres.

At midnight the railways, omnibuses and tramcars throughout the country came to a standstill. The public looked on and wondered.

For the first time a General Strike in Britain seemed a complete success. So successful was it that even the General Council of the Trade Unions itself seemed frightened.

The streets of the big cities of Britain were transformed during the night. In the morning there were no trams, trains or omnibuses plying for hire. Private car owners were picking up groups of people and taking them into the City to their work. Motor-cars which had not taken the road for years were unearthed and restarted, and the unwonted silence that hung over everything for some hours was suddenly broken by the churning of tanks as they moved to strategic points throughout London.

Troops fully equipped as in wartime also appeared guarding railway bridges. Cyclists seemed to appear by the thousand, riding up and down on their way to work.

The real fact was that the public had risen nobly to the contest. Although there was a complete absence of newspapers, they seemed to be animated by a stern national spirit to maintain order throughout this period of stress.

Only the B.B.C. functioned as a news and propaganda association for the Government. There were wild rumours of riots in Birmingham, Glasgow, and Manchester. It was said that there had been shooting in the streets of these cities. The calm voice of the announcer at the B.B.C. dispelled a good many fears.

For the first time broadcasting was proving itself as a great national institution in such an emergency.

The Government took over the offices of the *Morning Post*, intending to issue an official news-sheet from there under the editorship of Mr. Winston Churchill. This office was surrounded by police, and a national news-sheet did appear. It was entitled *The British Gazette*, and consisted of two pages of matter only. But the workers also had their sheet. It was entitled *The British Worker*, and was printed by the Trade Union leaders.

On the Wednesday business in London seemed at a standstill. Many big concerns had given their staff indefinite leave. Even electricity had to be conserved, and at ten o'clock at night Piccadilly Circus was in darkness.

On Thursday the taxi-men of London came out on strike, thus helping to com-

THE NEW LONDON. The impressive exterior of the Shell-Mex building with its giant clock, and, on right, the new home of the B.B.C. in Portland Place are two examples of the new London which has arisen since the war. Changes are taking place so rapidly that the Englishman who returns after several years abroad scarcely recognises the old landmarks.

HUNGER MARCHERS IN LONDON. *Unemployed from all parts of Britain marched to London in October, 1932, to protest against cuts in unemployment pay.*

HUNGER MARCHERS IN LONDON. *The unemployed demonstration proceeded quite calmly until trouble was caused by a few agitators. Then the police made several baton charges, and many people were injured in the scrimmage.*

272 MILES AN HOUR!

SIR MALCOLM CAMPBELL *had taken Sir Henry Segrave's position as world speed king, and in 1931 he set up a new record of 246 m.p.h. Two years later he increased this to 272 m.p.h. at Daytona. Now in 1935 he plans to speed along Daytona Sands at 300 m.p.h.*

The early months of 1933 provided two sensations. LIEUT. NORMAN BAILLIE-STEWART
*was accused of selling information to the German Secret Service. Before the court martial
he was detained in the Tower of London. He was found guilty, and sentenced to three
years' imprisonment.*
*The trial of British engineers for espionage in Moscow also caused interest. The British
Government protested vigorously, and eventually all of the accused left Russia.*

WORLD ECONOMIC CONFERENCE. *Sixty-five nations sent representatives to the World Economic Conference, which opened at the Geological Museum, South Kensington, on June 12, 1933. It was held to find means of ending the world trade depression, but no agreement was reached. Here the King is seen inaugurating the ceremony.*

WORLD ECONOMIC CONFERENCE. *Delegates discussing the economic situation at the Geological Museum, South Kensington. Top photograph shows M. Paul Hymans (right), Belgian Foreign Minister, with M. Vasdias, Amsterdam. Below: The French delegation to the Conference.*

GREAT YEAR FOR ENGLISH TENNIS. In 1934, for the first time for twenty-one years, England won both the men's and the ladies' singles at Wimbledon. Fred Perry beat Crawford (Australia) by 6–3, 6–0, 7–5; and Miss Dorothy Round beat Miss Helen Jacobs (U.S.A.) by 6–2, 5–7, 6–3. England also retained the Davis Cup.

plete the dislocation of London transport. In the meantime thousands of volunteers were answering the Government's call.

Two hundred buses were taken out by these volunteers, who tried to help those pedestrians who were still struggling to and fro between their offices and homes. These buses, however, were attacked by angry crowds, which smashed the windows of some eighty of them.

There was a great scarcity of meat. Volunteers were called to assist in unloading carcases at the docks, whence they were carried to Smithfield in military lorries, escorted by armoured cars and soldiers in tin hats.

As each day passed immense damage and loss was inflicted on the trade of the nation. But the volunteer system arranged by the Government was working well. All the arrangements for feeding London and other big cities had been planned in advance, and although there was great inconvenience, there was no real suffering.

What was still more remarkable, the struggle was carried on, on both sides, with admirable temper. At the end of a week the trade union leaders knew that they were beaten. There was a rumour that Sir Herbert Samuel was in unofficial contact with the Government, the miners, and the mine-owners.

Hope of an early settlement sprang up in everyone. About 1 o'clock on May 12 the dispassionate voice of the announcer of the B.B.C. told Britain that the Trade Union Congress General Council had decided to terminate the General Strike that night.

But the chaos remained for some time. It was another five days before the railway men, dockers, printers and transport workers returned to work. The funds of the trade unions were exhausted, and their membership from this particular time underwent a rapid decline.

But the coal stoppage still went on. It lasted for seven months. Many iron works were brought to a stop. Other concerns had to import coal from abroad at heavy cost.

In the end the miners were completely defeated. The wage levels that they had to accept were in many cases cruelly low. Markets for British coal had been lost which were not easily recovered, and one-sixth of the miners found themselves permanently out of work.

It can now be seen that the General Strike was the preliminary raising of the curtain of that long, great slump which was now to follow.

II

The spectacular achievements in these depressed economic times were, curiously enough, in the air.

That great concern of which Britain is so proud, Imperial Airways, had come into being, and apart from regularly carrying passengers across the Channel, now extended its services to India and the Cape, South Africa.

Thirteen years ago the first small machine in the Paris route carried a pilot and two passengers. Then a year later came machines which carried a pilot and eight passengers. Following this came aircraft with two pilots and from nine to fourteen passengers. 1926 saw the introduction by Imperial Airways of a fleet of big three-engined air liners, which were the first of their kind, and each of which carried a crew of three together with nineteen passengers.

It was in 1932 that Imperial Airways

20

introduced the thirteen-ton, four-engined machines which, cruising at 105 miles an hour, carry a crew of four and have accommodation for thirty-eight passengers. Then came the speedy monoplanes of the Atalanta type for use on the African and Australian routes.

In its flying-boat service, too, Imperial Airways has led in construction and dependability. In 1924, when Imperial Airways began operations, the flying-boats then available carried six passengers at eighty-five miles an hour. By 1926 machines had been designed and built which carried twelve passengers at ninety miles an hour.

Then, in 1930, came the well-known three-engined "Calcutta" flying-boats for Mediterranean sections of the air mail route to India, which carry fifteen passengers and a crew of four, their total horse-power being 1,500. And now, to-day, on Mediterranean stages of the India and Africa air lines, Imperial Airways is operating the four-engined "Scipio" flying boats, developing 2,200 horse-power and carrying a crew of four, together with sixteen passengers and a ton of mails and freight.

Imperial Airways has a greater record of safety than any other air line in the world. By 1934 the total length of its air routes had increased from 1,000 miles (all within Western Europe) to more than 15,000, serving three continents and crossing no fewer than nineteen countries.

And in the course of this ten million miles of regular flying enterprise there have been but six accidents involving injury to passengers.

But it seems that every big advance in the air has been paid for by some terrible disaster.

The air disaster that shocked the world happened in 1930, when the British airship R 101, a sister ship of the R 100, set out on an experimental flight to India. Apart from the crew and many distinguished passengers, she carried some of the best brains in airship construction in Britain.

During the night the R 101 struck a hill near Beauvais, in France, and was completely destroyed by fire. Forty-eight of the fifty-four passengers and crew lost their lives, among those killed being Lord Thomson, Secretary of State for Air, and Sir Sefton Brancker, Director of Civil Aviation.

The shock of this disaster was such that the Government decided to abandon all further airship construction in this country. The R 100 was dismantled, and the airship research station at Cardington closed down.

Another spectacular development, also in the air, during this period was that of broadcasting.

How did this thing called broadcasting begin? The world total of listening sets is now estimated at about 40,000,000, and it is increasing at the rate of about 250,000 monthly.

Nearly half of these listening sets are in the United States. A quarter of this gigantic total represents the listening sets in use in Britain and Germany. The remainder are spread from Cape Horn to Kamchatka.

It was in 1913 that the Marconi Company were making their early experiments in telephony at Chelmsford. Even then many discoveries had been made about the application of electricity to the voice.

All early experiments, big and little, helped along the science of broadcasting. It had already reached an advanced stage when the Great War suddenly burst upon Europe, and broadcasting was shelved for the moment.

Early in 1919, however, the Marconi Company came back into the field, and Captain Round spoke from Ballybunion in Ireland to Cape Breton, 1,800 miles distant. Captain Round had a broadcasting set that used only 2·5 kilowatts, the electrical equivalent of power of the average motor-cycle.

It was in June, 1920, that Mme. Melba, the famous singer, became the first great radio star by broadcasting from Chelmsford through the characteristic enterprise of Mr. Tom Clarke, then news-editor of the *Daily Mail*. The story of how this broadcast came about is told in *My Northcliffe Diary*, by Tom Clarke.

"June 16, 1920: We had the Melba wireless concert last night. She went down to the Marconi place at Chelmsford. We had to arrange for a light supper for her of chicken and champagne. Soon after seven o'clock she started singing into a microphone hooked up with a 15 kw. set transmitting on 2,800 metres wavelength. I listened in at Blackfriars—frame aerial and telephones not enough to go round. We listened in turns. Melba's girl secretary was there. Her eyes nearly came out of her head as she heard the nightingale voice in 'Addio,' from *La Bohème*. 'It *is* Melba,' she cried in astonishment. I think she had not believed us up to that moment . . . To-day we are receiving messages from all parts. All Europe was the audience last night. Messages from liners at sea tell us how passengers listened to Melba far across the water."

A subsequent concert from Chelmsford was heard at Sultanabad in Persia, and in New York Harbour.

Broadcasting was born. Not only had a new science, a new entertainment, a new art come into being, but there was also the beginning of a new and great industry.

CHAPTER XIV

WHAT OF THE FUTURE?

The Great Depression—Breakdown of economic system—Crooked finance—Britain's financial crisis—Forming the National Government—Britain's recovery Preparations for King's Silver Jubilee—King Alexander's Assassination—Duke of Kent's marriage—A brighter future—Twenty-Five Years of Drama.

I

THE Great Depression was undoubtedly the real cause of the collapse of the gold standard in Britain. Since 1929 an economic blast had swept across the world. The whistle of that wind is still in our ears.

The extraordinary paradox was witnessed of huge piles of coffee being taken to sea and dumped overboard in mid-Atlantic. Rubber was burnt on estates in Malaya. There was a tremendous production of boots, shoes, clothes, motor-cars—almost every type of necessity and luxury—and yet a large number of the public was unable to avail itself of these things.

It was the breakdown of an economic system. The science of production had increased by research and applied methods to an extraordinary degree; the science of distribution had not kept pace with it.

Experts understood only too well the problems before them. The trouble was worldwide. The League of Nations estimated the total unemployed industrial workers in the world at 30,000,000, while producers, especially of foodstuffs and raw materials, could not obtain a price that would cover their costs of production.

Debtor countries were unable to meet their obligations to their creditors Debtor and creditor countries alike were hard put to it to make both ends meet, and Government after Government was brought to the verge of bankruptcy. Reparation payments and inter-allied debts could not be collected. The monetary system of the world, so painfully re-established on the gold standard during the previous years, fell once more into complete confusion.

Indications were obvious. In these years the financial world had to face a series of gigantic scandals which made the historic South Sea Bubble a minor affair indeed. In Britain there had been, some years previously, the bankruptcy and suicide of James White.

James White was a financier in the romantic style of Barney Barnato. An uneducated Lancashire man, he nevertheless used his native shrewdness to such ability after the war that very soon he was a man of millions.

Yet, in 1926, he died by his own hand, ruined. The depression had hit him hard, and he was attempting one big coup. It was an effort to control oil. Before White was through he had bought nearly £4,000,000 worth of shares. He needed nearly a million pounds to cover himself. Frantically he tried to raise the money. He failed.

But the financial panic that followed

THEIR ROYAL HIGHNESSES THE PRINCE OF WALES, THE DUKE OF YORK,
THE DUKE OF GLOUCESTER, AND THE DUKE OF KENT.

THE GREAT EVENT of 1934 was the wedding of H.R.H. the Duke of Kent, the King's youngest son, to Princess Marina of Greece. They became engaged whilst they were on holiday.

BUILDING *QUEEN MARY.* *The famous new Cunard liner, launched by H.M. the Queen
in September,* 1934, *has already had an eventful career. Work upon it was suspended on
December* 10, 1931, *owing to the economic conditions of the world, and was not resumed
until* 1934.

LAUNCHING QUEEN MARY, September, 1934. Her Majesty the Queen christened and launched Queen Mary, the world's largest liner, on September 26, 1934, at Clydebank before 250,000 people.

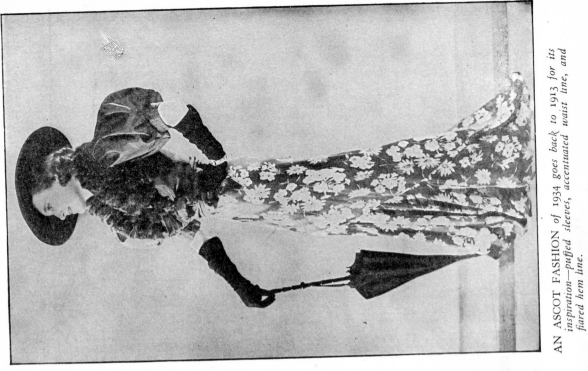

AN ASCOT FASHION of 1934 goes back to 1913 for its inspiration—puffed sleeves, accentuated waist line, and flared hem line.

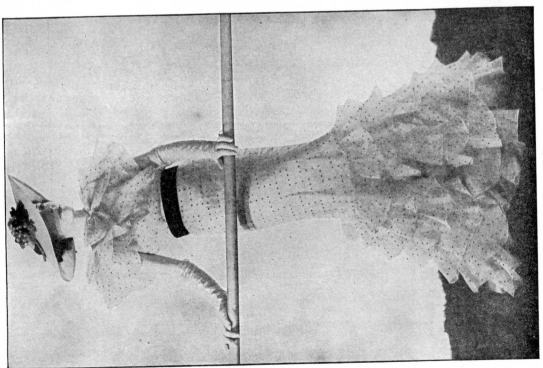

FRILLS AND FLOUNCES dating back to Victorian days are "modernised" for garden party wear in 1934.

KING ASSASSINATED. Europe was nearly plunged into war in October, 1934, by the assassination of King Alexander of Jugo-Slavia at Marseilles whilst on a State visit to France. Ironically, he had gone to France to discuss plans that might bring a more settled and peaceful Europe. This photograph shows the assassin being struck down.

the death of James White was nothing compared with the cataclysm that shook the City of London when the affair of Clarence Hatry reached its climax.

Hatry was the outstanding exploiter of the mad-money era of 1926-1929. The son of a German Jew, he brought his astute brain to bear upon the financial mechanism of modern times.

Starting with £60,000, he managed in four years to accumulate a £30,000,000 edifice.

But with Hatry, as with others, it was the same story. There came the moment when millions had to be raised quickly. To cover himself he forged some three-quarters of a million stocks.

The banks became suspicious. An inquiry was ordered. Hatry was arrested. By the time the tangle of crooked finance was investigated it was discovered that some £19,000,000 had been irretrievably lost. Hatry was tried and sentenced to fourteen years' imprisonment.

Then there was the great international financial catastrophe caused by the suicide of Ivar Kreuger, who controlled the great international Match Trust. His company had been floated with a capital of £26,000,000. A deal in 1927 with Poincaré put Kreuger on the heights. The Match King offered France £15,000,000 in exchange for a twenty-year match monopoly. Poincaré accepted.

Then, again, the slump. Soon this man of many millions found himself pressed for money on all sides. Kreuger resorted to a new device. It was a world in which paper represented money. Bankers seemed to have a wholesome respect for paper. Kreuger supplied them with plenty, bonds—all forged.

But even this colossal fraud could not save Kreuger. He travelled between Europe and the United States desperately trying to raise funds to stave off the inevitable smash. He failed, so in March, 1932, he committed suicide.

Some hours later financial panic raged in New York, Paris, and Stockholm. Another great bubble had burst.

II

While these financial crashes were occurring up and down the world and international monies were involved, Britain was desperately putting her own house in order. Foreign countries, faced with the prevailing depression, turned to the greatest money market in the world —London. Practically all countries kept large sums of money on deposit in London because it was considered the safest banking place in the world. Now these countries had need of these deposits. They swooped down upon their reserves.

In August, 1931, a serious run on the Bank of England began. The bank had not enough gold to stand the strain. It borrowed £50,000,000 in francs and dollars from France and America. But the drain was so severe that in a few days the £50,000,000 was almost exhausted.

Foreign advisers suggested pertinently to Britain that her huge unemployment dole should be cut. This was draining her of financial resources. Rather than face this unpleasant problem the Labour Government resigned and the National Government came into being. At once another £80,000,000 was obtained from France and America, but in a few days the foreign creditors had drained these coffers.

Therefore, on September 20, 1931,

Britain abandoned the gold standard. The Bank of England was empowered to refuse to give gold in return for its notes, and this meant that there was no guarantee that British money was worth a defined weight in gold.

The pound slumped heavily. It fell rapidly to the equivalent in gold of thirteen or fourteen shillings. But this had a remarkable effect. It cheapened British goods to the foreign buyer. Exports went up, and unemployment went down. In spite of all the outcry and criticisms of alarmists, the departure from gold brought greater advantages than disadvantages.

The year 1934 saw Britain emerging from the great economic war, as sixteen years previously she had emerged from the Great World War.

Despite the staggering burdens of debt and taxation—throughout this period the English had been the most heavily taxed nationals in the world—there were signs that a new and greater country was being born.

Slowly, but inevitably, a revolution had been going on in our midst. The enormous wealth of the country was being more equitably divided, industry was being properly organised, the old competitive system was giving way to co-ordinated efforts, and it could be seen by the discerning ones that, without barricades, bloodshed, assassinations, or all the stormy gutter politics of revolution, Britain was changing into a new, vigorous, and healthy country.

Evidence of the growing prosperity of Britain and the determination of the country to regain mastery of the seven seas was seen in the launching of the great new Cunarder on the Clyde on September 26, 1934. Provisionally called No. 534, there was a great shout of en-

thusiasm when, in the presence of the King and the Prince of Wales, Queen Mary christened the Cunarder "Queen Mary." As the giant ship slid down the slipway there was the feeling that a new era had opened for British shipping.

Something of the energy and optimism of Elizabethan days seemed to have been born again in the people.

And there was something of the spirit of Elizabethan adventurers in that galaxy of airmen and airwomen who raised themselves in the early hours of Saturday, October 20, at Mildenhall aerodrome, Suffolk, to begin the greatest air race in history. The pilots of the various machines, British and foreign, were competing for £15,500 in prizes offered in connection with the centenary of the State of Victoria, then being celebrated in Melbourne.

Jim and Amy Mollison, 12-to-1 favourites, were the first to hurtle into the darkness in their De Haviland Comet, a new type of fast plane of which much was hoped. Two minutes later, Roscoe Turner and Clyde Pangborne took off in their big Boeing, just as an orange-red sun edged over the horizon. The other machines, totalling twenty in all, also lifted from the ground in rapid succession. One of them, and the biggest of all, was a Dutch air liner owned by K.L.M. Company and nicknamed "The Flying Hotel."

The world was not long without news. Speeding non-stop from England, the Mollisons leaped sensationally into first place when they swooped into Bagdad, the first control point, towns ahead of the field. There Amy decided to have a hot bath and subsequently made a little speech to the officials gathered there.

Hardly had the dust of the departing

SCOTT'S GREAT
FLIGHT.

C. W. A. Scott and Campbell Black made aerial history in October, 1934, by flying from Mildenhall to Melbourne in 71 hours.

THE ROYAL WEDDING. *The scene in Westminster Abbey when the Duke of Kent and Princess Marina were married on November 29, 1934.*

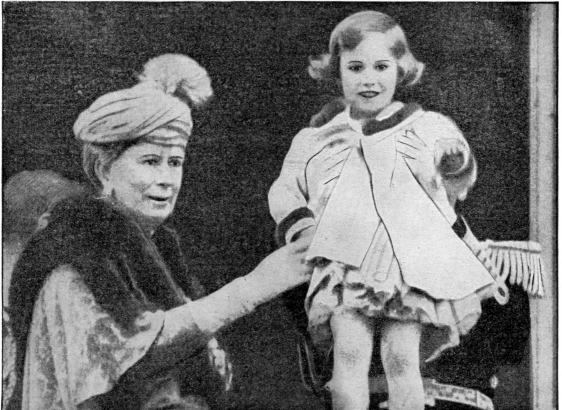

THE ROYAL WEDDING. *Thousands gathered outside Buckingham Palace to cheer the bride and bridegroom. The top picture shows them acknowledging the cheers. Below: The King holds up little Princess Margaret Rose to wave to the crowd.*

BRITISH TROOPS IN THE SAAR. *History was made in December, 1934, when British troops were sent to the Saar to maintain order during the plebiscite to decide whether that district should be returned to Germany. Although coldly received, the British soldiers were soon on friendly terms with the inhabitants.*

Mollisons settled on the Bagdad field when in dropped a second D.H. Comet, piloted by Flight-Lieutenant C. W. A. Scott and Captain T. Campbell Black. They left Bagdad close on the Mollisons' heels, and flew straight to Allahabad, second control point, to take over the lead. The Mollisons had landed at Karachi to refuel, and had taken off only to be forced back ten minutes later with landing-gear trouble.

On the second day Scott and Black were well in the lead with their D.H. Comet *Grosvenor House*. Behind them as they sped over the Bay of Bengal for Singapore were Parmentier and Moll, piloting the Dutch "Flying Hotel." This day also brought reports of hold-ups and disasters. Two Britishers, Gilman and Baines, had crashed in the mountains of Italy, and been killed. Others in the race were still in Europe.

The biggest sensation of the race came just before dawn of the third day, when Scott and Black flew their Scarlet Comet into Port Darwin. They had covered the last 300 miles over the sea on one motor, and risked death landing on a field made soggy by the first rain in seven months. Mechanics worked on the faulty engine, and soon they were off again.

Keeping up their sensational pace, Scott and Black flashed into Charlesville, refuelled, and sped towards the finish, where waiting thousands cheered their progress, reported over loud-speakers. With one motor dead, with only two hours' sleep since leaving England, Scott and Black triumphantly set down their scarlet torpedo in Melbourne at 3.34 p.m. In seventy-one hours eighteen seconds — just under three days—they had flown halfway round the world.

"The Flying Hotel," piloted by Parmentier and Moll, lost itself in the darkness near Charlesville. They landed with the help of headlights from hundreds of motor-cars. Nevertheless, they took second place on their arrival at Melbourne, the third place being taken by Roscoe Turner, flying a United States transport plane.

But the smashing of air records was not completed. Mr. O. Cathcart Jones and Mr. Kenneth Waller, flying a D.H. Comet, who arrived at Melbourne and took fourth place in the race, decided to turn round and fly back to England and set up a double record. They arrived back at Lympne aerodrome, near the Kent coast, on November 2. They had flown to Australia and back, 23,000 miles—nearly the circumference of the earth—in $13\frac{1}{4}$ days. They thus created seven new air records.

Preparations for the great Silver Jubilee of the King and Queen proceeded apace in these better times. A series of splendid events was arranged. Invitations to attend the celebrations in London were broadcast throughout the Empire. Welcome replies were received.

India decided to play a spectacular part in the celebrations. It seemed that the whole of the Empire would gather in London for this important event, the commemoration of the King's twenty-five years of reign over 493,000,000 subjects.

A programme was quickly drawn up. The Silver Jubilee celebrations were to be inaugurated by a Thanksgiving Service in St. Paul's Cathedral. Brilliant banquets and great receptions, and an Air Force, Navy and Army Pageant were also arranged. Altogether, the opinion was that these Silver Jubilee preparations would surpass in grandeur the Diamond Jubilee celebrations of Queen Victoria in 1897 and of her Jubilee ten years previously.

Shortly after this announcement came another, which revealed the genuine enthusiasm of the people of Britain for the Royal Household. The announcement appeared in the Court Circular. It was dated from Balmoral Castle, and read:

It is with the greatest pleasure that the King and Queen announce the betrothal of their dearly beloved son, the Prince George, to Princess Marina, daughter of the Prince and Princess Nicolas of Greece, to which union the King had gladly given his consent.

The courtship of the young couple had ripened during the visit of Prince George to Princess Marina's brother-in-law, Prince Paul of Jugoslavia, at the castle near Bled, amid the wild beauty of the Slovene Alps.

A few weeks later Princess Marina arrived in England and was given an enthusiastic welcome. Her brunette beauty and engaging smile appealed to all. In company with Prince George she proceeded to Balmoral, where the arrangements for the wedding at Westminster Abbey in November were discussed. Then Princess Marina returned to Paris to complete her preparations of the trousseau.

Although the announcement of the engagement between the Duke of Kent and Princess Marina came as a surprise to many, it was not unexpected to the friends of the Grecian girl. Only, the rumours in the early days were about the wrong man.

Visitors to the luxurious little flat in Paris where Princess Marina lived with her parents did not fail to notice a photograph which always stood on her table.

This photograph was of the Duke of Kent and the Prince of Wales, and was signed: "To Marina, from David and George." The visitors jumped hastily to conclusions. They went away rumouring among themselves that Princess Marina was going to marry the Prince of Wales. They did not know that the Duke of Kent, or Prince George as he was then known, had already captured the heart of the Grecian girl.

This photograph was the result of many meetings in London with Prince George. Often Princess Marina was to be found in Mayfair, a favourite dance partner of Prince George at the Embassy and other exclusive dance places. But even those who often saw them together did not guess that this was anything more than a happy friendship.

Early in 1934, Prince Paul of Jugoslavia, a man who had spent many years in England, and married Princess Marina's sister, sent an invitation to Prince George to visit him for a fortnight at his picturesque retreat at Bohinj. At the time, Prince George was still suffering from the strain of his heavy tour in South Africa, and could not immediately accept.

But when Prince George was at Cowes with the King and Queen at the end of the London season, he telegraphed to Prince Paul asking if it would be possible for him to spend a fortnight in Bohinj about September 15. Prince Paul immediately replied that he would be delighted, and Prince George set off from Croydon in his brother's aeroplane.

The shooting lodge of Prince Paul and the magnificent mountain scenery provided the ideal setting for two people to fall in love. Princess Marina was one of the guests of the little party that had been gathered together to meet Prince George, and very soon the two young people were taking long walks together over the mountain slopes and by the side of the blue water lakes.

The peasants of this glorious countryside saw the young couple together often. Very soon the village gossips were convinced that an engagement would be announced. A shepherd spread the story that he had gone into one of the little chapels among the mountains to pray. There he saw a young couple seated in silent reverence in the front row before the altar—and he saw the young lady, as she was leaving, light two candles in honour of the Madonna. The couple were the Duke of Kent and Princess Marina.

The whole world now knows how Prince George motored one evening to send a long telegram to the King asking his permission to marry the beautiful Grecian Princess. The King gladly gave his consent, for it has now become the axiom of our Royal Family that its members should be allowed to marry for love rather than tortuous motives.

And it can truly be said that this marriage with a Balkan Princess had no political significance whatsoever. As a member of the Jugo-Slavia Diplomatic Corps said, when the news was broadcast: "We are thrilled in our country because there is no suggestion of political reasons for their marriage; just plain love for one another."

Nevertheless, the Duke of Kent's marriage further unites our own Royal Family with a family which is related to nearly all the Royalties of Europe. Princess Marina's grandfather, King George of Greece, was the brother of Queen Alexandra. Her grandmother was the Grand Duchess Olga of Russia. Her aunt, the wife of King Constantine, was the ex-Kaiser's sister, and a granddaughter of Queen Victoria.

Through her sister, Princess Marina is also related to the Royal Family of Jugo-Slavia, and through her cousin to King Carol of Rumania.

Yet, even at the moment when this loyalty to the British Throne was manifesting itself in this country, and the preparations for the great celebrations proceeding with enthusiasm, tragedy again stepped on to the stage of world affairs.

King Alexander of Jugo-Slavia stepped ashore at Marseilles on the afternoon of October 9, 1934. He was paying a State visit to France.

King Alexander was greeted at Marseilles by M. Barthou, the French Foreign Minister. As the King and the statesman were driving from the docks a man ran out from the crowds lining the pavement, jumped on the running board of the closed car and, despite the efforts of the chauffeur, fired a number of revolver shots at point-blank range. Pandemonium ensued, during which three other people were killed and forty-five injured. By the time King Alexander could be got to a place of safety he was dead. M. Barthou died shortly afterwards.

On the same day that this terrible news was broadcast over Europe it was also announced that Prince George had been created Duke of Kent.

Tragedy also marked the lives of many British people in the year 1934.

One of the worst coalmining accidents for many years in Great Britain occurred near Wrexham; here explosion and fire took a toll of no fewer than 265 lives.

But in a manner as terrible, though more gradual, was the continued high number of persons killed yearly on the roads of Great Britain. This notorious scandal was at length made the subject of administrative measures.

A speed limit, though denounced by the mouthpieces of the motoring interests, was imposed in built-up areas which were defined by the presence of lamp-posts along the roads; the hooting of cars by night was forbidden; and an energetic Minister of Transport, who assumed office in the summer, introduced the salutary innovations of clearly marked foot-crossings in the Metropolis and asserted the rights of walkers to commit themselves to them at the peril of road traffic.

It became also increasingly evident how dangerous was the haphazard building of new houses along new main thoroughfares.

The shadow of the royal murder continued to loom over Europe, but in Britain it was dispelled by the splendours of the marriage celebrations of the Duke of Kent and Princess Marina.

The marriage itself at Westminster Abbey was one of the greatest popular pageants ever witnessed in this country. On November 29, 1934, the Royal couple entered Westminster Abbey, and knelt before the Archbishop of Canterbury. Behind them were Kings, Queens, Princes and Princesses, heading a brilliant congregation that included the greatest in the land.

The ceremony began. Throughout the Empire millions were listening, and by the miracle of broadcasting heard the responses, the "I wills," in perfect clarity. It is a fact that those in the Abbey on that great day heard less than those seated in their own homes.

The Royal couple repeated their troth to each other after the Archbishop. Then the Prince of Wales stepped forward and handed the ring to his brother. The Archbishop took it and returned it to the Duke, who placed it on Princess Marina's hand.

As the congregation seated itself for the Archbishop's address the six elder bridesmaids, statuesque in their simple white frocks, came into view, standing in a graceful group at the head of the nave.

While the Archbishop spoke the Royal bride and groom kept their eyes fixed on his face. They knelt together in almost complete immobility.

The National Anthem. The King and Queen moved forward and motioned to the bride's parents to join them. Together the parents walked with the bride and groom, behind the Archbishop, into the chapel for the signing of the register.

The Wedding March. The procession reappeared. The Duke and Duchess of Kent emerged from behind the screen. Hand in hand they walked together. The Duchess curtsied low to the King and Queen and smiled happily at each of her bridesmaids in turn.

Then happily, almost casually, the Royal guests walked from the church to the shouts of acclaim, the mounting crash of cheers outside.

Slowly the newly married couple drove through the streets, bowing to the plaudits of the huge crowds lining the pavements. Eventually, they reached Buckingham Palace. There was an even greater demonstration by the thousands who had congregated in the area facing the Palace.

The Royal Family came out on to the balcony. The King and Queen, the Prince of Wales, the Duke and Duchess

JUBILEE CAVALCADE

LONDON *had never before seen such loyal demonstrations as were given to the King and Queen during their Jubilee State Drive through the streets of the Empire's capital on May 6, 1935.*

LOOKING DOWN *on the amazing scene in Trafalgar Square, where thousands waited for hours to see the King and Queen's State Drive to St. Paul's Cathedral.*

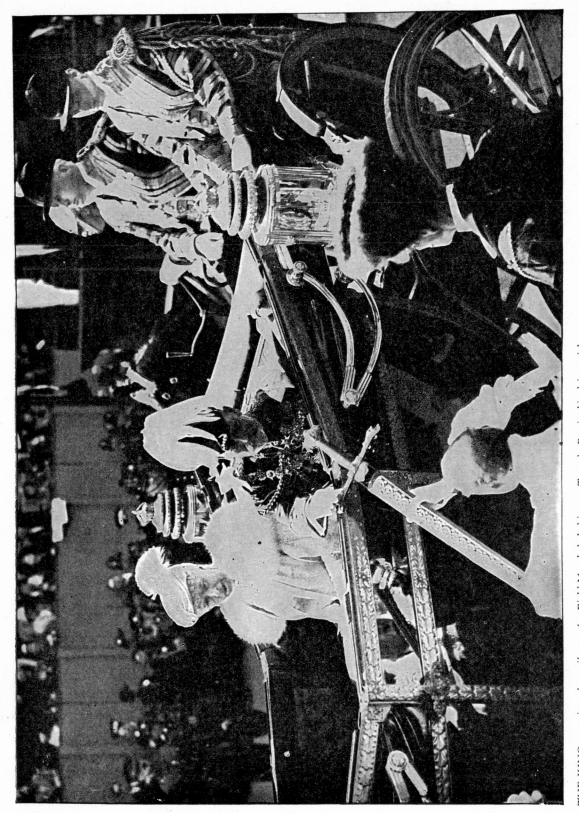

THE KING, *wearing the uniform of a Field-Marshal, halting at Temple Bar in his drive with the Queen to St. Paul's Cathedral to receive the historic Pearl Sword from the Lord Mayor in token of the City's homage.*

THE KING AND QUEEN, *with members of their family and their officers of State, during the Thanksgiving Service in St. Paul's Cathedral. An address was given by the Archbishop of Canterbury, and the entire service was broadcast throughout the British Empire.*

RAYS OF SUNLIGHT *lit up the impressive scene in St. Paul's, where the leading citizens of the Empire gave thanks for the continued reign of their King.*

AFTER THE DRIVE back to Buckingham Palace, the King and Queen and their family came out on to the balcony to acknowledge the cheers of nearly 200,000 people. "My very dear people . . . the Queen and I thank you from the bottom of our hearts for all the loyalty . . . and love with which . . . you have surrounded us," said the King in a broadcast to the Empire.

THE JUBILEE *was celebrated by rich and poor in every part of the country, and houses were decorated with flags and bunting. In Palace Road, in the East End of London, a tea was held for the poor children of the district.*

LONDON *was floodlit during the Jubilee celebrations, and several hundred thousand people thronged the streets every night. Traffic was banned in certain areas to facilitate matters for the sightseers. This photograph shows Buckingham Palace lit up by floodlights.*

of York, and also the Duke and Duchess of Kent. The cheers of the huge crowd rang out. There was a delightful incident when the King, smiling and obviously gratified by this great show of loyalty, lifted up Princess Margaret Rose so that the huge crowd could see her. The cheers rang out afresh.

The bride and bridegroom had a send-off on their honeymoon which they will never forget.

As they left Buckingham Palace members of the British Royal Family and of foreign Royal Families vied with one another in pelting them in confetti, rose petals and silver tokens.

The Prince of Wales, with the Duke and Duchess of York, the Earl of Harewood, Princess Alice and the Earl of Athlone, Prince and Princess Arthur of Connaught and the young Earl of Macduff, ex-King George of Greece, and other guests ran behind the honeymoon coach for some distance, still throwing tokens.

Princess Elizabeth, clasping her little sister, Princess Margaret, by the hand, Lady Mary Cambridge and Lady Iris Mountbatten, the other child bridesmaids, were also among those who scampered in pursuit.

Princess Elizabeth was highly excited and threw handful after handful of silver tokens and rose leaves at the Duke and Duchess.

The King had previously said good-bye to his son and his new daughter-in-law at the Grand Entrance. Awaiting the bridal pair was an open State landau, drawn by four of the famous Windsor greys, with two blue-coated postillions and two scarlet-clad outriders in front.

Through a lane formed by bridesmaids, still in their wedding dresses, pelting rose petals, the Duke and the Duchess made their way to the carriage. The Duke, who was bareheaded and wearing a dark brown suit, sat on his bride's left.

The Duchess was in her going-away costume of almond green tweed, trimmed with fur at the collar and cuffs, and a hat of the same material and colour.

In contrast with the splendour of their departure from London, the Royal couple were received at Himley Hall by the housekeeper and the butler. There was no ceremony.

The Duke and Duchess must have appreciated the simplicity of their welcome. They dined very soon after their arrival, alone, and then inspected the spacious building. Later, in a room converted into a cinema for the occasion of the honeymoon, they saw a film of their wedding.

The way was now clear for the Silver Jubilee celebrations of King George and Queen Mary. King George was approaching his seventieth birthday. Britain was emerging from the greatest economic slump in the history of the world The Throne had triumphed and was above the strife of politics and the manœuvrings for power.

Above all, the Empire looked upon the King as the symbol of its own unity. A splendid patriotism combined with a real devotion and an optimism founded upon the possibilities of the future brought the English nation to the year 1935.

It had been twenty-five years of great drama. No easy or comfortable time for the people. A period of great events, testing the endurance of every man and woman. But it was life, joyous and grim, lived to the full. There are few who will deny that those twenty-five years were well worth the living.

APPENDIX

A CHRONOLOGICAL LIST OF IMPORTANT EVENTS SINCE 1910

1910.

May 6.—Death of King Edward VII. Accession of King George V.

May 7.—King George holds his first Privy Council.

May 20.—Funeral of King Edward.

June 23.—Duke of Cornwall created Prince of Wales.

November 25.—Male Suffragist attacks Mr. Winston Churchill, Home Secretary, with a whip in a train.

December 3.—General Election.

December 18.—£4,000 aviation prize won by Mr. T. Sopwith.

1911.

January 3.—Sidney Street siege.

May 29.—Death of Sir W. S. Gilbert.

May 31.—*Titanic* launched at Belfast.

June 22.—Coronation of King and Queen.

July 13.—Investiture of the Prince of Wales at Carnarvon.

September 6.—T. W. Burgess swims the Channel.

November 11.—King and Queen leave for India.

December 12.—Durbar at Delhi.

1912.

January 17.—Captain Scott reaches South Pole.

April 14.—*Titanic* sinks after colliding with iceberg. Only 711 of 2,201 people aboard are saved.

1913.

February 19.—Mr. Lloyd George's house at Walton is damaged by bomb explosion. Suffragette accepts responsibility.

June 4.—Suffragette killed at the Derby.

October 11.—Loss of British s.s. *Volturno* by fire in Atlantic; 136 passengers drowned, 521 rescued.

1914.

May 22.—Government secures controlling interest in Persian oilfields.

June 25.—British battleships at Kiel; visited by German Emperor.

June 28.—Assassination of Archduke Francis Ferdinand at Sarajevo.

July 28.—Austria-Hungary declares war on Serbia.

August 1.—Germany declares war on Russia

August 3.—Germany sends ultimatum to Belgium. British Fleet mobilises.

August 4.—British ultimatum. Britain declares war on Germany.

August 16.—British Expeditionary Force lands in France.

August 20.—Germans occupy Brussels.

August 23.—Japan declares war on Germany.

August 23.—Battle of Mons.

August 28.—British naval victory in Heligoland Bight.

October 18.—Victory of the Marne announced.

November 1.—Battle of Coronel. German naval victory.

November 14.—Death of Lord Roberts.

December 8.—Battle of Falkland Islands. British naval victory.

December 25.—Informal Christmas truce. Fighting renewed at midnight.

1915.

February 20.—British and French warships attack Dardanelles ports.

April 25.—Allies land on Gallipoli.

May 7.—*Lusitania* torpedoed.

May 13.—Name of German Emperor struck off rolls of the Knights of the Garter, by command of the King.

May 23.—Italy declares war.

May 25.—Coalition Ministry formed. Mr. Bonar Law joins Government. Mr. Lloyd George appointed Minister of Munitions.

October 12.—Execution of Miss Edith Cavell.

December 15.—Sir Douglas Haig appointed to command British Army in France.

1916.

January 8.—Gallipoli completely evacuated.

February 21.—Battle of Verdun begins.

April 24.—Sir Roger Casement arrested.

April 29.—9,000 British troops surrender at Kut.

May 31.—Battle of Jutland.

June 5.—H.M.S. *Hampshire*, with Lord Kitchener aboard, sinks after striking a mine.

July 6.—Mr. Lloyd George appointed War Secretary.

August 3.—Sir Roger Casement executed.

August 30.—Hindenburg appointed Chief of German General Staff.

September 3.—Zeppelin brought down at Cuffley. Lieutenant Robinson awarded the V.C.

December 7.—Mr. Lloyd George succeeds Mr. Asquith as Premier.

APPENDIX

1917.

March 15.—Abdication of Russian Emperor.
April 5.—U.S. declare war on Germany.
June 15.—German air raid on London; 104 killed.
July 17.—British Royal Family becomes "House of Windsor."
November 6.—British capture Passchendaele.
December 10.—General Allenby occupies Jerusalem.

1918.

March 2.—Germany and Russia sign treaty of peace.
March 21.—German "push" on Western Front begins. Allied armies retreat.
March 23.—Paris shelled.
June 6.—Franco-British-American counter-attack successful.
July 16.—Ex-Russian Emperor murdered.
July 20.—Germans fall back across the Marne.
August 2.—Germans retreat south of Aisne.
August 30.—British cross the Somme.
September 17.—British troops invade Bulgaria.
September 25.—Bulgaria proposes Armistice.
October 1.—British occupy Damascus.
October 4.—Germany proposes an Armistice.
October 9.—British victory at Cambrai.
October 31.—Revolution in Vienna and Budapest.
November 3.—Austria accepts conditions of peace.
November 9.—Abdication and flight of German Emperor.
November 11.—Armistice granted to Germany.
November 21.—German Fleet surrenders to British.
November 24.—British troops enter Germany.

1919.

January 18.—Peace Conference meets in Paris.
June 15.—Alcock and Brown fly the Atlantic.
June 21.—Germans scuttle surrendered fleet at Scapa Flow
June 28.—Peace Treaty signed.
August 1.—Police strike.
August 25.—Inauguration of London-Paris air service.
September 26.—Railway strike begins. Settled October 6.

1920.

May 16.—Prince of Wales leaves for Australia.
July 10.—Death of Lord Fisher.
November 11.—Body of Unknown Warrior buried in Westminster Abbey. Cenotaph unveiled. Armistice Day commemorated by Two Minutes' Silence.

1921.

January 25.—Women sit for first time on jury in Divorce Court.
January 28.—R 34 becomes total wreck.

March 31.—Coal miners' strike.
July 22.—*Chu-Chin-Chow* played for last [at] His Majesty's Theatre. Record create[d] 2,238 performances.
December 6.—Irish Peace Agreement signed [in] London.

1922.

June 22.—Sir Henry Wilson assassinated in London by two Irish gunmen.
July 5.—Revolt in Ireland crushed.
October 23.—Mr. Bonar Law appointed Premier in succession to Mr. Lloyd George.

1923.

April 26.—Marriage of Duke of York.
May 28.—Mr. Stanley Baldwin succeeds Mr. Bonar Law as Premier.

1924.

January 22.—Mr. Baldwin resigns. Mr. Ramsay MacDonald becomes first Labour Premier.
April 23.—King opens British Empire Exhibition at Wembley.
October 29.—Labour Government heavily defeated at General Election.

1925.

March 28.—Prince of Wales leaves for Africa.
April 26.—Hindenburg appointed President of Germany.
December 1.—Locarno Treaty signed.

1926.

January 31.—British troops evacuate Cologne.
April 21.—Princess Elizabeth born.
April 30.—Coal lock-out and strike declared.
May 3.—General strike declared.
May 12.—General strike ends.

1927.

February 7.—New Prayer Book published.
March 22.—British troops in action in Shanghai.
May 12.—Police raid on Arcos House.
May 27.—Great Britain breaks off diplomatic relations with Russia.
September 26.—Britain wins Schneider Trophy.

1928.

January 6.—Thames overflows its banks. Several people living near the Embankment in London are drowned.
January 29.—Death of Earl Haig.
February 15.—Death of Lord Oxford and Asquith.

een of Afghanistan

s causes anxiety.

on becomes critical.

time at
d with
in

Craigwell House,

d becomes Prime

..anksgiving Service at
..ter Abbey.

22.—*Bremen*, German liner, wins Blue
Riband of the Atlantic, crossing in 4 days
17 hours.
September 7.—Britain retains Schneider Trophy.
September 20.—Clarence Hatry arrested.

1930.

January 24.—Hatry sentenced.
June 13.—Sir Henry Segrave killed.
August 6.—Unemployment figures exceed
2,000,000.
August 21.—Princess Margaret Rose born.
October 5.—R 101 crashes near Beauvais Forest,
France.

1931.

February 5.—Malcolm Campbell breaks world's
land speed record at 246 m.p.h.
March 14.—British Empire Trade Exhibition
at Buenos Aires opened by Prince of Wales.
August 24.—Labour Government resigns. Mr.
Ramsay MacDonald forms National Govern-
ment.
September 10.—Mr. Snowden, Chancellor of the
Exchequer, introduces Emergency Budget.
September 20.—Britain goes off the Gold Stand-
ard.
October 27.—General Election.
November 6.—New Cabinet announced.
December 10.—Work suspended on New Cunard
Liner No. 534.

1932.

January 24.—Mutiny at Dartmoor Prison.
February 10.—Death of Edgar Wallace.
July 21.—Ottawa Conference opens.
September 28.—Lord Snowden and Sir Herbert
Samuel resign from the Cabinet.
November 1.—Unemployment demonstration in
London.

1933.

January 30.—Adolf Hitler becomes Chancellor of
Germany.
February 27.—German Reichstag on fire.
March 20.—Trial of " Prisoner in the Tower,"
Lieutenant Baillie-Stewart, opens.
June 12.—World Economic Conference opens.

1934.

August 2.—Death of President Hindenburg.
August 29.—Duke of Kent's engagement to Prin-
cess Marina of Greece announced.
September 26.—*Queen Mary* launched by Her
Majesty Queen Mary at Clydebank.
October 9.—King Alexander of Jugo-Slavia
assassinated at Marseilles.
October 23.—Mildenhall to Melbourne Air Race
won by C. W. Scott and Campbell Black in
64 hours, 48 minutes, 49 seconds.
November 29.—Wedding of Duke of Kent.

1935.

January 13.—Plebiscite in Saar.
March 1.—Saar becomes part of Germany.
March 1 to 12.—Rebellion in Greece. Venizelos
flees to Italy.
March 28.—Duke of Gloucester's tour of Austra-
lasia ended.
April 6.—Cambridge won the Boat Race for 13th
year in succession.
May.—King George and Queen Mary return to
Buckingham Palace from Windsor
Castle.
Indian Princes arrive for Jubilee celebra-
tions.
Floodlighting of London begins.
May 5.—London crowded with people wishing to
take part in Jubilee celebrations. Hyde Park
kept open for two nights at request of the
King.
May 6.—State Drive to St. Paul's for Thanks-
giving Service. Public Holiday. Loyal cele-
brations throughout the Empire. The King
broadcasts a message of thanks to the
Empire. Chain of beacons lit throughout
Great Britain.
May 7-11.—King and Queen drive through
suburbs of London. Loyal demonstrations
outside Buckingham Palace and throughout
country.
May 9.—Loyal Addresses by both Houses of
Parliament to the King and Queen.